DINING OUT

A GLOBAL HISTORY

DINING OUT

OF RESTAURANTS

Dear Trina,

Bon Appetit!

Elliott

KATIE RAWSON & ELLIOTT SHORE

REAKTION BOOKS

To those who fed us

Published by Reaktion Books Ltd
Unit 32, Waterside
44–48 Wharf Road
London N1 7UX, UK
www.reaktionbooks.co.uk

First published 2019
Copyright © Katie Rawson and Elliott Shore 2019

Printed and bound in China by 1010 Printing International Ltd

A catalogue record for this book is available from the British Library

ISBN 978 1 78914 057 6

CONTENTS

PREFACE

People the world over eat outside the home as an unquestioned part of everyday life. At a roadside stand, in a fancy restaurant, on an aeroplane, at a fast-food joint, at a diner, a pizzeria, a neighbourhood hangout, from a street vendor, in a café, at a cafeteria, from a vending machine. The list is virtually endless and the number of restaurants in the world likely exceeds 15 million – Japan appears to have the most restaurants per capita: 91 per 10,000 inhabitants. In this book, we wanted to investigate the story of how dining out may have developed over the ages and throughout the world.

We have aimed to produce a global history of restaurants, which may appear to be a bold claim for one volume given the depth, breadth and length of the human experience of dining out. What we have done is both ask and answer questions, in vignettes and threads that are both synthetic and idiosyncratic, delving into many of the aspects of the development of the restaurant over the centuries. The book is as much about the history of working in restaurants as it is about the history of eating in them. It considers the distinctive features of places where people across the globe have dined out, from the first traces of what we know about people eating together in public. Relating a global history of restaurants through different facets – chefs, machines, reviews, international exchange – helps us to present restaurant history as a history not only of food, but of culture, economics and technology. We trust that this work will bring new insights into eating out by featuring people and innovations – many of which are not generally known – that have propelled us to the present phantasmagoria of the world of the restaurant. It is a book intended to help us reconsider, resituate and more deeply understand the people, restaurants and moments that are significant to the development of this central feature of modern life.

In Chapter One, we examine the long history of dining out beginning in the Bronze Age and ending with the first full-service restaurants in China in the twelfth century. In Chapter Two, we look at the dawn of the European restaurant in France in the eighteenth century, along with its variety of innovations, from specialized tables to guidebooks. In Chapter Three, we explore the democratization of restaurants across Europe and the United States as features of restaurant dining become an integral part of the lives of working women, the urban poor, artists, aristocrats and politicians. In Chapter Four, we consider the role of the chef, beginning in Japan and ending with Ferran Adrià in Spain, peering into kitchen inventions and interventions from the gas stove to molecular gastronomy. In Chapter Five, we turn to service, looking at three hundred years of waitresses and waiters in Japan, China, France and the United States. In Chapter Six, we consider how modes of travel – trains and cars – transformed restaurants. In Chapter Seven, we examine how mechanization, from the automat to the conveyor belt, transformed restaurant labour and expectations of eating in restaurants. In Chapter Eight, we compare notions of time in the late twentieth-century restaurant, looking at both fast food and slow food. In Chapter Nine, we end by explicitly taking up the notion of the global restaurant, investigating how food moves from one place to another, and how immigration and local palates shape what and how we eat over time. We hope you will enjoy the journey into this set of oft-told (and untold) stories about the history of restaurants, and that the contours and constraints of this book will encourage other stories and histories of restaurants around the world to be told. Bon appétit!

1

EATING AWAY FROM HOME:
THE LONG HISTORY OF RESTAURANTS

Eating out is such a familiar activity – one imagines that people must always have been doing it, and that the restaurant must be a very old part of human culture. A history of restaurants therefore is a history of many aspects of culture – social, technological, political, aesthetic and economic.

In the West, people are eating out more and more. Cooking a complete meal together at home can become a special occasion, one that celebrates family life. Much of the food we eat at home is either now taken out from restaurants, delivered to the door, prepared at supermarkets or bought at those same markets already processed to the point where we need only fire up the microwave to ready it for consumption. In many ways, eating at home is now an extension of eating out, rather than the other way around.

Historians of everyday life like to find origins, first examples: we like to know where the things that seem to have always existed began, and how they evolved into routine parts of human existence. The technological history of eating is a very long one: about 2.5 million years ago early hominins developed the practice of cutting and smashing food in order to swallow and digest it more easily. These practices meant less chewing, which enabled us to evolve smaller jaws and more articulable lips, allowing for human speech and better balance. Between 300,000 and 30,000 years ago, humans began cooking and agriculture burgeoned.[1]

People have taken food on the road or to work with them for millennia. They have also bought prepared food from vendors for thousands of years. However, restaurants seem to be a relatively new phenomenon. All of the elements of eating in a restaurant had to be invented. In the Western world, they only got their start around the time Europe began stirring politically from its reliance on hereditary nobility; however, that does not mean that the restaurant is necessarily an offshoot of democracy. The beginning of the restaurant in Europe certainly was bound up with the seismic changes in the world of the mid-eighteenth century – the political and social upheaval that would erase the monarchy, change the calendar and, at least temporarily, overturn the relationships between social classes that had been sanctioned by religion and precedent. But we will turn to the birth of the modern Western restaurant in Paris in the next chapter, because the first restaurants did not begin there. They began in twelfth-century China, which was itself experiencing a change in governmental structure and a boom in urban populations.

Eating out has always been framed by both social norms and economics. In this chapter, we consider the developments across the world that led to the restaurant, a cultural institution aimed at feeding appetites away from home.

In the ancient world, one would eat with a regular set of people on a daily basis; however, there were occasions when people expanded their group of dining companions. The occasions that changed people's dining behaviours, for both eating with strangers and eating in public, were travel (for work, religion, war, trade), negotiation (commerce, diplomacy) and celebration. Food and drink, taken together, by people who were not related to one another, was a feature of the most ancient societies of which we have a record. While the concept of a restaurant took much longer to develop, the theatricality of religious processions, and the special foods for special occasions, would be altered to form part of restaurant culture. These shifts in practice are the beginnings of behaviours that would transmute themselves eventually into such things as waiting to be seated, speaking to a waiter, looking at a menu and being served food cooked ostensibly just for you and your companions in a space that allowed for a private group to eat in a public or semi-private space.[2] To eat in a restaurant is to eat in public, interacting with people who are not related to us and who are performing a service for which they are rewarded.

In a moment, we will turn to the feasts and forums of dining; however, we begin where our material evidence of eating out begins, with workers. In the Copper Age (also known as the Chalcolithic, *c.* 3300 BCE), people began producing ceramic vessels at scale in northern Mesopotamia. These were initially made to distribute rations: they were even marked in cuneiform with a word that was later modified to become the word meaning 'to eat'. These bowls, with food in them, were given to people – in return for work – on a daily basis, a form that is more like a military or school cafeteria than a market or a tavern. These workers would have eaten together in places other than their homes, but it is unclear how we would characterize this as 'eating out' (there is no choice here, of food, of companions, of location, of time – making it seem a far cry from what we interpret as 'eating out' in the twenty-first century). Over time though, the ceramic bowls morphed into serving and eating dishes: they became more ornate, varied in size and reflected social status. In some ways, the earliest bowls are more familiar as tableware than the more elaborate vessels that followed them in these early millennia. At the same time, public eating changed as well. Large collections of even simple bowls in certain locations point to ceremonial or orchestrated crowds eating together. These collective eating practises edge closer to the experiences we are referring to when we talk about eating out.[3]

These forms of eating shift from strictly utilitarian to commensality. The archaeologist Susan Pollock describes what this means:

The word derives from the Latin *com* = together with, and *mensa* = table. On the most basic level, commensality is about eating and drinking together, but it is far more than just a physical act: it also comprises the myriad social and political elements entailed in those occasions. Underpinning commensality is co-presence.[4]

A Chalcolithic bowl decorated with deer and other incised schematic figures, c. 2500–2001 BCE, terracotta.

Attributed to the Nikias Painter, Attic red-figure bell-krater, c. 420 BCE, red-figure pottery. The symposium scene features banqueters wearing laurel wreaths and playing the kottabos game while a girl plays the aulos; a wreath hangs on the wall.

Georg Simmel, a German sociologist, pointed out what should be obvious: 'people cannot actually share food – what one person has eaten, another cannot.' He explains that sharing space, practices and portions of the same dish is a way to share experiences. This is commensality. Further, Simmel claims that commensal acts are 'an archetypal form of social practice'.[5] While the most obvious moments of ancient commensality are around religious practice (feasts, ceremonies and holidays), ancient commensality was not restricted to religious frameworks. Eating together as a secular practice becomes a central feature when we turn our gaze to ancient Greece – more specifically, to Athens.

The symposium is the most famous of the institutions of the 'consuming passions' of the classical period in Athens.[6] 'Symposium' derives from the ancient Greek for drinking together – the later Roman form was the convivium. The symposium moved the commensal nature of partaking in food towards a secular, social and sensual one that emphasized drink. Although drink may have been central, four other pieces of the historic restaurant

development start to come into focus: gender difference, sexual play, musical entertainment and conversation. When one combines the twin excesses of too much food and too much drink, aided and abetted by luxury foods and wines, one begins to see the seeds of the restaurants we know today.

The symposium was largely seen as a drinking party for men, a place where alliances and friendships were created and extended. It took place inside a private home, in a special room for men, the *andrōn*, which had a raised floor and could accommodate eleven to fifteen participants who reclined on their left elbows on two-seater couches. It was essentially a circle broken only by a door through which all of the people and the food came – the conversation seems to have been carried on in a ritual way, from left to right around and around and around. Small and intimate, with alcoholic beverages flowing, the space created was one within, cut off from the outside world.

The symposium started with the first of three kraters of wine – which was stronger than today's wine – diluted with water to the potency of a

Attributed to Lydos, terracotta column-krater (bowl for mixing wine and water), c. 550 BCE, terracotta black-figure.

Attributed to the Brygos Painter, terracotta kantharos (drinking cup with high handles): two female heads, c. 490–480 BCE, terracotta red-figure.

Attributed to the Painter of Brussels, terracotta kylix (drinking cup), mid-5th century BCE, terracotta red-figure.

Group of Karlsruhe, apulian red-figure dish with fish, c. 350–325 BCE, red-figure pottery.

modern glass of beer: the first krater was a toast to health, the second to love and the third and last to sleep. But that process was an ideal one: not necessarily how things proceeded, but perhaps a way to impose a kind of moderation on the guests who often went off the rails. In a fourth-century BCE play by Eubulus, Dionysus describes it this way: 'The fourth krater is mine no longer, but belongs to hubris; the fifth to shouting; the sixth to revel; the seventh to black eyes; the eighth to summonses; the ninth to bile; and the tenth to madness and people tossing the furniture about.'[7] The wine, which was supposed to loosen the tongue to enrich the conversation, was apparently just as often an excuse in itself to get together.

The symposium also included a feast, often of a special kind of food that inspired a special kind of passion: fish. Fish was more than a delicious food for those in attendance. It emerged as a new kind of food object – one thoroughly ensconced

in consumer culture and connoisseurship. Unlike many foods which were either so ubiquitous as to be uninteresting or part of rituals, fish at this moment in Athens were fully secular. The people at the symposium treated fish as critics would come to treat many foods over the next 3,000 years: as something to discuss, to assess, to debate, to pay outrageous sums for, to learn about and to opine over.[8] These discussions of fish were part of being together, of making social bonds, of working through political and economic alliances, of forming and enforcing non-kin relationships.

People who were not necessarily of the elite, who did not partake in the rarefied air of the symposium, had another kind of public space in which to eat and drink. The *kapēleion* or tavern was a place mostly for drink, but one could also get a little something to eat as well – the slightly more well-off individuals could buy wine in bulk to take away. These bars were scattered throughout

Athens. They were often owned by slaves and like pubs in London they had names: one mentioned often is the 'kapēleion of the bald man'. In Pompeii, these taverns reached a density that looks very much like that in cities of today. The excavation site of the Agora in Athens gives us a sense of what these taverns might have been like: researchers have uncovered a great deal of cookware (casserole dishes, pots, mixing bowls, mortars) as well as tableware (salt cellars, plates, small bowls and many drinking vessels), a flute, lamps and animal bones. At a nearby site, marble tabletops were found.[9] Those who hung out at these bars and taverns were excoriated in ways that likely ring true to modern ears:

> Even the most respectable of the young men are
> wasting their time in drinking and assignations
> and idleness and childish games . . . some of
> them chill wine at the *Nine Fountains*, there are
> some who play dice in the gambling-dens and
> many who loiter around the place where the
> flute-girls are trained.[10]

Games and music were features of both the rarefied symposium and the street life of Athens and other ancient Greek cities. In these spaces eating and drinking combined with music, conversation and sex. People developed rituals and technologies for eating together in public. They produced vessels for cooking, eating and drinking in mass quantities. They pursued luxury food and drink, like fish and fine alcoholic beverages. They indulged in excess. These places – from the symposium to the taverns – had almost all of the aspects of the modern world of eating and drinking in public.

Alimenti, formaggi from *Taccuino Sanitatis*, late 14th century, illustrated manuscript.

EATING IN CITIES

For more than a thousand years, the out-to-eat scene in cities across the globe looked somewhat like the ancient Greek one: taverns, teahouses and cafés, cookshops and food stalls, vendors and clubs. Large cities had a wide array of alternatives, open to a wider array of people.

For the lower classes, from Cairo to London, from Madrid to Kaifeng, places that are sometimes called cookshops were among the key venues the people got their food. Often working-class people in cities did not have their own kitchens (a trend that lasted into the nineteenth century); instead, they would get prepared food. While they could take this food home, the historical record implies that sometimes this food was consumed in public. The cookshops are remarkably similar across geography and time despite the great differences in the cuisine they would serve: they would each offer a single dish for the day, usually served in simple earthenware, in a

Adriaen Brouwer, *The Smokers*, c. 1636, oil on wood.

Walter Spencer-Stanhope Tyrwhitt, *Midan El-Adaoui: Cookshop in a Street Bazaar, from Cairo, Jerusalem, and Damascus*, 1912, illustration.

location that was 'a cellar or entryway', according to an eighteenth-century Spanish writer, which may only have had a soil floor, as the fourteenth-century chronicler Al-Maqrizi described.[11] These were not spaces for entertainment, for making food choices, for seeing or being seen – significant functions that the restaurant would come to serve; however, cookshops are clearly an important part of the eating-out scene that continues to this day in the form of food trucks and stalls, petrol station eateries and tiny takeaway or take-out joints.

Coffee houses, teahouses and cafés were significant spaces for socializing and ingesting local news along with beverages. These places were not restaurants in the sense of their service models or selections of food to order; however, they were significant in developing some of the politico-spatial elements that eventually were taken over by restaurants. Whether in Kashgar or Paris, venues that served tea and coffee were often places where the business of society, from gossip to insurrection, thrived.[12] In Venice the Caffè Florian, in continuous operation since it first opened in 1720, still plies its trade to tourists in St Mark's Square. In Uji, Japan, since 1160 Tsuen Tea has served as a hub for important citizens, like shogun Tokugawa Ieyasu (1543–1616), and is now run by the twenty-fourth generation of the Tsuen family.

In Europe in the early modern era, there was a tavern culture that was at least as highly developed

Jan Steen, *Merry Company on a Terrace*, c. 1670, oil on canvas.

Thomas Rowlandson, *Tavern Scene*, 1780–1827, watercolour.

as in ancient Greece. Public houses, taverns and ale houses dotted the landscape and were known more for their drink than for their food. Drinking was what mattered: both men and women drinking together and in public. Wine, cider, beer and ale or (a bit later) brandy and gin were the engines of these establishments. They were mostly explicitly forbidden to serve food or offer sleeping accommodation, or allowed only to serve cheese and bread.

There was also a tavern culture in China. As in ancient Greece, some of these places offered sexual entertainment (courtesans and prostitutes). To mark their offerings, they sported extravagant decorations: 'red and green balustrades, purple and green blinds, crimson and gilt lanterns, flowers and dwarf trees, elegantly-shaped chairs'. More humble taverns were made of bamboo with simple curtains. These taverns also required a certain amount of knowledge: one could go to the private rooms upstairs if one knew the routine. However, not knowing how to navigate these spaces often led not only to being laughed at, but to being charged more.[13]

From Paris to Hangzhou, it was possible to acquire the equivalent of modern takeaway meals. In Paris the typical kinds of foods that one would

Emperor Huizong of Song, *Literary Gathering*, c. 1100–25, ink on silk.

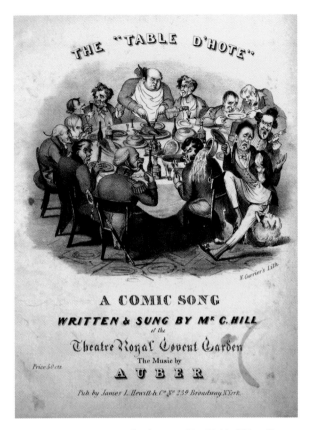

Sheet music cover image for the song 'The "Table D'Hote"', written by Mr C. Hill of the Theatre Royal Covent Garden (1900), illustration.

265 *Stuben* along the Upper Rhine and northern Switzerland.[14] In Paris and England, these kinds of regular, semi-private dining experiences were also common and continue to this day.

There were also completely public dining options. The 'table d'hôte' that popped up across Europe in the fifteenth century served a meal of the day at a set time for a set price. This kind of meal, where there was a fixed eating time and everyone dined together, both preceded and persisted after the invention of the restaurant. Food was placed on the table and the guests could partake of what was brought. If you came late, you probably did not get the choicest of morsels. A fixed price was set for the pleasure of dining at the table, whether you were hungry for a full meal or just wanted a little something on which to nibble. Many a table d'hôte had regular customers, but it was also an institution that made provision for travellers, as long as they could show up on time. In England, 'ordinaries', which usually catered to the working class, were basically tables d'hôte (offering a set time, price and meal). Most of these places were fairly simple, a step up – with seating and slightly more complex meals – from a cookshop. An elaborate example of an English table d'hôte or ordinary is Simpson's Fish Dinner House, which opened in 1714 near the Bank of England, London, and served a meal called a fish ordinary – a dozen oysters, soup, roast partridge, three more first courses, mutton and cheese – for two shillings.

eat for dinner – sausages, soups, poultry – had separate guilds of caterers. These establishments provided food to take away or eat immediately, but only the kind of food that conformed to the caterer's licence. To this day in Spain, patisseries are traditionally open on Sundays and provide rotisserie chickens specifically for after-church meals.

There were also clubs or communal halls. For example, in German areas of Europe, there were *Geschlechter-*, *Zunft-* or *Trinkstuben*. These places often required memberships and included a chart of rules, but in return the members socialized, ate and drank together. Usually, there was an official cook for the organization. At one point, there were

EATING OUT ON THE ROAD

For the past few thousand years, there have been food systems for travellers. On travel routes we see alternative roots of the restaurant from those that appeared in cities. Early travellers, be they officials in ancient China and Japan, traders along Mayan

Walter Bayes, *Rule's, 35 Maiden Lane, wc2, c.* 1940, pen and ink and watercolour on paper.

routes across what is now Mexico and northern Central America, or religious pilgrims from England to Ethiopia, relied on hospitality – not the hospitality industry, but the opening of strangers' homes. In many cultures, these acts were considered important social imperatives and often came with ethical obligations to serve generous amounts of food; yet eating on the road was always uncertain. In China, it was so uncertain that lavish feasts were held for people before they left – to send them off full and, in case of untimely ends, to say goodbye.[15]

Along silk and spice trade routes in North Africa, the Middle East, southern and eastern Europe, and central and south Asia, three structures emerged to serve the caravans of merchants moving goods and wealth between (to name a few) the Chinese, Indian, Arab, Sogdian and Roman regions: caravanserais, khans and inns. Like the cookshops, these places share features across time

Carl Hintner, *Stiftskeller St Peter in Salzburg*, c. 1900, photograph.

and geography – as well as having distinctive, culturally tied aspects. All of these spaces featured entertainment: dramatists, singers, musicians, poets and storytellers. At the same time, these were places for conversation and trade – as well as a moment's respite from the arduous journey across the Steppe. Khans and inns also often offered alcohol and sex services; caravanserais in Muslim areas did not usually offer these amenities. While large caravans would typically bring their own food, these stopping places would promote a vibrant food scene. Some places offered dining options where one was staying, while in other towns teahouses, taverns and cookshops popped up to serve food.

In northern and western Europe, beginning with the rise of imperial Christianity in the early middle ages, political, commercial and pilgrimage routes led to the rise of places to stay and eat. These locations divided into two camps (and are not unlike those stopping places that we see across eastern Asia as well): monasteries that provided lodging and independent inns. One of the oldest and most famous of the monastery eating places is in Salzburg, Austria, at St Peter's Abbey. In 803 Alcuin of York mentioned that Charlemagne dined there, and five hundred years later the Monk of Salzburg lauded the food service in poetry and song. By the 1760s St Peter's Stiftskeller (known as St Peter Stiftskulinarium since 2017) was a dining destination for the well-to-do.

Independent inns followed in the tradition of the caravanserai in offering prepared food and places to eat, talk and be entertained, but the arrival of pilgrims and merchants in these cases were more staggered than those on the Silk Road, where many of the customers would arrive together in caravans. At inns, while one might be able to get food at any time, the choice of what to eat (like in the cookshops) was usually fixed. Whatever had been cooked that day would be what was offered. Inns tended to have a reputation for a certain conviviality of a low sort and for terrible food, as Miguel de Cervantes, for example, reminds us:

> They set the table at the door to the inn, to take advantage of the cooler air, and the host brought him a portion of cod that was badly prepared and cooked even worse, and bread as black and grimy as his armour; but it was a cause for great laughter to see him eat, because, since he was

wearing his helmet and holding up the visor with both hands, he could not put anything in his mouth unless someone placed it there for him, and so one of the ladies performed that task.[16]

Later in *Don Quixote*, at another inn, Sancho asks what is to be had for dinner. The innkeeper tells him he can serve anything Sancho would like. A request for roast chickens is met with the unfortunate news that all of the chickens have been eaten by hawks. The second choice of pullets is also unavailable, all the pullets having been sent to the city. Veal, kid, bacon, eggs . . . all evoke a similar regretful negative response. Sancho finally exclaims:

Gustave Doré, *Don Quixote, Don Fernando, Dorotea, Cardenio, Lucinda, curate and barber eating together at inn*, from *Don Quixote of La Mancha* by Miguel de Cervantes (1880 edn), engraving.

'My God . . . why don't you just get down to
it and tell what you've really got, and stop all
this scurrying around.'
The innkeeper said:
'What I've really and truly got are some cow's
feet that look like calves' hooves, or a couple
of calves' hooves that look like cow's feet,
and they've been cooked up with chickpeas,
onions and bacon, and they just sit there,
saying 'Eat me! Eat me!'[17]

The food at these places varied as widely as
in restaurants today. In some it was terrible –
cheese 'full of mould and worms', maggoty meat –
and in others it was wonderful, including delicious
trout, strawberries, roast veal, broccoli and dessert
that confirmed 'already favourable' impressions.[18]
The food was often local – not simply because
people expected sausages in Bavaria and salmon
in Scotland, but because much of food procurement
was still a local activity. Spices might come from
abroad, but not much else. Most places had a
soup, three courses and dessert; however, fine
places might have up to fifty dishes across six
courses. The company and decor also varied,
from the classic large table with shared bowls
and bread used as plates, to more private parlours
with individual tableware and, for the finest
guests, silver.

THE FIRST RESTAURANTS

The places we have looked at thus far, from taverns
to tables d'hôte, from convivia and caravanserais
to cafés, are not quite restaurants as we know them
today. Restaurants in their fullest version, and in
the way we experience them now, rely on service
and choices. These features – and the restaurant
as an institution – took more than a millennium

to emerge from those first taverns, cookshops and
inns. It would take the growth of cities at the crossroads of a large-enough mercantilist economy that
hosted business travellers to warrant a fully formed
restaurant culture. That did not happen in the West,
but rather the first restaurants opened during the
Song Dynasty, around 1100 CE, in Chinese cities,
seven hundred years earlier than the emergence
of restaurants in Paris.

Why did restaurants start here? Perhaps the
most obvious answer is size: Kaifeng in the north
and Hangzhou in the south were cities that by
the end of the Song Dynasty exceeded 1 million
inhabitants each. Around the same time, Paris had
only reached the 300,000 mark while Milan had
200,000 inhabitants, Granada 150,000 and London
just about 100,000 souls. Second, the urban Chinese
population had money in small denominations.
Third, these enormous cities were massive centres
of trade that brought together people from numerous cultures. The notion that foods from other
places would be made available to travellers and to
people from those regions who made the city their
home became another impetus: the regional cuisine
that characterizes the restaurant culture in the
twenty-first century – 'authentic' foods from various parts of the world – was a fully formed part of
these two metropolises of Kaifeng and Hangzhou.
A fourth reason may be political: the loosening in
China of social orders that led to the emergence
of a society governed by a central bureaucracy of
scholar-officials rather than a hereditary aristocracy.
This group of people would have had power and
money, but may not have had the means, space
or desire to entertain in their homes. Moreover,
because one could move through the ranks by
manoeuvring politically, eating at restaurants
provided desired strategic spaces and occasions
to meet.[19]

The first recorded instances of restaurants are in Kaifeng, the capital of the Song Dynasty until 1127. These first writings and images of restaurants in this thriving city imply that they arrived into a scene already thick with the taverns, cookshops and stalls we discussed above. The restaurants were overwhelmingly speciality restaurants tied to regional cuisines. This is not surprising, since the city was a water-route crossroads, so in addition to bringing foodstuffs and other materials to market in the city, it also brought people, particularly merchants and bureaucrats. These travellers and transplants formed formal regional associations, and, after that, regional restaurants began to emerge. Song texts name southern, northern and Sichuan cooking. Eateries were created particularly to serve travellers from the south, who had a difficult time adapting to the tastes of northern food.[20]

Zhang Zeduan, *Qingming Scroll* detail, *c.* 1186, monochrome ink on silk.

The food scene in these cities was highly varied. Like today, one could eat at a food stall, a less formal or more formal restaurant, large or small. These various places also served a range of food: soups, stews, meats, vegetarian dishes, pasta, buns or wild game. They were often located in densely populated parts of the city. For example, one in Kaifeng known as Horse Guild Avenue, adjacent to the animal markets, was 'so lively that it was said that the smoke and heat of its lamps drove mosquitoes and black flies away'. In 1126 Meng Yuanlao describes this locale and its eateries in his memoir *Dongjing meng Hua*, or *The Eastern Capital: A Dream of Splendor*:

> North, along Horse Guild Street and outside of Old Fengqiu Gate, on the Angled Road of the Zoroastrian Temple lies the Prefect-north Pleasure District . . . In every single place, the gates are squeezed up against each other, each with its own tea wards, wineshops, stages, and food and drink.

> Normally, the small business households of the marketplace simply purchase [prepared] food and drink at food stores; they do not cook at home. For northern food, there are the Shi Feng style dried meat cubes made of various stewed items, of the House of Duan and the House of Li the Fourth, both found in front of Alum Tower; for southern food, the House of Jin at Temple Bridge and the House of Zhou at Ninebends are acknowledged to be the finest. The night markets close after the third watch only to reopen at the fifth. The more boisterous places stay open until dawn. Normally, even night markets in outlying, quiet places have such items as baked sesame buns stuffed with either sour bean filling or pork tenderloin, mixed vegetable buns, the

flesh of the badger and wild fox, stews of fruit-wings, blood sausages, and fragrant candied fruit. Night markets are held even in the worst snowstorms and on the darkest rainy days of the winter: found there are such items as meat strips in ginger and fermented bean paste, minced tripe with blood pasta, crystal fish paste, fried fresh liver, clams, crabs, walnuts, malt-sugar wheat gluten from Zezhou, crosshatch beans, goose pears, pomegranates, Japanese quince, Chinese quince, steamed glutinous rice balls, and soup made from salted fermented bean curd (*miso*). Only after the third watch do tea-sellers appear bearing their pots, seeking to satisfy those people of the capital, privately employed and government workers, who get off late and are able to go home only deep in the night.[21]

The clientele and offerings of eateries often matched their locales. For example, near one of the temples, among clothing and book shops, was a vegetarian teahouse-style restaurant. In an area with many brothels were also many southern restaurants.[22] Stephen H. West, a sinologist, speculates that 'while there is little information on the actual nature of the relationship between these regional restaurants and brothels, it seems predictable to find them together in parts of the city geared toward providing entertainment'.[23] Restaurants were often in entertainment districts, and many eating establishments included entertainment ranging from singing waiters to staged productions.

Many of these restaurants were quite large. West records one dumpling place that had more than fifty ovens, with four to five workers at each prep station, mixing, shaping and working the ovens. In 1147 Meng Yuanlao described these large restaurants:

Generally the largest restaurants were called 'partial-tea food.' They served such things as head stew, stalactite stew, pressed meat, baked sesame buns, lamb kid, large and small bones, kidneys in reduced sauce, brass-skin noodles, broad-cut noodles with ginger, twice-cooked noodles, cold noodles, chess piece pastas, and baked flour products. If one were to make it a 'full-tea' meal, then one added a head stew of pickled vegetables.

· · ·

In addition, calabash stew shops erected a scaffolding of heavy lintels and flowered posts that were bound together like 'mountain platforms' (*shanpeng*). On top of these they hung out sides of pork and mutton, twenty or thirty to the span. Just inside, the door fronts and shutters were decorated with vermillion and green; these were called 'gates of pleasure' (*huanmen*).

Each of these restaurants had a courtyard with eastern and western corridors, which were designated as seating compartments. When the guests sat down, a single person holding chopsticks and paper (*zhuzhi*) then asked all of the seated guests [for their order]. People of the capital were extravagant and unrestrained, and they would demand a hundred different things – some hot, some cold, some warm, some room temperature, some icy cold, as well as toppings of both lean and fat meats. Each person demanded something different. The waiter took their orders, then stood in line in front of the kitchen and, when his turn came, sang out his orders to those in the kitchen. Those who were in charge of the kitchen were called 'pot masters' (*dangtou*) or were called 'controllers of the preparation tables' (*zhuoan*). This came to an end in a matter of moments and the waiter – his left hand supporting three dishes and his right arm stacked from hand to shoulder with some twenty dishes, one on top of the other – distributed them in the exact order in which they had been ordered. Not the slightest error was allowed. Even the slightest mistake was reported by the guests to the head of the restaurant who would then curse the waiter, or dock his salary, or, in extreme cases, drive him from the place.[24]

In addition to the abundance of food, perhaps what is most striking in this description is the well-trained waiters. The image of these waiters singing their orders and balancing their many dishes seems modern, considering it is over a thousand years old.

The other stories of restaurants we have from this early period are from Hangzhou. The Song capital moved from Kaifeng to Hangzhou (known then as Lin'an) in 1132. Marco Polo arrived there just as the Mongol conquest was completed around 1275. He called the city Quinsai, which is a Persian variation on the Chinese word for 'capital'. Jacques Gernet, in his book *Daily Life in China on the Eve of the Mongol Invasion*, relies on the famous Italian visitor, who describes Hangzhou as 'the greatest city which may be found in the world . . . where so many pleasures may be found that one fancies himself to be in Paradise'.[25] Within the city were similar centres to those in the previous capital of Kaifeng, only with goods from further abroad: the Middle East and Southeast Asia.

In addition to banquet supply stores called 'tea and wine kitchens', which were basically caterers who took care of everything from food and wine to dishes and decor, there were also grand restaurants. (In France, we see a similar movement from caterers, called *traiteurs*, to restaurateurs). Marco Polo describes these places:

In the middle of the Lake, there are two Islands, on each of which stands a palatial edifice with an incredibly large number of rooms and separate pavilions. And when anyone desired to hold a marriage feast, or to give a big banquet, it used to be done at one of these palaces. And everything would be found there ready to order, such as dishes, napkins and tablecloths and whatever else was needful. These furnishings were acquired and maintained at common expense by the citizens in these palaces constructed by them for this purpose. Sometimes there would be at these palaces a hundred different parties; some holding a banquet, others celebrating a wedding; and yet all would find good accommodation in the different apartments and pavilions, and that in so well ordered a manner that one party was never in the way of another.[26]

Like in Kaifeng, there were also restaurants and teahouses, lavishly decorated 'with displays of flowers, dwarf evergreens, and works by celebrated painters and calligraphers to tempt the passers-by'; food was served on fine porcelain and lacquerware, and there was musical entertainment (the girls here sang, rather than played the flute as their Greek counterparts did).[27] In the circa 1300 Song compilation texts such as the *Meng Liang Lu*, there began to be, in addition to descriptions of the restaurants themselves, stories about people who did not know how to order properly in a restaurant:

After the order of seating hierarchy is settled, the wine sellers first lay out the 'viewing dishes' and ask how much [wine] is going to be purchased; afterward [waiters] exchange the [viewing dishes] for real dishes. There are some coarser folk who, unaware of proper practice, immediately set to with their chopsticks. They become the objects of scornful laughter.[28]

This notion of the country bumpkin, who strays into a culture for which he is not prepared, is a refrain that we will encounter on many occasions, from the inns of Europe that precede the restaurant, to the early nineteenth century, as Parisians learned how to behave through the use of travel guides and restaurant guides. Chinese guides of the eighteenth century also performed the same function for the new generation who frequented restaurants.

Despite the fact that the Chinese restaurant was fully formed almost a millennium ago, it took another seven hundred years to emerge in Europe. A great deal of food culture, from noodles to porcelain dishes, moved between Europe and Asia during the first thousand years of the Common Era; however, restaurants, with their waiters, menus, expansive food options, incredible decor and entertainment, did not migrate. Instead, European restaurants emerged suddenly. Moreover, they emerged, like Chinese restaurants, onto a scene rich with ways to procure food and to eat together in public, with inns and taverns, with clubs and teahouses, and yet largely devoid of menus, waiters, privacy or dining-out propriety.

2

THE RESTAURATEUR AND YOU: THE PRIVATE AND THE PUBLIC IN THE EARLY FRENCH RESTAURANTS

It is a Friday night, and you decide that you want to go out to eat. You could have planned ahead and made a reservation, but you didn't. Instead, you show up at a place you have never been before. A host shows you to your own table; a waiter, assigned to you, gives you a menu. You decide on a creamy pasta dish while your partner chooses a salad. Your food is prepared, maybe not from scratch, but just for you, plated just for you and brought to you. After enjoying (or not enjoying) your meal, the waiter brings you a bill, based on what you and your partner ordered and the price on the menu.

You probably do not reflect on these expectations when you eat in a restaurant. They are the characteristics that have defined the institution in China and been passed down and spread across the globe since the 1760s, when it debuted in Paris. Since that point, a restaurant has been defined as a place where you eat when you want to eat from a varied menu, within the limits of the opening hours of the establishment. A restaurant, at least initially, is a place where you are served by a waiter. And a restaurant is a place where you sit with the people with whom you came and where you pay after you have finished from a bill that includes no surprises. One of the great innovations of the restaurant is that it is about you, the person dining – a framing that restaurateurs and food writers have understood, shaped and proclaimed from the first soup-serving instances of this new way to eat out.

FINE AND DELICATE MEALS

> 'Roze, rue Saint Honoré, Hôtel d'Aligre, the first Restaurateur, offers fine and delicate meals for 3–6 livres per head, in addition to the items expected of a restaurateur.'
> – *Almanach*, 1769[1]

In the beginning, the restaurant was not a place, but a food: a restorative broth. Recipes for these broths appear in eighteenth-century cookbooks and medical texts, most outrageously proposing stewing meat and bones with jewels and gold, but more commonly suggesting the broths be a long-cooked, very condensed consommé.

In the 1760s an enterprising Frenchman opened the first dining establishment serving 'restaurants', that is, broth, to diners individually, at any time. There is debate around who this first restaurateur was: for two centuries, a man with the moniker Boulanger was credited with the invention; however, in the early 2000s, evidence of a different first restaurateur – Mathurin Roze de Chantoiseau – arose. The stories of the two men – which do not vary that greatly – reveal the nature of these new businesses.

The story of Boulanger – told to English-reading audiences first in 1803 by the journalist Francis William Blagdon in *Paris As It Was and As It Is* – is one of economic and political expediency: 'in 1765, one BOULANGER conceived the idea of *restoring* the exhausted animal functions of the debilitated Parisians by rich soups of various denominations.' Blagdon says this man did not have a licence to be a caterer or *traiteur*, so he set up an expensive soup shop whose 'articles were served up without a cloth, on little marble tables', with surcharge for the nice experience. 'Novelty, fashion, and, above all, dearness, brought them into vogue.'[2]

While the details of this story – the name of the restaurateur, the unlicensed food preparation – are not historically verifiable, the tale itself does describe key aspects of the first restaurants: consommé shops with great decor, higher prices and a well-heeled clientele.

The empirically grounded version of this story – researched and told by historian Rebecca Spang – highlights similar aspects. Mathurin Roze de Chantoiseau was, similarly, neither a chef nor an experienced *traiteur*, but an entrepreneur: he ran a journal, and he engaged in political reform. It is in his 1765 *Almanach* that he first lists himself as a restaurateur. The business he created served 'exclusively those foods that either maintain or

re-establish health'.[3] The first restaurants presented themselves as *maisons de santé* (health houses). Advertisements in the 1770s – from printed notices in newspapers to the signs that hung above restaurant doors – promised aid for the weak or weary and relied on discourses, from Latin slogans to health-condition-specific menus, to develop a scientific and medical rationale for their food businesses.

However, these were not clinics: they were more like spas – while health was important, beauty, image and the fashionability of certain ailments were at the centre of these claims. These new businesses focused on providing restorative cures to individuals. The clientele was more wealthy than those who had frequented taverns, and included women, whose constitutions were often deemed delicate, as well as men who were sensitive – which was praise at the time, connoting that they were aware, intellectually engaged and refined.

Since the goal was restoration, the space was designed with the idea that the experience was as central as the food: people sat at tables alone; dining was available at any time; the rooms were beautifully decorated; the china was delicate and the service was individual and discreet. While this version of the restaurant only lasted a decade or so before it expanded into the breadth of places we now think of as restaurants, the ethos it developed – of hospitality as individualized and aesthetic – continues to shape restaurants today. Even fast-food chains that proclaim to make food 'your way' and invest in the latest trends in fonts and finishes hew to this model, which stands in contrast to the communal or utilitarian experiences that had typified dining out since its inception.

The restaurant expanded from these elegant consommé purveyors along two paths. Some of the original restaurants began expanding their menus – adding light fare like fruit, cheese or simple chicken

Moonik, *Hôtel d'Aligre or Hôtel de Beauharnais located at 15 rue de l'Université Paris 7th distinct in France*, 2011, photograph.

dishes. Other establishments, that had been *traiteur-caterers*, for example, began picking up elements of the restaurant, such as replacing communal tables with individual ones and offering à la carte menus and food at any time.

By the late 1780s we see the rise of the grand restaurants in Paris that became the archetypal model of what a restaurant is. Between 1789 and 1793 the first grand restaurants of Paris – Trois Frères, La Grande Tavene de Londres, Boeuf à la mode, Cadran bleu, Méot and Robert – opened their doors; they teemed with a sparkling array of silver, mirrors and chefs. The transformation of inns, taverns and cafés into restaurants led most clearly to the diverse restaurant scene we know today. This transformation was shaped as much by changing working

and living arrangements as ideas about leisure and beauty. However, it was the grand restaurants – their popularity and glamour – that in part account for the expansion of restaurants across the world.

PALAIS-ROYAL AND DINING PALACES

It is not unusual to find novelists, travel writers and others describing the early restaurants of Paris as palaces. Large mirrors, fine china, novel lighting and luxe furnishings typified these palatial venues. In a little over a decade, the restaurant had moved from a spa-eatery to a dining spectacle. The area where this was most apparent was the Palais-Royal, an entertainment district that became filled with early restaurants.

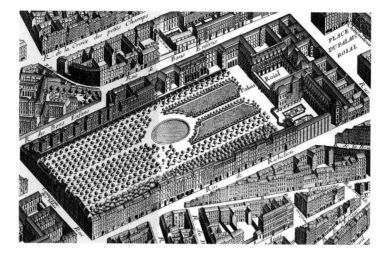

Claude Lucas after Louis Bretez, *View of the Palais-Royal as depicted on the Turgot map of Paris*, 1739, ink on paper.

The Palais-Royal, located near the Louvre, was built in 1633 as a palace for Cardinal Richelieu and was originally called the Palais-Cardinal; after his death in 1642 it became the property of the king of France – and stayed in royal hands for 150 years. In the 1780s it underwent a transformation from a private palace with a public theatre to a public arcade with more entertainment venues, drinking and dining establishments, and gardens open to all for strolling. During this time, it also became the heart of Paris's burgeoning restaurant scene.

La Grande Taverne de Londres, which opened in 1782 in the Palais-Royal, was, in the words of the food writer Jean Anthelme Brillat-Savarin, 'the first to combine the four essentials of an elegant room, smart waiters, a choice cellar, and superior cooking.'[4] Blagdon encapsulates the interiors of this quintessential luxurious French restaurant:

On the first floor of a large hotel, formerly occupied, perhaps, by a farmer-general, you may enter a suite of apartments, decorated with arabesques, and mirrors of large dimensions, in a style no less elegant than splendid, where tables are completely arranged for large or small parties. In winter, these rooms are warmed by ornamental stoves, and lighted by quinquets, a species of Argand's lamps. They are capable of accommodating from two hundred and fifty to three hundred persons, and, at this time of the year, the average number that dine here daily is about two hundred; in summer, it is considerably decreased by the attractions of the country, and the parties of pleasure made, in consequence, to the environs of the capital.[5]

The interior of the restaurant was not unusual; nor were its 318 dishes compared to other restaurants. However, the man who ran La Grande Taverne de Londres made it stand out. The restaurant was founded and operated by Antoine Beauvilliers, who was previously a royal chef and subsequently wrote one of the cookbooks that established the French national cuisine. As the former pastry chef to the brother of the king, Beauvilliers is a classic example of a restaurateur who brought to the bourgeois table the style and bearing that previously only the aristocracy had enjoyed. In fact, after the Revolution, he was almost executed for his courtly ties – however, his fine, public hospitality as a restaurateur saved him (or at least the well-connected new guard who ate at his restaurant wanted to keep his meats on the table rather than see his head on the chopping block). As a chef, he transformed French dining, bringing sauces, stuffing and a range of techniques, heretofore only available to nobility, to the new upper class, which included merchants, entrepreneurs, artist-intellectuals and American travellers. Dressed in uniform, including a royally bestowed sword, Beauvilliers would move around his restaurant chatting up the guests in multiple languages, remembering what they liked, recommending delicacies and wines, endearing himself to customers and padding their bills.

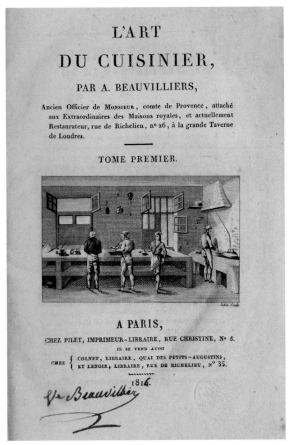

Title page from *L'Art du cuisinier* by Antoine Beauvilliers (1754–1817), engraved by Jubin, 1814.

Near the Palais-Royal, three years after Beauvilliers set up shop, a restaurant with a quite different lineage and menu appeared on the scene: Les Trois Frères Provençaux. The three brothers of the restaurant's name were not brothers at all, and neither did they come from Provence. Rather, they were from Marseilles and had married three sisters. But they brought to Paris the splendid *brandade de morue*, a salt cod dish from Provence. Initially, the restaurant was modest in its decor, without white tablecloths and with very little silver. However, by the turn of the nineteenth century, the restaurant was the first stop in Paris for many foreigners on the grand tour, especially for Americans, who admired its furnishings as much as its food and who perhaps felt it easier to experience France in a way that seemed to demand less classical training than visits to historic sites and museums. One of those travellers, Caroline Mathilda Stansbury Kirkland, described the restaurant in the following way:

> At the Trois Frères Provençaux, for instance, which is one of the best, you are seated at a table covered with damask fine enough for royalty, with napkins to match, all of an extreme purity and whiteness. You have silver forks and spoons to as many plates as you can contrive to use in succession; your food is all served in silver dishes, quite hot, and the cuisine is of the greatest delicacy, as well as variety. All about you are immense mirrors, statuary, flowers; fruits in elegant baskets of china or molu, and whatever luxury can devise to enhance the pleasure of dining.[6]

This one establishment so embodied the notion of the French restaurant that it was imported to the first World's Fair in the United States, the Centennial Exposition in Philadelphia of 1876. However, in Paris it competed with a litany of fine-dining

Eugene Lami, *Interior of Les Trois Frères Provencaux restaurant with Its Restoration Era Decor, from Winter in Paris, France*, 1842, engraving.

establishments as well as cafés and tables d'hôte newly turned into restaurants. To navigate (and promote) this pristine pastime and fashion, a new kind of writing emerged.

'A GUIDE TO THE WAYS OF EATING VERY WELL'

Aiding and abetting the development of the restaurant as the hallmark of French culture – that could be visited with delight and exported abroad – was the emergence of a nascent publicity industry that would help cement the notion of what counted as a classic example of the institution. What we now call food writing – articles, essays and books about chefs, foods and eating – came into being

alongside restaurants (and chefs and modern haute cuisine). This food writing in late eighteenth- and early nineteenth-century France took two courses: there was the rise of professional writing about food, and there was a flood of personal writing about food, especially in letters (the blogging and Instagramming of its day). Guidebooks, listings and reviews of restaurants abounded. While different modes of gastronomic writing emerged, they shared the feature of usually being one-part observation and one-part spectacle – which leads to fascinating, sometimes conflicting descriptions of the splendours of Paris's food scene.

Many of the vivid images we have of the restaurant world come from the man who birthed journalistic food writing (and did much to shape and ensconce the genre of the review): Alexandre-Balthazar-Laurent Grimod de La Reynière. While Roze's *Almanach* catalogued, described and advertised restaurants, it was Grimod who developed the world of gastronomy – a form of writing, critique and culinary interest from the eater's perspective (that may remind us of the discourses around fish at the symposia in ancient Greece). In 1803 Grimod first published the *Almanach des gourmands*, subtitled 'A Guide to the Ways of Eating Very Well'.[7] His *Almanach* included reviews of products based

on tasting contests he conducted with a group of unnamed jurors. He would also publish reviews of restaurants. His writing is a mix of sarcasm, overstatement and insightful critique. Many of his claims about ways of eating and what it means to eat were adopted by later famous gastronomes like Brillat-Savarin (who seems to have almost plagiarized Grimod's work, though he was a more eloquent and less acerbic writer).

Grimod, like Beauvilliers, moved between the modes of eating of the *ancien régime* and the new world of food. Grimod was a child of aristocrats,

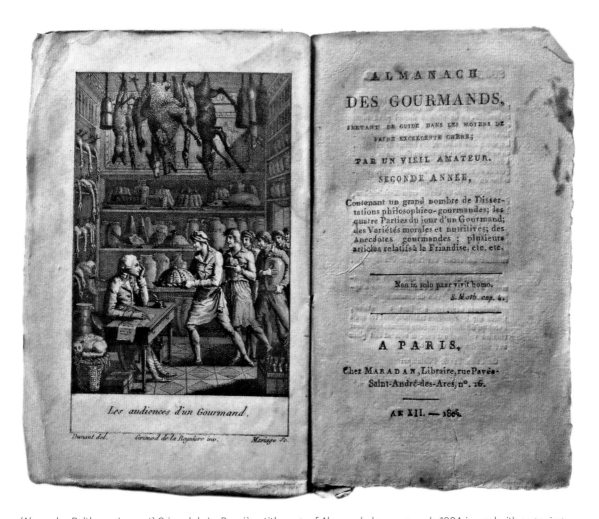

(Alexandre-Balthazar-Laurent) Grimod de La Reynière, title page of *Almanach des gourmands*, 1804, journal with engravings.

So-called funerary feast, organized by Alexandre-Balthasar-Laurent Grimod de la Reynière (1758–1837).

but had a chequered upbringing, in part due to being born with webbed hands. In his youth, a story developed that pigs had eaten his hands, and as a child, he was christened as the god-child of poor farmers. Grimod seems to have responded to this – and to being shuttled around to various schools and homes – as a launching point for an unconventional career that often simultaneously mocked and explored how elitism functioned. As a young man, he used his parents' home to stage large, spectacular dinners that included dressing up pigs and having them seated at the table; that introduced his family as farmers and grocers; and that included large, peasant audiences who paid to watch the 22 notable guests eat. In response to these antics, his parents had him arrested. His arrest led him to a monastery, where he was taught about food and where he had gloves with mechanical fingers made so that he could write. In the tumultuous years of revolutionary and post-revolutionary France, Grimod used his position as an insider-outsider to develop a network and reputation for guiding people in new ways of eating.

Grimod developed the criteria for what constituted a great restaurant: it had to be able to fulfil one's fantasy and desire. He helped to cement in the minds of his readers the restaurant as a place apart, a place with its own rules, where learning to read the menu and to order the right foods and wines developed into an act of taste that took effort to perform correctly. His first *Almanach*s took readers on a tour of Paris's dining establishments and food purveyors. Later editions abandoned this promenade style and organized the businesses by type. The texts were how-to guides for new experiences, such as ordering food, eating dishes in the correct order, using utensils properly and tasting focused on the chief aspects of a dish (a kind of instruction not unlike that given when learning to taste wine). They were

also guidebooks, which rated foods and places. The reviews were submitted to a panel of judges Grimod organized called tasting juries. His initial group spawned a number of other gastronomic societies, whose legacy we can still see in organizations like the Diners Club World's Fifty Best Restaurants Academy. Like restaurant critics of today (think the fearsome critic in Pixar's 2007 film *Ratatouille*), Grimod was known as much for his bite as his bites. After Beauvilliers refused to submit to one of his judgings, he stopped including the restaurant in his guide, despite the fact that it was one of the most renowned restaurants in Paris. Grimod's models set the stage for a variety of food writing to emerge over the next century, from tomes on the culinary arts to gastronomic treatises, food journalism (written by authors such as Charles Dickens) and reviews.

LIGHTS, TABLES AND OTHER INNOVATIONS

The late eighteenth and early nineteenth centuries were an age of advanced automata and inventor worship, and a time when society was becoming more interested in how technologies could serve people. This obsession with innovation drove many of the elements that made restaurants emerge and thrive, from the expansion of cities and the Industrial Revolution to the development of delicate sauces and the printing of menus. Gas lighting, as much as liberty and entrepreneurialism, built the restaurant. In part, advances in lighting built the modern city and made the evening a place for all kinds of activity. Oil lamps and candles – alongside expanses of mirrors – illuminated the first restaurants. At the *fin de siècle*, William Walton described the Parisian restaurant scene by focusing on these lights:

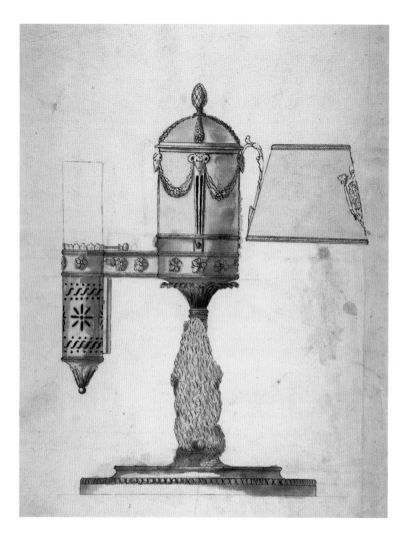

Unknown artist,
*Argand Lamp
with Shade,*
c. 1800–1900,
pen and wash.

[Paris] swarms with cafés, – that of the Caveau, of the Grotte Flamande, of Foi, the Café Italien, the Café Polonois, of Beaujolais, and the Café Mécanique, and nearly all these cafés are very nicely lit in the evenings by the lamps a la Quinquet, which give a very bright light, but which require a great deal of care on the part of the attendants.[8]

Set onto the Parisian and world stage at the same time as the restaurant – 1765 – the Quinquet lamp transformed lighting. Until this point, lamps were often dim or excessively smoky. The Quinquet lamps were the result of significant improvements by Aimé Argand, who developed a new style of wicks and chimneys, and Quinquet, who developed the curved chimney as well as a Parisian market for these new lamps. Now lamps could burn brightly, illuminating all kinds of places – including cafés and the nascent restaurant. Henry Smith Williams's *The Wonders of Science in Modern Life* (1912) described the lamp in a section titled 'The Banishment of the Night'. While this title might seem hyperbolic, the lamp did transform Parisian nightlife. By 1820 gas lighting was being used across Paris, and by 1900 there were 50,000 gas and electric street lights across the city. Because the streets became safer and public interiors became more pleasant, especially in the trendy new restaurants and the cutting-edge cafés, going out for dinner transformed from an act of obligation or merrymaking to an avocation. Moreover, the lighting allowed restaurants to be places where people could see and be seen.

Once in these well-lit spaces, patrons were seated at individual tables, which were perhaps the most basic, consequential and quickly acculturated innovation of the restaurant. Even with fine dining at the same time, the idea of the banquet – with many people around a large table – would have been the norm. The individual table was central to descriptions of eighteenth-century French eating establishments: the tiny marble tables of chic cafés, the white tablecloths of grand restaurants. However, perhaps no tables were more commented upon than the tables at the Café Mécanique.

This café, which opened in 1786, was in the Palais-Royal. Set among theatres, casinos and budding restaurants, the Café Mécanique was a piece of theatre in and of itself. Instead of servers bringing coffee to your table, the tables were mechanized. The idea of a mechanized table – a predecessor of vending machines and automat eateries – sparked the imagination of many ladies in Paris, Thomas Jefferson and a line of writers into the twentieth century. People describe the mechanical table in subtly different ways. Blagdon, in his *Paris As It Is and As It Was*, wrote that,

> Before the revolution, I remember, in the *ci-devant Palais Royal*, a coffeehouse called *Le café mécanique*. The mechanical contrivance, whence it derived its name, was of the most simple nature. The tables stood on hollow cylinders,

the tops of which, resembling a salver with its border, were level with the plane of the table, but connected with the kitchen underneath. In the bar sat a fine, showy lady, who repeated your order to the attendants below, by means of a speaking-trumpet. Presently the superficial part of the salver descended through the cylinder, and reascending immediately, the article called for made its appearance.[9]

While this seems a fairly accurate representation, the descriptions of other writers become subsequently more fantastical, reaching their peak in this version from Marjorie Coryn's 1945 novel *The Marriage of Josephine* (Josephine Napoleon, in case you were wondering):

> At the Café Mécanique one could, by dropping one's coin into a slot, obtain little meat pies or slices of pate, already neatly wrapped in paper . . . Here he changed two hundred franc assignats for metal discs the size of silver franc pieces. He examined the cupboard-like compartments that lined the room, each with a notice on the door describing the nature and price of the contents. Many of them were empty, bread for sandwiches being unobtainable. The little meat pies were the best value for one's money, though apt to become a bit monotonous in the end. He dropped his coin into the slot he had chosen. There was a whirr of mechanism, and the cupboard disgorged two little paper-wrapped packages into the basket hung beneath to catch them. He picked them up and dropped them into his Pocket.[10]

Coryn's wildly inaccurate, almost steampunk description of the nineteenth-century café draws on the machinations of mass-industrial twentieth-century automats rather than the science of the Enlightenment.

The most detailed, accurate English description of the Café Mécanique comes from Shelby Thomas McCloy in his book *French Inventions of the Eighteenth Century*. After tracing the lineage of the restaurant, from the inventor Monsieur Belleville to Monsieur Tantes, the entrepreneur who made the Café Mécanique famous, McCloy describes the scene:

> Little frequented during the summer, it was crowded in winter by numbers of both sexes and all classes, who flocked there for their evening diversion. Unfortunately the room was small and could not accommodate all who came. In common with other cafés of the period it carried a stock of current newspapers, and mention is made that one had to arrive early in the evening to be certain of reading them. On Sundays, on account of the crowds, the papers were locked up.
>
> In this Café were a number of marble tables, each resting on two hollow columns or supports that communicated with the cellar where the food was served. To obtain service, a customer would pull a chain on one of the table legs or cylinders, causing a bell in the basement to ring. Then a valve would open on the table and the patron would give his order, evidently by speaking tube. The order would then be filled by a dumb-waiter which rose by the column. The proprietress (*limonadière*) was at the cashier's desk on the main floor and was able at any time to communicate by a speaking tube with the servants in the cellar. The service appears to have been largely in drinks, even as it is in French cafés today.[11]

What might be most interesting about this description is that the café became so crowded the proprietors had to lock up the newspapers. Others concur that it was so busy that people waited outside.

The café was a spectacle of French invention. It also inspired engineers from beyond France. The British inventor James Smithson (founding donor of the Smithsonian Institution in Washington, DC) recounted the café in his descriptions of the eighteenth-century scientific revolution. Thomas Webster's *An Encyclopædia of Domestic Economy* (1815) includes a section about the mechanisms of the Café Mécanique, saying that its methods are 'now frequently used at coffee-houses and taverns in London' and 'might be adopted with advantage in some private houses'.[12] According to Thomas Jefferson's biographers, Monticello was one of those private houses. After a visit to Paris, Jefferson was inspired by the café to build his own dumb-waiter system. In addition to being a delight and a novelty, the mechanism captured the kind of labour-saving aspiration that drove much of this moment of invention.

Perhaps one of the simplest references to the café comes from the author Julian Barnes:

> I walked to the Palais Royal feeling impressed with myself . . . It felt as if everything was coming together, all at one. The past was all around; I was the present; art was here, and history, and now the promise of something much like love or sex. Over there in that corner was where Molière worked; across there, Cocteau, then Colette; there Blucher lost six million at roulette and for the rest of his life flew into a rage when the name of Paris was mentioned; there the first *café mécanique* was opened; and there, over there, at a little cutler's in the Galerie de Valois,

Charlotte Corday bought the knife with which she killed Marat.[13]

'There the first *café mécanique* was opened.' This simple sentence, set in a litany of Parisian experiences, reflects the way that this particular place, with its gimmicks and grand crowds, continues to capture the imagination.

SEEING, SPECTACLE AND SECRECY IN EARLY RESTAURANTS

The spectacle of the Café Mécanique as McCloy and others describe it was not only the automation, but the attendant crowd. Seeing and being seen were at the heart of restaurant dining in late eighteenth- and early nineteenth-century Paris. In a restaurant, a young woman could discreetly order a meal that fit her tastes and eat it without interacting with strangers. At the same time, she could examine the world around her and often her own image, and people could see her. Seeing without interaction comes up in many descriptions and illustrations of the time. The most forlorn version of this is in images of people standing outside restaurants, looking in. Auguste Luchet describes such people as

> Sometimes rushing, sometimes slow, they stop from time to time, pausing beside vents exhaling balsamic odors from the justly famous kitchens of Véfours and Vérys . . . they stare at the symmetrical arrangements of foie-gras pâtés and galantines, lobsters, partridges, pheasants, and who knows what else . . . like a cat who wants something on the other side of the window.[14]

For the diners themselves, looking is part of the experience. Blagdon's description at Beauvilliers' Grande Taverne de Londres is a standard one:

'We will take our seats in this corner, whence, without laying down our knife and fork, we can enjoy a full view of the company as they enter.' For women, the experience was often even more exciting, as the American traveller Caroline Kirkland describes:

> Dining at a restaurant is one of the novelties of the lady-traveller in Paris. Taking a sandwich or a plate of oysters at Thompson and Weller's is a considerable feat, and some of our ladies at home roll up their eyes at the boldness which can venture thus far. But to sit down in a public room, to a regular dinner of an hour's length or more, is quite another affair, and it really requires some practice before one can refrain from casting sly glances around during the process, to see whether anybody is looking. But these restaurant dinners are very pleasant things when you are once used to them . . . withal, though there may be twenty other parties dining at as many tables within sight, yet nobody looks at you, or seems to know that you are there. One waiter takes you under his especial care, and the different courses are served with the precision of clock-work, everything being as neat and elegant as possible. One feels at first as if it was a transgression; but after a while this subsides into a feeling of agreeable abandon, unalloyed by any sense of naughtiness; and a dinner at a restaurant becomes one of the natural events of a Paris day.[15]

At the same time that early European restaurants emphasized visibility and spectacle, they also created and provided even more private spaces in the form of *cabinets particuliers*. These were private rooms, often on the upper floor of a restaurant, that were decorated and serviced like the tables in the larger dining room, but these rooms had a door.

Cabinet particulier (private room) at a grand restaurant, published in *La Semaine des Familles* (1863–4), printed etching.

The room often included lounging furniture, like a divan, as well as a table. The waiter would generally knock before entering. These rooms were used for a variety of reasons – politics, business, romantic affairs – and offered diners the liberty to speak and act freely. Guy de Maupassant's *Bel Ami* has a *cabinet particulier* scene that demonstrates how these rooms allowed people to speak, eat and act with greater abandon:

He was ushered up to the second story, and into a small private dining-room hung with red and white, its single window opening into the boulevard. A square table, laid for four, displaying its white cloth, so shining that it seemed to be varnished, and the glasses and the silver glittered brightly in the light of the twelve candles of two tall candelabra. Without was a broad patch of light green, due to the leaves of a tree lit up by the bright light from the dining-rooms.

Duroy sat down in a low armchair, upholstered in red to match the hangings on the walls. The worn springs yielding beneath him caused him to feel as though sinking into a hole. He heard throughout the huge house a confused murmur, the murmur of a large restaurant, made up of the clattering of glass and silver, the hurried steps of the waiters, deadened by the carpets in the passages, and the opening of doors letting out the sound of voices from the numerous private rooms in which people were dining.

. . .

They sat down to table, and the waiter having handed the wine card to Forestier, Madame de Marelle exclaimed: 'Give these gentlemen whatever they like, but for us iced champagne, the best, sweet champagne, mind – nothing else.' And the man having withdrawn, she added with an excited laugh: 'I am going to get tipsy this evening; we will have a spree – a regular spree.'

. . .

The Ostend oysters were brought in, tiny and plump like little ears enclosed in shells, and melting between the tongue and the palate like salt bon-bons. Then, after the soup, was served a trout as rose-tinted as a young girl, and the guests began to talk.

They spoke at first of a current scandal; the story of a lady of position, surprised by one of her husband's friends supping in a private room with a foreign prince. Forestier laughed a great deal at the adventure; the two ladies declared that the indiscreet gossip was nothing less than a blackguard and a coward.

. . .

And the conversation, descending from the elevated theories, concerning love, strayed into the flowery garden of polished blackguardism. It was the moment of clever double meanings; veils raised by words, as petticoats are lifted by the wind; tricks of language; clever disguised audacities; sentences which reveal nude images in covered phrases; which cause the vision of all that may not be said to flit rapidly before the eye and the mind, and allow the well-bred people the enjoyment of a kind of subtle and mysterious love, a species of impure mental contact, due to the simultaneous evocation of secret, shameful, and longed-for pleasures. The roast, consisting of partridges flanked by quails, had been served; then a dish of green peas, and then a terrine of foie gras, accompanied by a curly-leaved salad, filling a salad bowl as though with green foam. They had partaken of all these things without tasting them, without knowing, solely taken up by what they were talking of, plunged as it were in a bath of love.

The two ladies were now going at it strongly in their remarks. Madame de Marelle, with a native audacity which resembled a direct provocation, and Madame Forestier with a charming reserve, a modesty in her tone, voice, smile, and bearing that underlined while seeming to soften the bold remarks falling from her lips. Forestier, leaning quite back on the cushions, laughed, drank and ate without leaving off, and sometimes threw in a word so risque or so crude that the ladies, somewhat shocked by its appearance, and for appearance sake, put on a little air of embarrassment that lasted two or three seconds. When he had given vent to something a little too coarse, he added: 'You are going ahead nicely, my children. If you go on like that you will end by making fools of yourselves.'[16]

As the party's initial conversation suggests – 'the story of a lady of position, surprised by one of her husband's friends supping in a private room with a foreign prince' – *cabinets particuliers* were places where men and women could meet for illicit purposes. The legal system left a loophole for romantic affairs in restaurants. French men were not allowed by law to have mistresses in their homes, nor to have public liaisons or second homes for their mistresses; however, the private cabinets – which sometimes even included second stairways so a couple did not have to arrive together – made meeting and extramarital interaction possible. Blagdon says that

In these asylums, Love arranges under his laws many individuals not suspected of sacrificing at the shrine of that wonder-working deity . . . In them too, young lovers frequently interchange the first declarations of eternal affection; to them many a husband owes the happiness

of paternity; and without them the gay wife might, perhaps, be at a loss to deceive her jealous Argus, and find an opportunity of lending an attentive ear to the rapturous addresses of her aspiring gallant.[17]

Private rooms also allowed for political groups, for spies, for people who needed a private space outside of the home to meet, but for whom public meetings were interdicted by French law. In fact, restaurants became spaces for sedition precisely because state monitors were planted in cafés and theatres, but not in restaurants.

BILLS AND BILLS OF FARE

Late eighteenth- and early nineteenth-century restaurants had copious options on their menus. Before the restaurant, a menu was simply a card that would describe what one would be eating. In the restaurant, it became a vision of options. The description of the menu below is neither unusual nor outlandish. The experience put choice and abundance on display. At the same time, the items had prices so that one could make a meal to fit one's budget.

Good heaven! the bill of fare is a printed sheet of double folio, of the size of an English newspaper. It will require half an hour at least to con [*sic*] over this important catalogue. Soups, 13 sorts. Hors-d'oeuvres, 22 species. Beef, dressed in 11 different ways. Pastry, containing fish, flesh and fowls, in 11 shapes. Veal, amplified into 22 distinct articles. Mutton, confined to 17 only. Fish, 23 varieties. Roast meat, game, and poultry, of 15 kinds. Entremens, or side-dishes, to the number of 41 articles. Desert, [*sic*] 39. Wines, including those of the liqueur kind, of 52 denominations, beside ale and porter. Liqueurs, 12 species, together with coffee and ices.[18]

Nonetheless, the act of ordering from a menu necessitated a learning curve. Literature of the time abounds with humorous stories of people taking half an hour to read a menu or ordering ludicrous meals because they did not know what the items were or even how to begin putting together a meal. It was part of the waiter's job to help guests order, but there was also advice literature – as well as the writing of gastronomes – available to help one pre-pare in advance. Travel writers of the time note both their fascination and their trepidation in the face of these menus.

For us today, it may seem less impossible to decipher a menu than for the early restaurant to be able to make all of the dishes on the menu. How,

in an era before refrigeration, did these restaurants stock such plenty? One answer is: they didn't. Menus often included a code for what was not being served on a particular day owing to unavailability (strawberries in December, for example). The waiter might also let you know that an item was not available. Further, many options – especially as French haute cuisine developed – were variations in cooking method with the same ingredients. While some restaurant customers were gastronomes, most were not. In fact, just as the fish frequently served in restaurants today may not correspond to turbot or cod, there was a question of what exactly one was getting at some restaurants. This is most vividly illus-trated in the various nineteenth-century cartoons and lawsuits about cat meat in Parisian kitchens.

In addition to the menu, the bill arose as a central point of discussion and experience in

Thomas Rowlandson, *Dinners Drest in the Neatest Manner*, 1811, hand-coloured etching.

Louis Brion de La Tour, *Assassination of Michel Le Peletier*, 1793, stipple engraving.

François-Aimé-Louis Dumoulin, *Death of Le Peletier St Fargeau*, 1793, engraving.

restaurants. From descriptions of several of the major restaurants in post-revolutionary Paris, we learn that women – specifically the wives of restaurateurs – were usually in charge of the money. Of La Grande Taverne de Londres, we are told,

> On the left hand, as you pass into the first room, rises a sort of throne, not unlike the estrado in the grand audience-chamber of a Spanish viceroy. This throne is encircled by a barrier to keep intruders at a respectful distance. Here sits a lady, who, from her majestic gravity and dignified bulk, you might naturally presume to be an empress; revolving in her comprehensive mind affairs of her vast dominions. This respectable personage is Madame Beauvilliers, whose most interesting concern is to collect from the gentlemen in waiting the cash which they receive at the different tables.[19]

The author Honoré de Balzac, who describes menus and bills in great detail in his literary works, is said to have had a deal with Madame Véry, of the famed Véry's, whereby he would write his tip, sign his bill and have it sent to his publisher.

Balzac's characters don't have as lovely setup. They are, instead, often besieged by their bill. For example, in *Lost Illusions*, the young poet Lucian Rubempré, having recently moved to Paris and even more recently been rejected by the woman he followed there, decides to have a meal at Véry's:

> A bottle of Bordeaux, oysters from Ostend, a dish of fish, a partridge, a dish of macaroni and dessert – this was the *ne plus ultra* of his desire. He enjoyed this little debauch, studying the while how to give the Marquise d'Espard proof of his wit, and redeem the shabbiness of his grotesque accoutrements by the display of intellectual riches. The total of the bill drew him down from these dreams, and left him the poorer by fifty of the francs which were to have gone such a long way in Paris. He could have lived in Angoulême for a month on the price of

that dinner. Wherefore he closed the door of the palace with awe, thinking as he did so that he should never set foot in it again.[20]

Bills even become the centre of political discourse, as the murder of Louis-Michel Le Peletier demonstrates.[21] On 20 January 1793, between his first and second course, Le Peletier became the French Revolution's first martyr. A wealthy man, a Jacobin and a magistrate in the Paris parliament, he was a regular at Fevrier's, a restaurant in the Palais-Royal. After voting for King Louis XVI's death sentence, Le Peletier went to dinner – and while eating was accosted and stabbed by a former member of the Royal Guard.

Both the restaurateur Dominique Fevrier and the restaurant's two waiters, Lepine and Durant, gave testimony about his murder. Apparently, Lepine had just gone to the kitchen to get the next course, when the assassin rushed in and allegedly plunged a sabre into Le Peletier's chest. The restaurateur fought with the assassin to no avail – he escaped into the streets of Paris. The story was told and retold, taking on symbolic and hyperbolic details. His meal was frugal; his last words heroic. His single assassin multiplied to a group.

However the most interesting variation presents Le Peletier not as a man killed while having a meal, but as a man killed while trying to pay his bill. This is not factually accurate – Le Peletier was a regular at the restaurant, so probably paid his accumulated bill weekly or monthly, and the restaurateur himself (who was settling someone else's bill when the stabbing occurred) and the waiters testified that he was seated at his table. This mythic detail, then, is about politics: who owes, and who pays. It is a claim about the responsibility and follow-through of the Jacobins as opposed to King Louis XVI, who was represented as lavish, someone who left the French people with the tab. However, in our understanding of restaurant history, perhaps it is just as interesting that by this time, the idea of the bill – an example of personal accounting – is so tied to the restaurant that it makes sense to weave it into the tale of a murder.

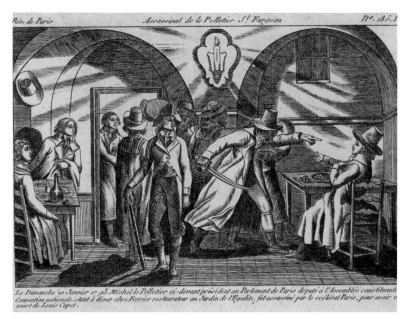

Unknown artist, *Assassination of Le Peletier St Fargeau, Sunday 20 January 1793*, 1793, engraving.

Cooks preparing food behind two long counters in the kitchen of Delmonico's restaurant at the northeast corner of Fifth Avenue and 44th Street, New York, 1902.

RESTAURANTS BEYOND PARIS

La Grande Taverne de Londres, Les Trois Frères Provençeaux, Véry's and the Grand Véfour are symbolic of what would become – for all of the world – the blueprint of the French restaurant, soon not only a tourist destination and fixture of Paris but a major export product. In some ways, the French restaurant became truly French in its exportation to other countries, most notably to England. La Grande Taverne de Londres paid homage to a French fascination with the English public houses, and French food, prepared in English restaurants by chefs trained in Paris, completed this act of trans-channel fascination.

The French restaurant spread widely and rapidly – for example, by 1812 Brussels had one, by 1819 it had seven; however, one the the earliest and most spectacular versions was not in Europe, but America. Giovanni Del-Monico was born in 1788 in the Swiss Canton of Ticino and became a sea captain whose schooner carried tobacco from Cuba to Cadiz, then wines to New York and lumber back to Cuba. He stayed in New York after 1824, setting himself up as an importer and rebottler of wine, and changed his name to John. His brother Pietro, who was a pastry chef in Bern, would become Peter in New York in 1826, when he and his family joined his brother. This wealthy pair – they possessed about $20,000 in capital – first opened a café and pastry shop. A sign painter mistakenly spelled their name as Delmonico, and the family used that form of the name from then on in all of its various restaurant locations.

A ladies' luncheon occupying all the tables in the dining room of Delmonico's restaurant, at the northeast corner of Fifth Avenue and 44th Street, New York City, 1902.

From a small shop with a few pine tables serving coffee and cakes to the model for all of the nineteenth-century restaurants in the United States was a step of just four years. By 1830 the Del-Monicos opened the first restaurant in the United States at 25 William Street, New York, and the next year they invited their nephew Lorenzo to join them. This establishment introduced French cuisine that utilized American-grown ingredients, which had not been widely used before, and delivered this cuisine with care and attention to each individual diner. Initially displeased with the state of American agriculture and the options in the market, the Del-Monicos created their own farm in Brooklyn, so that they could source what they needed in terms of quality and variety. Belgian endive, aubergine and artichokes – *Chicorée au jus*, *Aubergine farcie* and

Artichaux à la Barigoule – were among the 371 selections on the eleven-page menu of 1838. For businessmen, the restaurant became the place to gather for an elegant, hot meal at lunchtime. For almost an entire century, the Delmonico's restaurants set the standard for upscale dining in the United States.

When the family opened their new building at the corner of Beaver and South William Streets in 1837, John Del-Monico welcomed almost the entire press corps of New York to a preview dinner while standing between marble pillars that he had imported from Pompeii to grace the front of his new establishment. The press notices he received for this event were entirely favourable. The restaurant was built according to classic lines, with three floors of dining; the third floor was reserved for private dining rooms. The cellar claimed to hold 16,000 bottles of wine. The restaurant had cost the unheard-of sum of $100,000 in a city that had just become the largest in North America. But the key to its success was undoubtedly the food and its preparation.

The Del-Monicos used the fresh abundance of good ingredients and the latest French cooking and presentation techniques to teach Americans about taste. They were the first to employ a side-by-side translation of the menu in French and in English as they eased their adopted countrymen into the world of fine dining. Like many of the immigrant groups who came to the u.s., the Del-Monicos kept in touch with the old country, devouring the latest cookbooks and importing what they could not reproduce from local ingredients:

> Today a new *aide cusinière* brought the last inventions of the Rocher de Cancale, the Trois Frères Provençaux, and the princely laboratories of Talleyrand – tomorrow, a new invoice of pâtés of Strasbourg, Toulouse or Angoulême, or the arrival of a Clos de Vougeot or Chambertin, unscathed by its then supposed enemy, the sea.[22]

Following his clientele uptown with successive moves, Lorenzo Del-Monico and subsequent generations of Del-Monicos would develop the restaurant to its greatest reach at four locations in Manhattan. They employed Charles Ranhofer, a French-born and -trained chef, from 1862 until 1894, except for a short interruption in the late 1870s. Ranhofer, who began his American career at the only New York rival of Delmonico's in the second half of the nineteenth century, Maison Dorée, then presided over the finest restaurants in the country, published

an all-encompassing cookbook and was the first to inhabit the status of celebrity chef in the United States. He invented baked Alaska to commemorate the purchase of that territory, was involved in the creation of lobster à la Newburg and taught the next generation of American chefs. He was an early member and president of the Société Culinaire Philanthropique, the oldest association of chefs, cooks and pastry chefs in the United States, which was founded in 1865 by a group of French chefs for the promotion of French cuisine in the United States. (The scp is still very much in existence.) Delmonico's was, like the first Parisian restaurants, the inspiration and the model for the restaurant in the United States.

Even as London and New York extended the reach of restaurant culture, Paris remained its epicentre. Just over half a century after the English observer Blagdon described the early restaurants of Paris, an American saw them again through his own spectacles, and the same three establishments – Véry's, Trois Frères Provençaux and Véfour's – still stood at the top of the list. 'These are the places to test the renown of French culinary art, and the depths of your purse.'[23] The middle classes were now a new audience for the restaurant, and several establishments sprung up in the mid-century: the Tortoni, the Café Riche, the Maison Dorée and the Café Anglais. Restaurants across Europe served French food; however, the accoutrements of French service, linguistic markers and decor had more staying power than the cuisine. While the grand restaurants continued to sparkle throughout the nineteenth century, pubs, clubs, cafés – and an expanding urban population – would play an increasingly important role in shaping the restaurant.

3

ELITE EATING AND THE
DEMOCRATIZED RESTAURANT

By the 1850s, eating in a restaurant was available to a wide range of people, as this lovely vignette by the American James Jackson Jarves presents:

> To see the French eat one should visit the restaurants of lesser magnitude and fame, particularly on a Sunday, where the rush to dinner, as no one dines that day under his own roof, is absolutely fearful to a lover of a quiet meal. Infants, dogs, and nurses, all have a seat that day, and the amount consumed would indicate considerable preparatory fasting . . . A family enters, consisting of father, mother, maiden sister, two children under five years of age, and a dog. All the tables are filled. They turn to go out. The restaurateur rushes forward, intercepts their retreat, and promises a table 'toutsuite.' He sees one party have called for their bills, hands them their change, and plumps the new comers into their warm seats, with an array of broken bread, dirty glasses and all of the debris of the previous meal before them. Once seated, with bonnets and hats hung up, they are considered as fish fairly hooked. The 'garçon,' with a dexterity and rapidity peculiarly his own, whisks away the soiled table-cloth and dishes, and in an instant has replaced them with snow-white linen and porcelain. Now commences the 'tug of' eating. Each member of the party, except the dog who gravely occupies his chair, too well bred to manifest impatience, plants a napkin under his or her chin, of the dimensions of a moderate-sized table-cloth. The females pin the extremities to each shoulder, so that in front they have much the appearance of being in their shrouds. The 'carte' is studied, orders given, and content and pleasure reign. At these family feasts children are literally crammed, indulged with wines and all of the delicacies called for by adult taste, their parents delighted in proportion to the quantity they consume . . . The waiter has a dozen calls at once – the same dish perhaps ordered dressed in a dozen different modes – he is to remember each mode and each table – to supply every change of course, omitting nothing required, and at the end of the meal he has to recall every dish,

William Spalding and T. Packer, *Matilda Gorger; or, Mullicatawny Soup, a Mackerel' and a Sole'*, 19th century, lithograph.

Vincent van Gogh, *Interior of a Restaurant in Arles*, 1888, oil on canvas.

the quantity and the quality – and there may have been twenty different articles called for at one table – that the 'addition' may be made out. What wonder then, if in the confusion of orders, he at times mistakes his napkin for his handkerchief, and unconsciously wipes the perspiration from his brow, performing with it the next instant the same service for your plate, or rushes in from the 'cuisine' with six dishes piled pyramidically in his hands, a roll of bread under each arm, and the latest called for 'addition' between his teeth.[1]

In the nineteenth century, in Europe and the United States, the formal restaurant, and in particular the French restaurant, maintained cultural dominance. However, dining out was an experience that expanded in a variety of contexts and social roles: middle-class diners would go out for Sunday dinner; people from all social strata would dine out as a way of attending to business and for pleasure; and places emerged for both artistic and political elites. Taverns, cafés and pubs took up service models of restaurants, and new havens opened to the working class and for the middle class – lunch rooms, ice-cream emporia and pizzerias. The roles of women expanded to fill all the occupations in the restaurant; they no longer just minded the till, but became central customers. An exuberant blending of categories reached beyond the French ideal while still retaining it as a model to which to aspire. In order to understand how restaurants came to be spaces for everyone and were transformed by that diversity of people, we will begin with the stories of the restaurant as a space for consumer fantasy both about and by the upper class.

CELEBRITY AND CELEBRATION DINING

The Café Royal in London is a good example of how French fine dining cultivated and maintained cultural cachet. Founded in 1865 by the French immigrants M. Daniel Nicolas and Célestine Thévenon, the Café Royal fulfilled the expectations of the elite by offering French cuisine, prepared by French professionals in sumptuous surroundings; it was a restaurant where the leading lights of London's aristocracy would gather to eat and to be seen. As Andrew P. Haley puts it, dining right was a 'public declaration of class membership'.[2]

The Café Royal saw the right litany of famous diners come through its three dining rooms (the Restaurant, the Grill Room and the Brasserie): two future kings of England – Edward VIII and George VI – Winston Churchill, James McNeill Whistler, Oscar Wilde, Gustave Doré and so on. While this list spans almost a century, catalogues of the famous, powerful, talented, wealthy and beautiful patrons who visited were not uncommon aspects of nineteenth- and early twentieth-century reporting on restaurants.[3] The parading of names reinforced the demand for the restaurant, creating a feedback loop for the elite and a beacon for those wishing to be so.

People used the Café Royal as a space to meet people worth meeting, to hold forth, to have audiences. Not all of these meetings ended well, as the stories of Oscar Wilde at the Café Royal prove. He began his time there at the Grill, eating and drinking frugally with his artist colleague Whistler. However, as his fortunes rose he began to frequent other fancier dining spaces there. Wilde enjoyed the food: 'He overfed like a schoolboy in a tuckshop with an unexpected sovereign in each hand,' wrote his biographer Arthur Ransome.[4] Wilde became the consummate gourmand, who would confer with the chef before each course and order the most exquisite wines in the cellar.[5] He also used the space for entertainment and company. He regularly went to the boxing matches that came to be held there and first dined there with his lover and friend Lord Alfred Douglas in 1892. After Douglas's father, the Marquess of Queensberry, left a note at the restaurant 'For Oscar Wilde, posing sodomite', Wilde met with several of his friends, including Frank Harris and George Bernard Shaw, to seek their advice. He opted to sue Queensberry for libel, which led to Wilde's eventual prosecution and imprisonment for sodomy. During the trials, the Café Royal shows up more than a dozen times: Wilde met there with lovers, editors and friends. Further, it was presented as a place where the couple purposefully met in public. For example, the trial testimony included a postcard with a claim from Douglas to his father that he 'made a point of appearing with [Wilde] in many public restaurants, such as the Berkeley, Willis's Rooms, the Café Royal, &c., and I shall continue to go to any of these places whenever I choose and with whom I choose'. For Wilde, then, the Café Royal was a place to be in the company of other artists, like Whistler, of editors and theatre producers, of theatrical audiences, of society onlookers and of friends and lovers. It was a place to do work, to have a good time eating or watching live boxing, and to cultivate a following in the press, in the arts and in society. Unfortunately, as we will see in San Francisco as well, the public side of these spaces that allows people to be available and to be celebrities also

William Orpen, *The Café Royal, London*, 1912, oil on canvas.

Hubert Clerget,
*Louvre - Place
Vendôme, Hôtel
Continental (At
the Restaurant),*
c. 1800s,
watercolour.

allows their business to be followed by private eyes, testified to in court and made even more public than they may have wished.

However, most of the society sightings and lures of restaurants had more impact on perceptions of how to enact social class and how to be a conspicuous consumer than they had on people's privacy or freedom. Where we most clearly see this transformation in conspicuous consumption, with dining at the centre, is in great hotels. Near the end of the nineteenth century, a new group of celebrity chefs, hoteliers and maîtres d'hôtel became the guardians and gatekeepers to the world of restaurant cuisine. The Waldorf-Astoria Hotel opened in 1893 in New York; three years later, the Palace Hotel in St Moritz; while 1897 saw the opening of the Vier Jahreszeiten in Hamburg, the Naples Grand Hotel Excelsior and the London Connaught Hotel. The next year, the Ritz opened in Paris.

But it was the Savoy Hotel, opened in London by Richard D'Oyly Carte in 1889, that set the international standard for restaurants. The great hotelier César Ritz came to be its manager and he brought

with him the maître chef Auguste Escoffier, and Louis Echenard, a master of wine, as maître d'hôtel. The Savoy sparkled with glittering parties. One of the most famous was the Gondola dinner, hosted by champagne millionaire and Wall Street financier George Kessler, in July 1905. Venice was recreated in the old forecourt, lit by four hundred Venetian lamps, with a silk-lined gondola decorated with 12,000 fresh carnations, a 1.5-metre (5-ft) birthday cake, and arias sung by Enrico Caruso. The grand hotel restaurants were huge operations that relied on the newest kinds of industrial efficiencies at the dawn of the twentieth century. At the Savoy, the scale of the enterprise was such that it provided its own power and water, and roasted its own coffee. It also served a wide range of dishes including Indian, Russian and German cuisine as well as fine, canonized French and English dishes.[6]

What the Savoy, the Ritz, the Waldorf-Astoria and the numerous other grand hotels had in common was a clientele. Escoffier created dishes for Sarah Bernhardt, Lillie Langtry, Dame Nellie Melba and the Prince of Wales, later Edward VII. Royalty

Joseph Pennell, *Waldorf Astoria Hotel, Thirty-Fourth Street and Fifth Avenue* (original location), *c.* 1904–8, crayon and pencil on brown paper.

Raimundo de Madrazo y Garreta, *Masquerade Ball at the Ritz Hotel, Paris*, 1909, oil on canvas.

patronized the Savoy in such numbers that the special bell heralding their arrival had to be abandoned,
and by 1914 the Savoy Grill had established itself as a
rendezvous for leading stars, impresarios and critics.

The notion behind these extraordinary palaces
was that they were a place to eat and be seen away
from home, and to hold parties away from home,
which would in many ways be similar to those that
the wealthiest merchants of the world, royalty or
the new celebrities would have held in their own
domains before the end of the nineteenth century.
In fact, many of the hoteliers and their great chefs
either made their names as caterers to the wealthy or
continued to provide the service of their restaurants
and hotels to their famous guests remotely.

It was the partnership of the hotelier and the
chef that cemented the notion of the grand restaurant into the twentieth century, and nowhere was
that collaboration more perfectly matched than in
the talents of Ritz and Escoffier. Their common goal
was the marriage of fine cuisine and fine service:
the perfecting of how the food was prepared and
the elegance with which it was served – and the
repetition of that act and its multiplication in many
different places throughout the world. From Rome
to New York, from London to Budapest, the same
quality and the same result was to be expected
from the same recipes. Dining in the restaurants of
grand hotels became something akin to a spiritual
experience for generations of the powerful who had

The American writer Mark Twain (1835–1910) being celebrated by the Pilgrim's Club at the Savoy Hotel in London. Ernesto Prater, *Mark Twain, Illustrazione Italiana*, xxxiv/29 (21 July 1907), photograph.

Gondola dinner party at the Savoy Hotel, July 1905.

Max Cowper, *The Grand Foyer of the Savoy Hotel Restaurant in London*, c. 1900, colour illustration.

conquered the financial, the royal or the artistic worlds. César's wife Marie Louis Ritz describes the ceremony of crêpes Suzette:

> The hush that descends upon the waiters as they gather like acolytes round the blue flame, the deft gesture of the sacerdotal maître d'hôtel as he pours the rich liqueur into the copper dish, the aromatic smoke which rises suddenly, fills the onlooker, the prospective diner, with a feeling of proper respect, and he tastes the first mouthful with something like religious fervor. In the matter of wine the same thing holds good. The shape and size and fineness of the glass, the manner of the waiter as he pours the wine, all contribute to the ultimate enjoyment of the taste.[7]

At the beginning of the twentieth century, many examples of the first great wave of classic French restaurants had disappeared – such as Rocher de Cancale, the Trois Frères Provençeaux and the Café Very – but the next wave of temples of cuisine took their place: Voisin's, Paillard's, the Tour d'Argent, Durand's, Henri's and the Ritz. An Englishman, when asked where he might choose to dine, answered: 'Breakfast chez Henri at the Gaillon, dine at the Ritz, and sup at Durand's.' But there was also a new idea on the horizon, embodied by Maxim's, where the food was taking second place

Jean Cocteau, *Pablo Picasso, Moïse Kisling and Paquerette enjoying themselves at café La Rotonde, 105 Boulevard du Montparnasse, August 1916*, photograph.

to the spectacle of music hall celebrities, former ballerinas and other members of the entertainment world, many of whom would arrive at the restaurant only after midnight, and who were its main attraction. In addition to the after-theatre scene, restaurants became the haunts of writers and artists (not unlike Whistler and Wilde at the Café Royal): in Paris, La Rotonde was frequented by Pablo Picasso, Gertrude Stein, Ernest Hemingway, F. Scott Fitzgerald and T. S. Eliot. Franz Kafka and Max Brod dined at Prague's Café Montmartre. Further afield, the Literary Café (Literaturnoe Kafe) in St Petersburg, founded in 1816, may have been frequented by Dostoevsky and Chernyshevsky and was the site of Alexander Pushkin's final meal in 1837, before he died in a duel. Restaurants and theatre, restaurants and writers, restaurants and the demi-monde, were connected in the nineteenth and twentieth centuries to one another as they had been in China in the eleventh, twelfth and thirteenth centuries: in both cases the two worlds were physically located cheek-by-jowl. However, in the nineteenth century, these spaces of celebrity – homes for the elite and the famous – were transforming the idea of what a restaurant could be. Moreover, the reporting on these upper-crust people, their habits and habitus, drove a movement towards restaurants as spaces for class theatre, power-building assembly and in-demand leisure.

MEETING AT RESTAURANTS

While the upper classes splashed out on fine dining in the nineteenth century as a display of their refinement, restaurants serving the upper-middle class – politicians, businessmen, merchants, lawyers and publishers – emerged as important spaces not only for dining but for meeting. We can see this in clubs in England, restaurants in San Francisco and hotel

and department store restaurants in Russia, Mexico and China.

Like their French counterparts in the mid-eighteenth century, the British upper-middle class had few places to gather in public in the early nineteenth century. Public houses – pubs – were ubiquitous, but as the century wore on fewer and fewer wealthy people were to be found in them. Clubs would play an increasingly important role through the century, and not just in London. More than a hundred clubs with 60,000 members were counted in New York in 1886. Describing the role and roots of clubs in his expansive book *Clubs and Club Life in London; with Anecdotes of its Famous Coffee Houses, Hostelries, and Taverns, from the Seventeenth Century to the Present Time* (1872), John Timbs says:

> our elegant Essayist, writing with ages of experience at his beck, has truly said 'all celebrated Clubs were founded upon eating and drinking, which are points where most men agree, and in which the learned and the illiterate, the dull and the airy, the philosopher and the buffoon, can all of them bear a part.'[8]

Timbs discusses the more salient features of a club: namely that they often revolved around shared politics and sometimes around shared art. While many early clubs simply met at restaurants or taverns, by the mid-nineteenth century some clubs had their own spaces and with that often their own chefs. At more well-to-do clubs, those chefs specialized, as one might imagine, in French cuisine. While there were many kinds of clubs from which to choose, some of the most long-lasting and influential were the Beefsteak clubs. Beginning in the early eighteenth century, the Beefsteak Society was initially a space for men who fancied themselves wits. At a time when the Church and the state held

Honoré Daumier, *Coffee House Politics*, from 'The Good Bourgeois', *Le Charivari*, 21 April 1864, lithograph on newsprint.

significant power, these clubs 'constituted havens of aesthetic play and free conversation', often harnessing laughter for critique.[9] These clubs created spaces for people to rehearse political claims, to organize dissent or engagement, to explore new ideas and make connections. They did so under the guise as well as the experience of eating. Ned Ward, in 1709, described the instance of some joiners of the Beefsteak Society:

> Orders were despatched to the superintendent of the kitchen to provide several nice specimens of their Beef-steak cookery, some with the flavour of a shallot or onion; some broil'd, some fry'd, some stew'd, some toasted, and others

roasted, that every judicious member of the new erected Club might appeal to his palate, and from thence determine whether the house they had chosen for their rendezvous truly deserved that public fame for their inimitable management of a bovinary sliver which the world had given them . . . When they had moderately supplied their beef stomachs, they were all highly satisfy'd with the choice they had made, and from that time resolved to repeat their meeting once a week in the same place.[10]

These kinds of clubs, which were spread across England, colonial and early republic America, as well as other British colonies, used restaurants (and taverns) as spaces to facilitate new and more accessible artistic and political action. Over time, they were also established as spaces that changed restaurant history, as we will see with the Reform Club in Chapter Five.

On the West Coast of the United States, in San Francisco in the 1840s and 1850s, two restaurants acted as signifiers of the rising political role of restaurants. In 1849 a restaurant along classic French lines, the Poulet d'Or – which quickly became known as the Poodle Dog (either because it sounded that way to non-French speakers or because the owner had a pet poodle) – opened for business. In many ways, it followed the pattern of its East Coast forerunner, Delmonico's, though in a lower key. When it opened one could get a multi-course French meal (soup, fish, meat, vegetables, salad) that ended with 'fruit in season'. Wine was included and locally made. The restaurant's ability to use fresh ingredients makes it seem thoroughly Californian in addition to French. By the 1850s the restaurant was fully ensconced in the thriving local agricultural economy, utilizing ingredients such as city-raised chickens and oil from olives grown and pressed just a few miles away.[11]

The restaurant had the backing of financier François Pioche, who aimed to create a world-class city, with world-class cuisine, out of San Francisco.[12] The restaurant, like Delmonico's, would move several times in its history, eventually settling in relatively luxurious accommodations in a six-storey brick building. The first floor had a public dining room where 'a man could safely take his wife and daughter to dine in elegance' and the sixth floor had a 250-person dining hall complete with space for an orchestra as well as a smaller more intimate banquet room; however, the second through to the fifth floors held private dining suites, outfitted,

The wine list from the Ritz Old Poodle Dog, San Francisco, undated.

like their French counterparts, with beds and scandals. According to James R. Smith, 'bribes formed the basis for the businesses' ability to keep their upper rooms in operation and scandal free . . . A lady might dine with her husband downstairs on Sunday knowing full well he may have been upstairs on Saturday night.'[13] At the same time, the dining room, banquet areas and even private suites became spaces for under-the-board rather than under-the-sheets meetings.

A political graft scheme, which involved the Poodle Dog in the early twentieth century, demonstrates other ways in which restaurants became spaces of political manoeuvring: the French restaurants relied on the city for their liquor licences; they were also places where politicians often conducted after-hours business. In 1906 two politicians – Eugene E. Schmitz and Abraham Ruef – colluded to deny the restaurants their licences and then advised them to retain Ruef as their lawyer. Of course, he immediately got the licences reinstated;

however, the misconduct was rooted out because, perhaps not surprisingly, an editor of a major San Francisco newspaper was a regular at another French restaurant and heard the story. Ultimately, Ruef was prosecuted.[14] This story illustrates not only how restaurants could become part of political manoeuvring, but how restaurants acted as central spaces for people to meet, unearth political intrigue, listen to general gossip and even garner power.

The same year that the Poodle Dog opened, another restaurant that had a thriving political and business scene opened in San Francisco: Norman Assing's Macao and Woosung, perhaps the first Chinese restaurant in the United States. Norman Assing, a prominent San Francisco merchant, was an elected community leader, chosen as head of the Chew Yick Association, one of the first Chinese mutual aid societies in America. Assing claimed to be an American citizen, naturalized in Charleston, South Carolina: while technically only 'free white persons' could be naturalized, some courts did naturalize Chinese people, and it remains unclear whether Assing achieved that status. At his Macao and Woosung Restaurant, he held banquets at which he entertained local politicians, philanthropists and police officers. He would work with officials and power players in Chinese and white San Francisco society to improve resources for Chinese immigrants. He often represented the Chinese American community on formal occasions, and served as an interpreter. He commonly petitioned for the rights and naturalization of immigrants and spoke out publicly. He used the space of his restaurant and his position as a successful business owner to shape political, social and economic discourse.[15]

Echoing the French revolutionary tradition, restaurants across the world were spaces for political planning. In a posh setting in Moscow, reminiscent of the grand hotels like the Savoy and the Ritz, the restaurant played a more successful role in a revolution that still reverberates a century later. The Metropol Restaurant combined many of the interwoven facets that marked restaurant culture at the dawn of the twentieth century: celebrity, spectacle and politics.

The founder of the Hotel Metropol, Savva Mamontov, being a patron of the arts, decided to create not just a hotel, but a cultural centre, with a theatre, exhibition halls, indoor stadium and restaurants in addition to hotel rooms. Mamontov engaged the best architects, painters and sculptors in the creation of the Metropol. The project took six years to complete, opening in March of the fateful year of 1905 with all the trappings of its earlier counterparts in Western Europe: an Art Nouveau building with electricity, hot water and telephones in the rooms; refrigerators; and elevators. Elite visitors flocked to the Metropol Restaurant, especially the evening after Nicholas II signed the Manifesto promising to convene the Duma and grant democratic freedoms to the Russian people on 17 October 1905.

The audience raised toasts to freedom; people congratulated each other and were in high spirits. The great singer Fyodor Chaliapin was among the guests. At the request of the visitors, Chaliapin, captured by the public enthusiasm, climbed up onto a table and sang a cappella the famous Dubinushka, a folksong, which was considered very seditious at the time. After that, Chaliapin took his hat, walked round the room, and collected an impressive amount of money, which he later handed over to the revolutionary workers.[16]

The Bolshevik Revolution broke out in 1917 and the hotel was seized by cadets who were forced out by the Red Guard after a six-day siege was ended

Agustín Casasola, *Zapatistas at Sanborns Restaurant, Mexico City*, 1914, photograph.

by an artillery attack. The Metropol became the residence of the leaders of the Bolshevik Party and the Soviet state. The restaurant, where until recently the elite had enjoyed French cuisine, was turned into a meeting room. But the restaurant reclaimed its connection to the outside world when, in 1925, it was the site of the First Moscow International Chess Tournament.

Such political uses of restaurants exploded across the twentieth century. In Mexico, during the Revolution, the Zapatistas used a soft-drink dispenser at a branch of Sanborns to act as a meeting space – one of the most iconic and widely circulated images of Emiliano Zapata and his comrades was shot there. In China in 1929 the Cathay Hotel, now the Peace Hotel, opened in the Sassoon House on the Bund in Shanghai. It was an amalgam of Eastern and Western styles, built for Sir Victor Sassoon, a prominent British businessman. Like other grand hotels, it saw a parade of famous guests: Charlie Chaplin, Bernard Shaw and Noel Coward among them. The ninth floor, which housed the restaurant, became the space for the wheeling and dealing that shaped the economic and political fate of much of Asia after the Second World War. During the Cultural Revolution, it became a place where the

Gang of Four (Jiang Qing, Zhang Chunqiao, Yao Wenyuan and Wang Hongwen) carried out some of their planning. While by the 1970s women like Jiang Qing would have a seat at the dining and political tables with men, how women came to be at those tables – and literally at tables in restaurants – is equally a political and a social story.

LUNCH AND LADIES

Men may have been using fine-dining restaurant tables to conduct their after-work affairs, but the revolution in restaurants came not in these dinner-time bastions of power but in lunch and the role of women. The nineteenth century saw women, one of the first targeted audiences for restaurants, come into being as a central customer base. Women's experiences in cities changed the face of dining out. As restaurants expanded across Europe and the Americas in earlier eras, women as customers had been mostly absent or, by their presence, implicated as being of ill repute. However, the span of the nineteenth century saw an increasing number of wealthy women out in cities shopping and attending meetings. When it came to lunchtime, men went into the taverns, clubs and eating houses that were arrayed across the city.[17] Women did not have those options. Many fine-dining restaurants, clubs and taverns were run only for men – whether through menus and decor that catered to male taste (meat and dark wood) or through outright prohibitions on women entering the dining room. Mrs Blatch's experience at the Hoffman House in New York makes such exclusion clear. In 1907 the *New York Times* reported her exchange with a waiter, James C. Clancy, as he denied her entry:

'I am very sorry, but that is the regulation of the house, and we cannot make any exceptions in

its application. We do this for the protection of just such ladies as you are. We do it to keep out objectionable women; women of the type you would not like to have dining in the same room with you.'

'I have never been bothered by objectionable women,' responded Mrs Blatch: 'when I have been annoyed it has been by men. I do not suppose you make any effort to keep the objectionable men out.'[18]

Fougasse (Cyril Kenneth Bird), *'Of course there's no harm in your knowing!'*, from the 'Careless Talk Costs Lives' poster series issued by the British Ministry of Information during the Second World War, 1940, colour lithograph.

Eugène Atget,
*25, Rue des Blancs
Manteaux (Café,
rue des Blancs
Manteaux)*, 1900,
albumen silver
print.

Blatch sued the Hoffman House, but lost in a quick decision after she was mocked in the courtroom and her testimony was generally dismissed. According to the courts (in this case Judge Spielberg of the Fifth Municipal Court), restaurants could continue to require male escorts, though they were also instructed to offer dining areas for women, which they did.[19]

In America and Europe, dining options for middle-class women expanded rapidly between the 1870s and 1900s. The customer base expanded rapidly, too, as was described in the mass-market *Munsey's Magazine*: 'men are few, and woman rules . . . They swoop down in swarms when the luncheon hour arrives, and a man wandering into the places may well think himself an intruder.'[20]

Teahouses, ice-cream shops and lunchrooms catered to wealthy women as well as the increasing number of women in the professional workforce. Women had long worked in service positions and in agriculture and early industry; however, this period saw the growth of white-collar jobs for women, in particular clerical positions. Women-focused establishments emerged from this moment

Jules-Alexandre Grün, *Café Scene*, late 19th–early 20th century, pen, brush, ink and crachis, touched with lead white on wove paper.

Waitresses at the Room de Luxe, Glasgow, designed by Charles Rennie Mackintosh in collaboration with Margaret Macdonald for Catherine Cranston.

Agence Rol, *Réveillon 1912 (At a Restaurant)*, 1912, photograph.

in women's history in the city. These women shared a similar problem of finding places where eating would be pleasant and without social risk. Cafeterias, teahouses and ice-cream shops often served both men and women (and sometimes children), were not cost prohibitive and were clean and well-lit enough not to be risky while also being convenient. At some of these establishments, custom created segregated spaces: lone men standing at counters; women and couples seated at tables with a waiter.[21]

The aesthetics and menu options of these establishments transformed how restaurants looked, as they developed into the familiar and common forms that pervade today. While formal restaurants had long used mirrors, windows and high ceilings to enhance lighting and give a sense of depth, they also often included dark woods, velvets and other rich, heavy stylings. In spaces focused on women, the design choices tended towards lightness. Mirrors, windows, high ceilings, yes, but also bright

lighting, sheer fabrics, light colours and floral patterns.[22] Case in point are the Willow Tea Rooms in Glasgow, which were meant to be aesthetically engaging. Combining modern interiors with light refreshments, Kate Cranston commissioned Charles Rennie Mackintosh over a twenty-year period to design or restyle the interiors in all four of her Glasgow tea room establishments. At the Willow Tea Rooms at 217 Sauchiehall Street, Mackintosh created a *Gesamtkunstwerk*, of which the Room de Luxe was the main attraction: with its silver furniture and leaded mirror friezes, it offered a unique experience. At the Ingram Street location, Mackintosh created a Chinese Room which used a series of vertical and horizontal lattice-style screens, designed to reduce the height of the ceiling and increase the room's intimacy, along with vibrant colours as well as plastic design elements.

The menus at these restaurants were also lighter, similar to early Parisian restaurants, featuring cold

Agence Rol, *A Dinner at the Café Riche, 16 Boulevard des Italiens, 9th arrondissement de Paris*, 1908, photograph.

poultry, salads, soups and egg dishes. This coincided with changes in expectations for women's bodies and eating habits. A dating advice book from the time said that one did not worry about a woman driving up the cost of the dining bill because current fashion led women to be 'afraid of becoming corpulent' and to 'abstain from many things which they like'.[23] As we see with teahouses and ice-cream shops, in the British Empire and the United States, restaurants aimed at women often did not offer any alcohol.

As restaurants for female diners increased, so did the number of women owners in the restaurant industry. In the United States, between 1890 and 1930, the number of women restaurateurs increased from 2,400 to 40,000.[24] Many of these women, like Kate Cranston, framed their decision to run a restaurant as part of a social mission. As middle-class women moved into business roles, they also often brought with them discourses about how these restaurants were extensions of the home, creating a narrative that encouraged other women to eat out and maintaining models of being a 'lady', which may have given some women greater individual licence but were often bound also by subservience as well as class and racial discrimination. Jan Whitaker demonstrates how women put forth this mode of restaurant work as an extension of domesticity:

Mary Dutton, proprietor of the Chicago Ontra cafeteria chain begun in 1910, declared that the public restaurant was 'a home dining room on an enlarged scale.' For this reason, she said,

Walter Bayes, *The Phoenix Eating House, Braintree, c.* 1940, watercolour.

a woman in this field would 'become so interested in seeing that everything is provided for the comfort and enjoyment of her guests, that she will forget the long and unusual hours which restaurant work necessitates.'[25]

As nice lunch options expanded in the last decades of the nineteenth century, so did the dinner options for women – and men. Going out to eat began to be a social pleasure for a wider range of people; it was not just for the wealthy, but for the middle class, too. Initially there were few options for middle-class dining in the evening, in part because women were not expected to be dining out and middle-class men had a wider range of options (like clubs and taverns). However, as dinner dates became a popular leisure activity, lunchrooms often extended their days, staying open late to cater to these couples. Further, non-formal, non-French restaurants – restaurants with food from other cultures (Chinese, Italian) – became destinations for this new class of diner.[26]

BEYOND FRENCH FOOD

Despite the fact that French dining defined *the restaurant* in the European and American context in the nineteenth century, features of the restaurant spread into eateries of all sorts – and fine dining stretched beyond French cuisine. Moving beyond the French involved changing foods, expanding what could be considered good cuisine, and also changing registers and discourses. It literally involved moving from French-language menus, which were common far beyond the borders of French-speaking countries, to English, German, Italian or whatever language the patrons spoke.

Restaurants with local colour, local foods and local traditions were established in the early nineteenth century; however, it was in the late nineteenth century and early twentieth century that these types of places became what was expected of a restaurant, instead of elite, French-inflected dining. In Lieutenant Colonel Newnham-Davis's *Gourmet Guide to London* of 1914, in addition to reviewing Simpson's in the Strand, the Ritz and the Café Royal, he devotes several sympathetic reviews to restaurants like Romano's, whose chef, in addition to having mastered French cuisine, 'had an open mind with regard to the cookery of other nations. The *mouzakkas* . . . from his kitchen are the best I have eaten outside of Bucharest. He makes a groundnut soup . . . [from] Nigeria . . . quite admirably, and Romano's is the only restaurant I know of in Europe where one can eat a Malay curry cooked as it is cooked in Malaya.' At Goldstein's, our critic wondered how anyone could eat the entire panoply of dishes at this kosher restaurant as he praised the kugel, the pickles, corned beef and almond pudding, 'one of those moist delicacies that I thought only the French had the secret of making'. He also praised a Chinese restaurant and those Italian restaurants in Soho that 'jostle the French restaurants in every street'.

Germany and Italy both showed a similar pattern to Britain and the United States: the restaurant was imported from France through the introduction of grande cuisine by chefs trained in Paris, and this was then followed by the development of middle-class and lower-class versions of the restaurant in the latter half of the nineteenth century. Germans adopted the word 'restaurant' into their language after 1850, and it was used to designate those establishments that followed the example of the Café Royal or Delmonico's. Previous German terms referred to inns or taverns and they were superseded, at least in legal terms, by the words *Gastwirtschaft* or *Gaststätte* for those restaurants that developed for the middle class. After 1840 Berlin, Hamburg, Frankfurt am Main and Munich would all boast formal restaurants, many of them connected to the rise of the luxury hotel, but they also saw restaurant features, like printed menus and table service, moving into these middle-class dining establishments. From Italy, the evolution of pizza is a great example of the transition from street-food to restaurant in a kind of eatery that was not for the upper class.

In the twenty-first century, pizza is eaten by people of every class and in every country. However, less than two hundred years ago it was the food of poor people in Italy. The movement of pizza from street-food stalls to sit-down dining was a transformative moment for this dish, which was to become a worldwide eat-out sensation.

The first pizzerias, where people would buy pizza and eat it at the store – a pizza restaurant – are documented in 1799. We know this because the owner of an early pizzeria, Gennaro Majello, ran into trouble. Majello had closed his restaurant because the French troops (Naples was occupied at the time) would eat without paying. Without income and needing to pay the pizzeria's rent, he was falling deeply into debt and was seeking clemency. Majello did not invent the pizzeria – he just helped it onto the historical record. In 1807 Naples had 55 pizzerias – we know this because they were inventoried by the government, since they did not belong to types of businesses already being taxed.

Those same government records present the people who ran pizzerias as being on the lowest rung of the business ladder (alongside those who cooked offal and vended fruit). Most of the people who opened pizzerias were of modest backgrounds; running the business was a stepping stone into a higher economic class. Pizzeria owners sometimes worked with pizza hawkers, who would sell pizzas on the streets (some, oddly, on consignment). They would call out their topping, and when a hungry Neapolitan asked for a slice, the hawker would set up a wooden board and cut one. These pizzas were generally not of the best quality and may even have been responsible for a cholera outbreak. Some pizzeria owners provided their hawkers with ways to rewarm the pizza, but the vision of hot pizza delivery was some two centuries off. Pizza eaten in a pizzeria was considered to be, generally, of much better quality.

Women were also part of the pizzeria trade. They sometimes owned pizzerias (by law, only if widowed, unmarried or permitted by their husband). They often worked in them by serving tables, making dough, preparing other menu items or keeping the books. In addition to the restaurant and hawking economy, there was also a thriving women-led, pop-up street pizza scene. Typically once a week women would set up a cylindrical burner and cook pizzas for people to buy. This was an underground economy (unregulated and untaxed) that provided important income for women and offered locals pizza. In fact, the success of these female entrepreneurs may have led directly to the development of the pizzeria.[27]

Like taverns, cafés and inns after the advent of the restaurant, other purveyors of food adopted the selling of pizza over time, so that a restaurant that had sold macaroni might add pizza to its offerings or a shop that had only sold wine and no food might add a few tables and a pizza oven. The pizza oven was the most difficult and contentious part of a pizzeria. The oven had to either be built or modified from an existing structure; if it did not include the correct kinds of ventilation or was not well maintained, it would cause fires or excessive smoke. Health and safety inspections were a regular part of the life of a nineteenth-century pizzeria owner.

Francesco de Bourcard, 'The Pizzamaker', in *Customs and Practices in Naples and its Environs Described and Illustrated* (1853).

Complaints from neighbours were also frequent, as most of these shops were in what would now be called 'mixed-use developments' – but in cities this was simply life: living, dining and working in close quarters.

Pizzerias began serving in the late morning and were often open until midnight offering hot meals. Usually they did not separate the kitchen from the dining area, so the customer would come in, place their order and watch it be made, speedily, from the prepared dough and ingredients, and placed in the oven. These customers came from many different classes, though they did not all buy pizza in the same space. The very poor would have bought their pizza from a hawker, but for people with three soldi instead of just one, there was a neighbourhood restaurant to patronize. The working-class pizzeria may not have had chairs, like many counter-service cafés and diners in the United States, northern Europe and Asia (sitting down is, historically and globally, a privilege). Middle-class families would have been seated, with waiting staff to serve them, sometimes even in a separate dining room, depending on how large and fancy the place was. There were also pizzerias that served both working- and middle-class patrons. For example, Port'Alba had a standing section downstairs (where the kitchen was) that was cheaper, often serving students and workers, and a seated section upstairs that catered to the bourgeoisie. Even royalty eventually fell for pizza, it seems. In 1889 Queen Margherita of Savoy ate and reportedly enjoyed pizza from a local pizzeria in Naples owned by Raffaele Esposito. The story that is oft repeated is that the pizza Margherita is named for her, utilizing ingredients that resembled the colours of the Italian flag. By this time pizzerias were not only in working-class neighbourhoods, where they had originally begun, but were located across the city.[28]

The pizzeria, as a takeaway place and as a full-service restaurant, travelled with Italian families as they emigrated. As southern Italian immigrants settled in New York, they built tenement store-front pizzerias on the East Side and little apartment pizzerias (with two tables, hot pizza, wine and beer) in Harlem. In the United States, as in Italy, the pizza trade was at first more working-class, but expanded to include middle-class patrons, initially bohemians at the turn of the twentieth century, but by 1915 white-collar male and female commuters had become part of the New York pizzeria clientele.[29]

POOR PEOPLES' RESTAURANTS

For the poor as for the middle class, eating in restaurants may have started around the middle of the nineteenth century. These establishments were almost always self-service and the food was not necessarily cooked to order. We have a marvellous description of one such establishment – a cross between cafeteria, tavern and takeaway shop – from a mid-century novel written in German in Philadelphia. Mike Clapmann's Tavern and Restaurant was run by an Irishman, serving German food to men and women, black and white, in a rickety building on the southern outskirts of the city:

> Upon entering the front room, which was really the dining room, one was taken aback by the extraordinary fittings of the restaurant: the buffet table was filled with the richest selection of dishes, exactly like that of the fashionable restaurants of Chestnut Street. The only difference was in the kind of foods, in the bowls in which they were kept and in the art and manner in which they were dispensed. In two rows, one behind the other, stood twenty large, big, shiny red clay pots and in each one was stuck a large

tin ladle. In one was pickled pigs' knuckles, in another giblet stew, in a third pork and sauer-kraut, in a fourth white beans, in a fifth yellow pea soup, the sixth apple butter, the seventh mashed carrots and potatoes, in the eighth plum jam and in the others marinated oysters, fish and meats of most different kinds, fried liver and potatoes boiled in their skins, and on top of that 'Fruchtkuchen' ('pies') of all possible combinations.[30]

One could eat at Mike's in two ways: either bringing along a dish from home to fill with the restaurant's food (for takeaway), or eating inside using the restaurant's tin plates. A ladleful cost one cent (this price per amount model was and continues to be a popular method for less expensive restaurants).

In crowded urban areas where there were no kitchens in apartments or flats, people had to buy their food already prepared; much of this kind of eating was basically takeaway. In some ways, the nineteenth-century urban experience in the United Sates was not unlike that in eleventh-century Cairo: cookshops by other names were the most common form of eatery. Additionally there were small taverns and restaurants in tenement houses, boarding-house dining rooms and low-end oyster houses.

There was also a great deal of food sold and eaten on the streets. Fish and chips is a good example of this. The classic fish and chips of British fame started out as two separate fried dishes; the fish-seller was an itinerant who hawked his fish and bread for a penny at the pubs or sold from a stall. The chip-sellers sold to the very poor, often from the front room of a home, using lard that had often turned rancid, to people who either ate the chips in the back room or took them away, like the fish, wrapped in newspaper. It is unknown when the two dishes were joined together, but Joseph Malines is

generally credited with having opened the first true restaurant to serve fish and chips in London in 1864. Fish also became significantly less expensive at this time because of advances in boats, such as the invention of the steam trawler, and the growing practice of packing fish in ice, allowing there to be more saleable product. This meant that fish as well as chips were affordable for the poor and working class.

As it became cheaper to procure and ship food, dining changed across the spectrum. A notable example of this, which also demonstrates the complicated nature of class in restaurants in the nineteenth century, is the consumption of oysters, which was part of both high-end and low-end dining.

SOPHISTICATED AND SAWDUST
RESTAURANTS WITH OYSTER SHELLS

As the American-born British poet T. S. Eliot evokes in 'The Love Song of J. Alfred Prufrock', oyster houses could be shady places:

Let us go, through certain half-deserted streets,
The muttering retreats
Of restless nights in one-night cheap hotels
And sawdust restaurants with oyster-shells:
Streets that follow like a tedious argument
Of insidious intent

Oyster houses were often located in the basements of buildings, a practical decision because oysters needed to stay cool and ice or other cooling methods were easier to control in the basement. However, these basement spaces were also often low-rent, rustic affairs. While most oyster houses lacked table service, they did have important waiting staff – employees who shucked and distributed oysters in the front of the house, on demand. Additionally, most oyster houses served beer, wine or spirits, which depending on the place would be meted out by a barman or delivered by servers.

Most oyster houses, then, were not aimed at the well-to-do. But Thomas Downing's Oyster House in New York developed a reputation as a place for powerful men as well as women to come and eat oysters. How reputation is established is complicated; however, it appears Downing began initially with an incredible knowledge of oysters and a real commitment to having the best oysters on offer. Born as a free black man in Virginia, Downing grew up working with oysters. When he came to New York in 1819 he began an oyster business, initially selling the oysters he raked from the Hudson River. Succeeding in a dense marketplace of oystermen,

he eventually bought both a more upscale building for his establishment and a series of buildings with cool basements that had continuous flowing water in them to keep the oysters fresh. The restaurant flourished owing to both Downing's continued curation of the oysters and his excellent job at working the front of the house.

In addition to raking at least some of his own oysters (until 1835), Downing also established strong relationships and a reputation for discerning taste with the other oysterers in New York. For example, he would go out early in the morning and board incoming vessels in order to buy up their choicest oysters. On open water, he would taste the wares, buy the best product and transfer those oysters to

Keystone View Co., *Express Shipments of Oysters Leaving Oyster House, Baltimore, MD, USA, c.* 1905, photographic print on stereograph.

M. Fanoli after Richard Caton Woodville, *Politics in an Oyster-house*, 1851, lithograph.

Charles N. Morris, *St Nicholas Restaurant: Shell Oysters Received Daily by Express*, c. 1873, colour engraving.

Walker Evans, *Second Avenue Lunch, New York*, 1931, gelatin silver print.

Agence Rol, *Réveillon 1912 (At a Restaurant)*, 1912, photograph.

his boat; then, to help out the oysterer, he would go to the place where they were auctioning off the rest of their haul and bid up the price without really intending to buy the inferior oysters. Practices like this kept him popular with his suppliers and in control of the best oysters in the city.

Those delicious oysters developed a following, beloved by Charles Dickens and Queen Victoria as well as a litany of celebrated – though now forgotten – New Yorkers. Like Delmonico's, Downing's eventually transformed its interior from that which one would expect in most oyster houses to the mirrored, curtained, chandelier-studded interior that high-end clientele (including women) expected. It also expanded its menu from whole or shucked oysters to oysters in an array of preparations. Major

business and political transactions occurred at Downing's, while Downing himself curated the crowd and the spaces they sat in as carefully as he did his oysters. Downing was also involved in politics and social movements – in particular as an active abolitionist, though this was not a central part of his business persona.

While the East Coast was awash with oyster houses – so many that the trend depleted many eastern oyster beds – the Mountain West was having its own oyster boom. Rocky Mountain oysters are not oysters at all, which may seem obvious: the Rocky Mountains are, at their closest, over 800 kilometres (500 mi.) from the Pacific coast. Rocky Mountain oysters are in fact a foodstuff one does not need to ship – traditionally, therefore, these 'oysters' were

Agence Rol, *Interior of restaurant 'La cheminotte'*, 1921, photograph.

sheep testicles. However, fresh oysters – real ones from the sea – were ridiculously popular in mining-town restaurants in the Rockies during the gold and silver rushes between the 1840s and 1880s. They turned up in advertisements, newspaper articles and menus next to champagne and selling for high prices ($1 per oyster at the time; adjusted for inflation that would be $30 today). One might assume that these oysters were canned, but they were not. They were fresh – their purveyors proclaimed it, their high prices reflected it and we can trace their commercial routes. So how was this possible? Thanks to trains, packaging innovation and new forms of refrigeration.

Oysters came packaged in two ways: in the shell and as shucked meats. The shucked oysters were put into pails, topped with water and sealed. They were then placed in larger wooden tubs packed with ice, or conversely they were packed in larger tubs and then a core of ice was placed into it. These iced, shucked oysters could be marketable (that is, fresh enough to sell) for a week to a month, enough time to get from the East Coast to Colorado. Whole oysters were packed in thirty-gallon barrels. They were packed so tightly, through a process of shaking down and adding materials to snug the top of the barrel, that the shells could not open. They could last up to two months, if in appropriate transit (which

Ben Shahn, *New Orleans Restaurant*, 1935, photograph.

would again include ice). The oysters were then put on trains and sent towards their destinations across America. Thus oysters became a central feature of mining food – both on the half shell and in extravagant preparations like the hangtown fry, an oyster and bacon omelette.

For these miners, who were overwhelmingly from classes that on the East Coast would be eating at down-and-out oyster joints rather than Downing's, the experience of oysters was about conspicuous highs of consumption. This led to outrageous prices as well as a booming business in oyster scams, like putting canned oysters on a shell and calling them oysters on the half shell.

From working-class men eating in sawdust-strewn basements to miners eating dollar oysters in the mountains and the well-heeled slurping oysters on velvet chairs, the nineteenth century was a period when dining in a restaurant became accessible, with local variation, for a much wider group of people. In this moment, we see the wide divergence that restaurants would take – the importance of decor, menu choices and service styles in establishing the clientele of a place. We will continue to explore these aspects, moving on in the next chapter to the thing that the Del-Monicos and Thomas Downing understood: the importance of cuisine and, in particular, the people who become the conductors of cuisine – chefs.

4

THE MENU AND THE CHEF

'When a customer receives a dish, they get food and design at the same time,' says elBulli chef Ferran Adrià.[1] The food – and much of the design – at most restaurants is created by chefs. From early restaurants in Paris started by former royal chefs to modern restaurants founded by immigrants, the people running the kitchen are often seen as the heart of the restaurant. Unfortunately, the word paired most often with 'chef' is now 'celebrity'. In the media-saturated twenty-first century, this means that many of the chefs we know are people who make media appearances or perform shows as much as they are people who make food or menus. This cult of personality isn't new, but in all periods, it has obscured the innovative work that chefs do. In this chapter, we look at five influential chefs who worked across five centuries, shaping cuisines and kitchens. The chef and the menu are often inextricably bound and form the core identity of a restaurant. What these chefs served tells us about how they understood their customers, how they used the kitchen and how they shaped food preparation.

MAKING MENUS, MAKING CHEFS: KAISEKI

In the 1650s in Kyoto, the cultural capital of Japan, a wealthy person might go to a nice teahouse and have a meal. Having tea was a ceremonial experience. It usually involved a set guest list and a stated occasion. While the tea ceremony was central to these gatherings, they also included a specially prepared meal. If you were planning to host the tea in Kyoto, perhaps to celebrate your newborn nephew, you would have three top places from which to choose. These prominent teahouses served elaborate meals in somewhat sparse settings with carefully cultivated service. Each came from the lineage of the man who developed the Japanese tea ceremony, Sen no Rikyū (1522–1591); however, the meals you would get would not be the same. His sons – Sosa, Soshu and Sensō – each developed different techniques, which they taught to their apprentices and used to cultivate a following for their schools of cooking. These were defined by their proprietary and secret cooking techniques, and were named after the chefs who developed and perpetuated them.[2] Each school of cooking was known, in part, based on its menu: not only the dishes served, but how those dishes were prepared, from the way they made stock to the way they cut burdock and the aesthetics of plating. How these chefs related both to ingredients and to customers' experiences demonstrates aspects of what it means to be a chef.

The cuisine these Japanese chefs developed was part of a proto-restaurant. People would go to a public establishment to receive an individual private meal. Eventually this gave way to a system with two types of venue: ones that looked more like restaurants, specializing in what came to be known as kaiseki cuisine, and teahouses with long-time relationships with caterers (which still exist today). The shifting culture of the sixteenth century turned the minimalist simplicity and purposeful frugality of the early tea ceremony food into an elaborate event cuisine, laying ground for kaiseki cuisine; however, those changes manifested differently in Kyoto and Edo (now Tokyo). Japanese restaurants writ large developed out of both high and low teahouse culture in the late seventeenth century; however, the formal teahouses of Kyoto and Edo were where the best-known lineages of chefs emerged in Japan.[3] Kyoto and Edo cuisine developed differently based on their customers' preferences, which reflected their socio-economic status. In Kyoto, whichever school one chose, the cuisine that emerged foregrounded aestheticized simplicity and the importance of creating a memory-laden and memorable encounter. In Edo, the cuisine emphasized the power and wealth of the customers, while maintaining aspects of rustic cooking.

Notepad with diagram by Chef Ferran Adrià of Spain, 29 September 2011: an insight into how his food and cooking systems are choreographed.

Making the Menu in Kyoto
10th Month, 17th Day, Noon
Miso soup course
    Tofu
    Vegetables
    Fish roe
Pickle course
Citron Miso
    Lotus leaf plate of Kyoto ware
    with a cinnabar flat bowl over it
Rice course
Grilled on cedar planks
    A large layered box brought out
    Sea bream
    Oysters
    Chestnuts
    Green onions
Sweet course
    Grilled rice cake
    Cold pepper miso, sugar

Kubo Shunman, *Two Young Men and Several Women Dining at a Tea-house on the Bank of the Sumida River, c.* 1788, diptych of polychrome woodblock prints, ink and colour on paper.

Fermented soybeans
Later course
Persimmon
Kelp roll

The menu above comes from the high-tea-culture tradition in Kyoto at the moment when it was turning into kaiseki. Sen no Rikyū, the founder of the kaiseki tradition, developed a ritual that involved simple food to accompany ceremonial tea. In the years after his death his tradition was continued both by blood and adopted relatives,

people who came into his business and became part of the family. Multiple schools of cooking arose from Rikyū's lineage. In the fourth generation, three schools of cooking from the three brothers mentioned previously (Sensō, Sosa and Soshu) came to cover the most prestigious collection of teahouses, caterers and eventually restaurants. We will look at just one of them, the Urasenke.

This school was established by Sensō Sōshitsu (1622–1697). Sensō was mainly what we might think of as a caterer: he provided individuals and teahouses with meals prepared for special occasions. In Japan

Utagawa Kunisada and Ichiransai Kunitsuna, *Two Court Ladies (Goten Jochu) and a Geisha at a Restaurant*, after 1844, triptych of polychrome woodblock prints, ink and colour on thin paper.

today, traditional teahouses still rely on caterers providing delivered food. The customer chooses from a menu; the order is given to the caterer along with a sense of timing for the tea and entertainment at the teahouse; and the food is delivered fresh, course by course. Kaiseki developed as a dining experience that had a specific order for the six to eight courses and traditional dishes to be served; however, Sensō was one of the chefs establishing this tradition, so his meals are less codified than those of his successors.

At the heart of Sensō's style was the idea that the food should be connected to the moment – to the season, the attendees and occasion. In order to lead guests to think about these specific aspects, he chose ingredients and servingware that sent sensory, historical and linguistic messages. For example, at a meal that was meant to be a celebration of a new supply of tea, he served foods – lobster and rice cakes – that would traditionally be served at New

Year's celebrations. At other meals, Sensō would use servingware renowned in poetry and annals to serve his dishes creating visual variations with his own additions: putting an unusual red rectangular tray in the middle of his great-grandfather's (Rikyū) round cherry-leaves-and-flowers motif (*yoshina wan*) serving set. The idea was to simultaneously draw on the long history of the tea ceremony, while tailoring the experience to the exact foods, celebrations and celebrants of the moment.

The menu at the beginning of this section is for a good-luck meal. Sensō played with both words and culinary forms to foreground the theme and frame the occasion. The miso soup, which normally had two ingredients, included three, signalling abundance. The sweet course was a riot of senses – the light, sweet cake with sugared pepper miso contrasted with sticky, salty, black fermented soybeans. The final course, another play in contrasts, ended with *kobu*, a nod to the word *yorokobu*, which means 'joyous'. This kind of gesturing wordplay, familiar from Japanese poetry, was common practice at the high-end Japanese table.[4]

Sensō's idea, as a chef, was that the people eating together would be in communion, sharing experiences and memories. The meal was meant to throw into relief both memories they shared historically and those being made in the moment of the dinner. Chef Sensō is an early example of what would become, in Japan and across the globe, high-end cuisine. He played with variations and juxtapositions of colour and texture, with plating and combination and with expectations around food, in order to create aesthetic and emotional effects.

As we will see later, this attention to the meal as an event and to the manipulation of gustatory and visual expectation is echoed in the tasting menus of chefs like Ferran Adrià four hundred years later.

MAKING THE MENU IN EDO

While Kyoto dining traditions were poetic, multi-coursed events, Edo cuisine was much more about class and comfort. The cuisine in Edo – the earlier name for Tokyo – emerged for the *daimyo*, people who were wealthy hereditary landholders, as well as people who had advanced through the military system. While their interest in tea ceremony cuisines

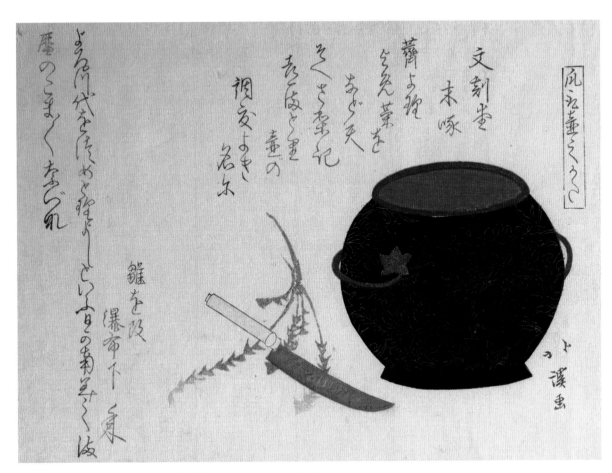

Totoya Hokkei, *Vase and Kitchen Knife*, 1816, polychrome woodblock print, ink and colour on paper.

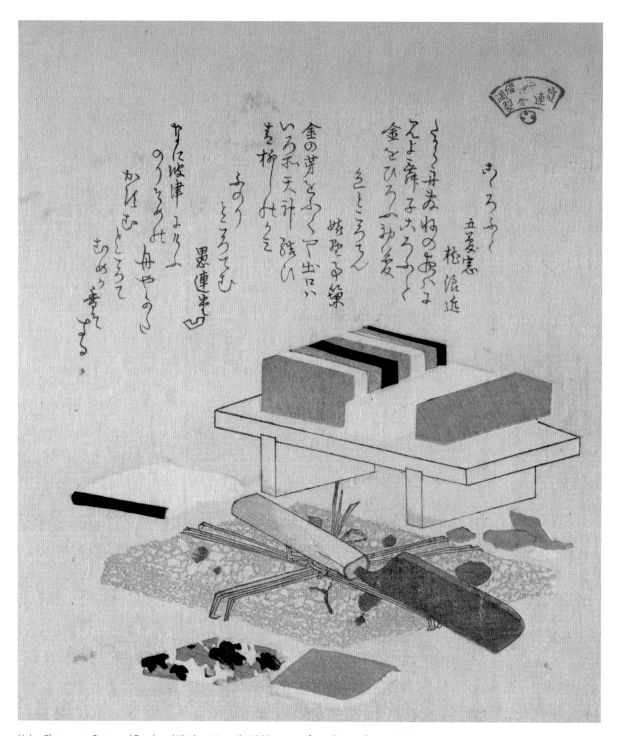

Kubo Shunman, *Seaweed Food and Kitchen Utensils*, 1800s, part of an album of woodblock prints, ink and colour on paper.

came out of the Kyoto traditions, they were forming a new cuisine, one that was not about performances of culture and communion, but about ostentation that signalled their place as rightful inheritors within an older order. The Kyoto and Edo traditions are examples of two of the modes of restaurant consumption that rose and fell in popularity. In this vein, they are like the first Parisian restaurants, performing abstemious health, while places like the Grand Hotel in Monte Carlo were performances of red-and-gold ostentation.

Chef Kobori Enshū was one of the major players in establishing this cuisine. He developed meals with many courses, often including high-end ingredients, served on very fine china, which he commissioned and sometimes even named (putting a new-money twist on Rikyū's tradition of dishes with lineage). His menus were outlandish, often serving many species of birds, fish and shellfish in a single sitting. He developed fifty ways to cut a carp, including elaborate knife techniques that became part of a named, branded and sought-after 'secret'

system of transmission that presaged the proprietary knowledge of twentieth-century restaurant franchises. While Sensō's dishes were served hot or cold when they were prepared, at just the right temperature, Enshū's dishes are more like the ones we see on European tables until the late nineteenth century: visually elaborate, but not temperature sensitive. Cooled food was seen as a sign of luxury because it implied the kitchen was far away from the dining area.[5]

These Japanese chefs prefigured aspects of the sociology of cuisine that continued into the twenty-first century. Their cuisines responded to cultural claims, to their customers and to the sensory experiences of food. It is the attention to dining beyond taste that is at the heart of restaurant cuisine: how food looks, the dishes it is served on, the way that it interacts with the rest of the menu and the timing of its service are what make restaurant dining unlike regular home dining. Restaurant dining is experiential and often aesthetic – even when that aesthetic is a properly placed pickle!

An early 17th-century serving dish (*Hirabachi*) with circular patterns (*Botan-mochi*), made from stoneware with a natural ash glaze (Bizen ware).

Hishikawa Moronobu, *The Kitchen of a Joroya*, c. 1680, monochrome woodblock print, ink and colour on paper.

Hishikawa Moronobu, *A Banquet in a Joroya*, c. 1680, monochrome woodblock print, ink and colour on paper.

Utagawa Hiroshige, *Teahouse at Hirokōji, c.* 1835–42, polychrome woodblock print, ink and colour on paper.

ESCOFFIER AND SOYER: INVENTING THE MODERN KITCHEN

Alexis Soyer (1810–1858) and Auguste Escoffier (1846–1935) are alternately bestowed with the moniker of first celebrity chef – along with a litany of famous predecessors in Europe and Asia. Instead of looking at the celebrity of chefs, perhaps a better question is: what did these chefs do that made them renowned? How did they change what it meant to cook and eat in a restaurant? In the cases of Soyer and Escoffier, they were leaders in organizing and using kitchens, and their contributions still structure the kitchen today.

In nineteenth-century Europe, cooks had a shorter lifespan than their contemporaries in other fields, and vegetables and meats had a shorter usable lifespan than foodstuffs today. Both of these sets of truncated lives were due to the technologies available or unavailable in the kitchen. The higher mortality rate of cooks was caused by constant exposure to coal fires; the decay of food by lack of refrigeration. While scientists of the nineteenth century should be given credit for many of the underlying technologies that improved kitchens, the people who ran those kitchens – chefs – were also key inventors. Soyer and Escoffier, who are often discussed in terms of their splendid cooking, their fancy guests and their fanciful lives were, in fact, key innovators in kitchen technology – transforming restaurant cooking not only with their flourish, but with their attention to detail and their material and managerial inventions.

E. Tutkovits, *Peeling Vegetables: Grande brasserie restaurant Walsheim, Strasbourg*, early 20th-century postcard.

After rising through the Paris restaurant scene of the 1820s as a teenager, Alexis Soyer became the chef de cuisine at the Reform Club in London. Soyer had long been both an inventive chef and a tinkerer; however, the position at the Reform Club allowed him to create a modern kitchen. The Reform Club, a political club established in the wake of the parliamentary reform movement to make that body more representative, hired Soyer as its chef in 1837 and at the same time began building the premises for the club. Soyer worked with the architect to design the then-futuristic kitchen space. Its most significant contribution was in the 'sophisticated control of temperature'. Not surprisingly, it had a large oven; however, the oven was flanked by boiling stoves, soufflé ovens and a steam closet, among other cooking devices, in order to best use its excess heat. Soyer also developed a set of movable metal-lined shields that could keep the heat from other parts of the kitchen and reflect it back onto things that needed to

be kept warm. The kitchen also used water and ice in ingenious ways, such as running ice-cold water over and under boards, ceramics and marble to keep fish and vegetables cold. Most significantly, though, the new kitchen used gas stoves.

Soyer (who died at the age of 48) worked his way up in a restaurant kitchen in an era when the conditions of those kitchens regularly killed the people who worked there. Burning large amounts of coal in enclosed spaces (even decently ventilated ones) produced excessive amounts of carbon dioxide. This resulted in a build-up of carbon dioxide in the cooks that inhabited these kitchens – a condition that led to kidney failure, lung conditions and other deadly illnesses. The great chef Antoine Carême (who also died young) expressed how obvious the problem was (and then, true to form, nevertheless romanticized the work of the cook), saying 'The charcoal kills us, but what does it matter? The shorter our lives, the greater our glory.'[6] The gas

CHARCOAL STOVE AND HOT PLATE.

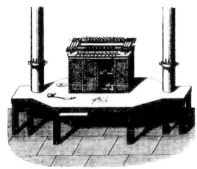

KITCHEN TABLE AND HOT CLOSET.

Fig. 2.—SECTIONAL VIEW OF THE KITCHEN DEPARTMENT OF THE REFORM. CLUB

'Reform Club Kitchen Arrangements', *The Builder*, vol. IV (18 July 1846), illustration.

stove was one development that led to a cleaner and less dangerous kitchen.

In 1802 Zachäus Winzler became the first person recorded to cook on a gas stove, which he himself built. Other tinkerers and scientists worked on similar inventions during the first decades of the nineteenth century.[7] However, in 1836, it was James Sharp who developed, patented and began the first factory production of the gas stove. This occurred just in time for Soyer to be smitten, and to put it into the design of his modern restaurant kitchen.

In addition to being safer, the gas stove also allowed Soyer and his cooks to control heat in ways that were previously more difficult. Wood and coal stoves had steadily improved over the nineteenth century, allowing for the beginning of subtle distinctions as well as a consistent temperature. These innovations in hob cookers led to the development of the mother sauces, which are stock-and-roux bases cooks modify to make a large range of specific sauces for dishes in French cuisine. These sauces were the foundation of much restaurant cuisine at the time. The gas stove made manipulation and consistency of heat even more accessible, eventually becoming the home and restaurant hob of choice across the world. (Worth noting here, though, is the reluctance and resistance of French chefs towards the gas stove when first developed.)

While the Reform Club kitchens were renowned for their impressive manipulation of fire and ice, chef Soyer also introduced many small but transformative kitchen gadgets. For example, he developed

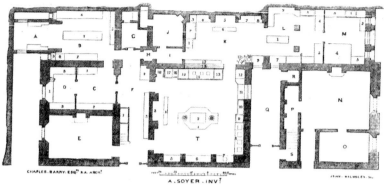

Fig. 1.—PLAN OF THE KITCHEN DEPARTMENT OF THE REFORM CLUB.

GAS STOVES, BAIN MARIE, &c.

BAIN MARIE, SINK, AND HOT PLATE.

FISH SLAB.

ICE DRAWERS AND DRESSER.

THE DINNER LIFT.

'Reform Club Kitchen Arrangements', *The Builder*, vol. IV (18 July 1846), illustration.

the kitchen sink catch or strainer. Clogging drains with food detritus had long been a problem in kitchens and it often took a long time for kitchen staff to clear them. Soyer came up with the simple but ingenious idea of having a strainer that set into the drain, which would catch the materials so they did not travel into the pipes. He was also an early inventor, adopter or adapter of the kitchen timer.

SOYER'S TABLE

Potage à la Comte de Paris.
Potage à la purée d'Asperges.
Saumon de Severne à la Mazarin.
Rougets gratinés à la Montesquieu.
Le Chapon farci de Foie gras à la Nelson.

Saddleback d'Agneau de Maison à la Sévigné.
Les Olives farcies.
Salade d'Anchois historiée
Thon mariné à la Italienne.
Sardines à l'Huile de Noisette.
Sauté de Filets de Volaille à l'Ambassadrice.
Petites Croustades de Beurre aux Laitances de Maquereaux.
Cotelettes de Mouton Galloise à la Réforme.
Turban de Ris de Veau purée de Concombres.
Les Dotrelles aux Feuilles de Vignes.
Le Buisson d'Ecrevisse Pagodatique, au Vin de Champagne à la Sampayo.
La Gelée de Datzic aux fruits Printaniers.
Les petits Pois nouveaux à l'Anglo-Français.
Les grosses Truffes à l'essence de Madère.

Les grosses Asperges verdes, sauce à la Crème.
Risolettes à la Pompadour.
Les Croquantes d'Amandes pralinées
aux Abricots.
Le Miroton de Homard aux Œufs de Pluviers.
La Crème mousseuse au Curaçao.
La Hûres de Sanglier demi-glacée, garnie
de Champignons en surprise.
Les Diabolotins au fromage de Windsor.

If we examine a menu from the Reform Club for 9 May 1846, we can see how Soyer's modern kitchen manifested on the table. The meal outline above was a private dinner at the club (rather than just a regular menu). These kinds of private meals were quite common in both public and club restaurants (and still occur today). The coursed menu is not surprisingly in French and includes quite extravagant dishes.

Soyer discusses the menu in his 1847 book *The Gastronomic Regenerator*. A quarter of the dishes have sauces that each, as his text demonstrates, have their own vagaries of heat and timing – for example, his brown sauce (the base of many other sauces) must be heated, simmered, cooled, boiled, simmered, strained, warmed and cooled, then boiled, simmered and cooled again. He also served a jelly and a mousse that would have needed to be chilled before being served. In line with his desire to explore food technologies, he developed a dish that involved an unusual piece of serving equipment, the pagodatique.

The pagodatique's appearance in the Reform Club dining room is a story about the adoption of Chinese dining practices in the West. Soyer had learned that it was a custom in Chinese dining rooms to have simply cooked fowl served:

surrounded by three or four small saucers, each containing different ingredients, spices and pickles, suited to the dish they partake of; each person takes a wing or fillet . . . Then they cut it in small pieces, on their places, and dip them into the different sauces, until they produce a favorite seasoning to their taste.[8]

Soyer thought it was ingenious, allowing a chef to serve a main course with a range of sauces or accompaniments and allowing the diners to make their own decisions or try all of them. In the 9 May 1846 menu, he served crawfish with truffles and a champagne sauce in the pagodatique. In his book, he lets readers know that they could acquire one of these serving dishes from him or the sole manufacturer with whom he collaborated, thus presaging the vast array of celebrity chef cookware tie-ins we see in the twenty-first century.

While a seeming novelty, *le Buisson d'Ecrevisse Pagodatique, au Vin de Champagne à la Sampayo* demonstrates not only Soyer's practices, but how restaurant chefs often operated. For the vessel, he adapted international chefs' practices to the place he inhabited, which meant employing a method of composing a dish that differed from precepts of the tradition in which he had been trained. However, Soyer's dish is not composed of the foods from the Chinese banquets that were the inspiration behind it. Instead, the contents of the dish are fully European – only the form of the dish is Chinese inflected. This particular pagodatique dish includes an ingredient (truffles) that he had planned to use in a different dish; however, he was not able to procure the rest of that dish's ingredients for that meal. When a storm made it impossible to import ortolans (a songbird one eats bones and all), he took the truffles he had sourced for the first recipe and adapted it into this new dish. To highlight the alluring exoticism, instead of serving a dish with multiple sauces and garnishes in side dishes (as the inspirational Chinese meal did), Soyer worked with a European china manufacturer to make an object with an orientalist aesthetic and gave it an orientalist name. As is a common feature of restaurants (from McDonald's to elBulli) the visual and tactile experience of the dish is as important as the flavour.

While the pagodatique dish did not become a mainstay of the Reform Club, it demonstrates Soyer's ability to understand and survey, and adapt and combine, available ingredients with novel forms. Soyer's discourse around procuring food and his role as a chef innovating with ingredients presages chefs of the twenty-first century. His self-proclaimed 'culinary laboratory' is not unlike that of elBulli's innovative and renowned chef Ferran Adrià, to whom we turn at the end of this chapter. In *The Gastronomic Regenerator*, Soyer discusses at length where and when he procured his ingredients for the 9 May 1846 menu above:

The tradespeople received their orders a week previous to the dinner. The finest mullets I ever saw, as well as the Severn salmon, were obtained at Grove's, in Bond Street; the remainder of the fish was from Jay's, Hungerford Market. At seven o'clock the live Severn salmon was brought to me, it having just arrived direct from Gloucester, and was boiled immediately, being just ten minutes before the dinner was placed upon the table, and was eaten in its greatest possible perfection. The finest of the poultry came from Bailey's, Davis Street, Grosvenor Square, and Townsend's, Charles Street, Haymarket. The foie gras and some very fine fresh French truffles came from Morel's; the hors d'oeuvres, from Edges and Butler's, Regent Street. The saddleback of lamb came from Newland's, Air Street, Piccadilly, the Welsh mutton from Slater's, and the young green peas and a very expensive dessert came from

Solomon's, Covent Garden. My being so minute in mentioning the name of the above tradespeople is not to advertise their fame in their different specialties, as that I believe they have already acquired, but merely to prove the trouble a real gourmet will take to furnish his table.

This attention to where his food came from might remind us of twenty-first-century menus, which include the names of farmers and fishermen who grew or caught the food on offer. This is not to give Soyer too much credit (his works in general read like a man who could use a little *more* humility). He is, though, part of a lineage of restaurant cooks and chefs who had made their careers by working at the intersection of cutting-edge technology, broad and often international food traditions, and fine ingredients.

ESCOFFIER AND THE NEW AESTHETICS
OF DINING

Born in the same year as the elaborate menu we just discussed, Escoffier seems almost like a latecomer to the work of transformative nineteenth-century chefs. However, he is perhaps the most famous for his contributions to the professional kitchen and the phenomenon of the celebrity chef. In Europe, Escoffier made two innovations with regard to how restaurants function: the kinds of food he prepared (his menu) and the organization of his kitchen (the *brigade de cuisine*). These two contributions are intertwined.

We begin with an example of the first: Escoffier's *prix-fixe* menu from the London Carlton dining room. For twelve shillings and six pence (around £100 per head today, about the cost of dinner at the contemporary Ritz Carlton in London), diners would get:

Melon Cocktail
Velouté Saint-Germain
Truite de rivière Meunière
Blanc de poulet Toulousain
Riz Pilaw
Noisette d'agneau à la moelle
Haricots verts à l'Anglaise
Pommes Byron
Caille en gelée à la Richelieu
Salade romaine
Asperges d'Argenteuil au beurre fondu
Mousse glacé aux fraises
Friandises

This menu showcases a variety of cooking styles
and a range of temperatures, to which we will
return. This menu could seem not unlike Soyer's –
it has a jellied dish; it has a salad; it has asparagus;
it has lamb, fish and chicken. However, even when
one accounts for differences in scale (a planned *fête*
versus a *prix fixe*) the composition and ordering
of courses are not quite the same. This reflects the
biggest change between Soyer and Escoffier, even
if it is one not immediately apparent from the
menu: namely, how the food was made and served.

   Take, for example, Soyer's self-titled *Salade de
Grouse à la Soyer*– a meat and egg salad. It is fancy,
even fanciful. Compare this to Escoffier's mantra:
Faites simple (Keep it simple). Escoffier simplified
dishes, presentations and the structure of the meal:
fewer courses, fewer garnishes, fewer ingredients.
And all of this while increasing flavour and drama
at the table.

   Over the course of the nineteenth century the
high-end dining table transformed from aristocratic
to haute. While that might not seem like a great
leap, the difference between being well born and
fashionable is significant. As a side note, the term
haute cuisine didn't make it into English until the

Auguste Escoffier (1846–1935), 1930, photograph.

1920s, but *haute bourgeoisie*, referring to the upper
middle-class, was introduced in 1888.[9] The *haute
bourgeoisie* were really the focal point of high cuisine
by the latter half of the nineteenth century. Their
aesthetics simultaneously echoed and eschewed the
practices of earlier aristocracy. In France Antoine
Carême developed the style of cooking that became,
for the next century, haute cuisine in the Western
world – updated and popularized by Escoffier.

   In some ways, Escoffier reflected wider changes
in aesthetics. His table next to Soyer's would be like
a Van Gogh or a Monet next to a Romantic painting.
While both might be beautiful and dramatic, the
ways they employ colour, composition and stroke
are entirely different. The modern paintings, like
Escoffier's dishes, are less busy and more invested

in the arresting and new use of the pared-down ingredients of painting: light, colour and stroke. Likewise, Escoffier's table had fewer dishes on it and showed a greater investment in highlighting single ingredients and dishes served at the specific moment of maximum sensory pleasure.

Peach melba is a good example of the importance of simplicity in Escoffier's recipes. It requires a perfectly ripe peach, blanched, skinned and sprinkled with just a touch of sugar; vanilla ice cream; and pureed raspberry with a little powdered sugar. The recipe has four ingredients, two of which are sugar. It is almost obscenely simple. Despite and because of this, according to Escoffier, 'Any variation of this recipe ruins the delicate balance of its taste.' As the dish rose in popularity, Escoffier complained of editors and writers who showed 'carelessness' in publishing recipes that strayed from the original, often including more ingredients. He said that they would 'take liberty' but not take 'the trouble of doing the proper research', leading to a dessert that 'could hardly satisfy the palate of a real connoisseur'.[10]

Peach melba would be served in a dessert course. While it might be odd to note, this is one of the aspects of fine dining that was important for Escoffier's contribution to the restaurant. In the 1880s, while at the Grand Hotel in Monte Carlo, Escoffier adopted a new style of service, which required that each course be brought out and served individually. Escoffier was committed to serving dishes at exactly the right temperature – and often with dramatic flair that emphasized his kitchen's precise timing. In the most outstanding cases, this included flambéing ingredients tableside (a move which called for excellent, well-trained front-of-house staff – and is the reason why the international maître d' contest of today includes flambéing a pineapple). To execute these meals, servers left

the kitchen with every order of a course for each person in the party at precisely the right time. It required pacing the preparation so the next set of diverse dishes would also be ready at the same time. The pace of dining, from kitchen to customer, was changing.

In the eighteenth century and much of the nineteenth, fine food was often cold food, or at the least, room-temperature food. Tables were set elaborately: meat and lard sculptures of the Parthenon; crystalline palaces of sugar; many, many dishes of a variety of animals, chutneys, pies and other victuals. The food was set up, the diners seated, and while dishes might be added and removed, there was not the same kind of course-based experience. Early restaurants were often places where food was not cooked to order – those rich consommés of the first Parisian restaurants were often reheated or kept warm; other foods that were popular in these places, such as poached chicken, salads, bread and cheese, were often served cold or at room temperature. This is in part because kitchen space was at a premium and figuring out how to deal with the demand for single servings was daunting. Escoffier, following in the path that Carême had begun, started serving food that was purposefully and needfully hot. In particular, the role of sauces made the timing of serving food of essential importance.

Today it may be a given that there are five mother sauces in French cuisine. However, initially there were only four, christened by Carême in his cookery texts of the 1830s: *béchamel*, *espagnole*, *velouté* and *allemande*. (They are all roux with, in the order above, milk, beef/veal stock, chicken/fish stock or chicken/fish stock plus eggs and cream.) Over the course of his career at grand hotels across Europe and at the Savoy, London, Escoffier developed a new iteration of French cuisine, which drew from Carême as well as other European traditions.

In 1903, with the publication of Escoffier's *Le Guide culinaire, aide-mémoire de cuisine pratique*, he bestowed to the culinary world a new order of five sauces: *béchamel, espagnole, velouté, hollandaise* and *sauce tomate*. (*Allemande* was demoted to being an offspring of *velouté*.) These sauces are used, in turn, to make hundreds of others – the exact right sauce for the dish. It would be fair not to over-venerate the sauce, as it also had to be put on a perfectly prepared dish. For example, Escoffier would not have his steak grilled or his chicken broiled by gas – only wood and highly pure coal would give it the features it needed.

Escoffier's attention to the detail of each dish gave him a well-earned reputation, but this trait also initially gave him a headache. While kitchens had long been places of bustle, they were not necessarily places of organized precision. To be successful, Escoffier had to work with a well-oiled machine, made up of a large group of people. To do so he turned to, and perhaps perfected, a new way that kitchens were being organized, drawing on nineteenth-century military and industrial techniques. One of Escoffier's major contributions was the codification and canonization of the *brigade de cuisine*.

BRIGADE DE CUISINE

The kitchen management system Escoffier championed helped make it easier to get dishes to customers on time and at the correct temperature. The *brigade de cuisine* is a form of kitchen management, used even today, that divides the making of meals into stations. Professional kitchens, harking back at least to those of monarchs in the fifteenth century, divided kitchen duties into separate tasks: someone was in charge of bread, meats or elaborate sugar sculpture, or had the duty of washing dishes; however, these tasks were assigned kitchen by kitchen,

only sometimes with a codified logic and rarely with a designated space. When restaurants in Paris first began – often run by people who had been chefs to the wealthy before moving to serve them in public spaces – they brought with them some of the kitchen organization of great houses and castles. However, kitchens were often small and the pace of a restaurant was frenetic (as it is today). In the press, people worried about the cleanliness of kitchens and often described their atmosphere as chaotic (in some ways, again, as it is today).

The *brigade de cuisine* tamed that chaos and became the blueprint for professional kitchen organization. This form has become so prevalent that even McDonald's has a modified *brigade de cuisine*. The basic idea is that each person in the kitchen has a job to do and a space in which to do it. A series of people, in a hierarchy, distribute orders. By everyone doing their specified job with the timing that is asked of them, orders – even complex orders for parties of twelve or more – are sent out at the same time and all at the temperature they should be. A classic (read: elaborate) *brigade de cuisine* is literally a brigade.

At the top is either an executive chef or a chef de cuisine. Smaller restaurants generally have only one person who does this job, but larger restaurants may have both positions. The chef de cuisine, in that case, would report to the executive chef. This person, who we will just call the chef de cuisine, is the leader of the kitchen. They are responsible for overall management, developing dishes and menus, overseeing procurement and hiring, and managing the staff – which includes giving the commands of the kitchen (that is, calling out the order to the right person at the right time).

Below the chef de cuisine is the sous chef. Deputy to the chef de cuisine, much of their job is in management. They make sure that the orders are going to the right place, that everyone in the kitchen is prepared for service and doing their job, that the dishes going out are the right dishes (in all ways). In contemporary kitchens, this person is also often responsible for such not-so-glamorous things as inventory. Like many positions of second-in-command, they hold a great deal of power.

The next set of chefs in the ranks are a group of cooks called the chefs de partie. They each have an element of cuisine they captain (which includes both cooking and directing lower-level cooks). These chefs include the *rôtisseur*, whose job involves much more than roasts: this person traditionally controls broiling, grilling and frying; the *poissonnier*, in charge of fish and seafood; the

entremetier, in control of vegetable and egg dishes as well as soups; the *garde-manger*, who manages cold hors d'oeuvres, salads, charcuterie and cheese, and usually oversees the pantry as well; the *pâtissier*, in charge of desserts, pastry, bread and pasta; and the *saucier*, who makes the sauces, heats hors d'oeuvres and finishes most of the dishes, and who is considered the most important chef de partie, ranking just below the sous chef.

They each have cooks (*cuisiniers*) under them. The *grillardin* and *friturier* (the cook who fries foods) are under the *rôtisseur*. Sometimes a *poissonnier* has an *écailler* (a person who preps shellfish). The *potager* (soup) and the *legumier* (vegetables) work under the *entremetier*. Sometimes

Felix Man, *Waiters Give Their Orders in the Main Restaurant Kitchen at the Savoy Hotel, London*, 1940, photograph.

Henry Bedford Lemere, *Savoy Kitchen Interior: View in the Kitchen at the Savoy Hotel*, 1893, photograph.

a *boucher* and *charcutier* work for the *garde-manger*. Sometimes the *pâtissier* has an army of people, such as a *confiseur* (for sweets and candy), *glacier* (ices and other cold desserts), *décorateur* or *boulanger* (bread, for example). Even more junior cooks (commis and apprentices) work for the *cuisiniers* and the chefs de partie.

There are also positions in the *brigade de cuisine* that do not prepare food for customers. These include the *marmiton* and *plongeur*, who mostly clean the dishes, utensils, pots and pans. The beloved *communard* makes dinner for the staff. Finally, the *aboyeur* communicates between the front of the house and the back of the house. Sometimes they distribute orders to the stations; at other times they simply report to the chef and sous chef. Escoffier modelled this format on military chains of command, with which he was quite familiar after spending seven years as an army chef. It was a system that worked and still works in many kitchens.

When orders came in at the Savoy for *Homard Carmélita*, *Poularde de Périgourdine* and *Pommes Byron*, the *poissonnier* would begin work on the lobster, the *rôtisseur* on the chicken, the *entremetier* on the potatoes and the *saucier* on the various sauces for each dish. They would employ the people at their stations to take on aspects of their part of the dish at the appointed time, and the sous chef would bring it all together. They could serve five hundred simultaneous dinners this way.

SQUARE PLATES, *PRIX FIXE* AND OTHER FINE POINTS

Escoffier's goal was always to create spectacular but streamlined meals. When he agreed to join César Ritz at the Savoy, he came not only with ways to run a kitchen and serve a meal that he

had been perfecting at the grand hotels, but with some thoughts on presentation that he had been developing during his decades in restaurants. One idea was small, but is an important part of understanding restaurants and their constant and recursive development. Like Sensō, Enshū and Soyer before him, Escoffier understood the impact of different kinds of dishes. He had long wanted silver square plates on which to serve hors d'oeuvres, and with this new position, he got them. When square plates re-emerged across menus in the early twenty-first century, they were both embraced and maligned, but what they were not was new. Changing shapes, colours and styles of servingware has been a way to encourage people to see and feel their food differently at least since the seventeenth century, and has been adopted by chefs like Soyer and Escoffier.

Escoffier also adapted a way of eating at fine-dining establishments that is still used today. In order to keep up with demand and still be able to create complex and stunning dishes, Escoffier took a page out of the book of the table d'hôte: he began offering a *prix-fixe* menu. These menus were a single price and included a set meal. They allowed the kitchen to prepare more easily and for the chef to suggest a meal that he believed would be right for the patron. While one can imagine that some part of a *prix fixe* is about balancing books and using up ingredients, it is also a practice that allows chefs to suggest a good meal to diners who do not have the expertise or will to navigate the menu.

For Escoffier, elegance was to be based on simplicity and the lack of extraneous details. He banished garnishes that were not edible or monumental forms of food presentation, and he simplified both menus and sauces. No more entrées that looked like Greek temples; food was to look like food. However, looking like food was not at all dowdy – instead it was full of life, movement and pops of colour. One cannot discuss Escoffier without demonstrating his own form of theatrical splendour – you will recall the description of the ceremony of crêpes Suzette by César's wife, Marie Louis Ritz, noted in Chapter Three.

Following in the tradition of menus Sensō created for seasonal and celebratory meals and in the tradition of Soyer's 1846 gastronomic blow-out, came Escoffier's red dinner of 1895 in Monte Carlo. The menu for the event worked the intersection of gustatory, visual and symbolic delight to celebrate the massive winning of a group of young men at a casino:

> Red smoked salmon and black caviar on
>   puff pastry, served on red napkins
> *Cliquot Rose*
> *Consommé au fumet de perdrix rouges*
>   (Red-legged partridge Consomme)
> *Supreme de rouget au Chambertin*
> *Laitance de carpes au écrevisses á la Bordelaise*
> *Cailles Mascotte*
> *Riz pilaw*
> *Chateau Lafite étampé 1870*
> *Poularde truffée aux perles noires du Périgord*
> *Salade de coeurs de la laitue rouge de Alpes*
> *Asperges nouvelles sauce 'Coucher de soleil par
>   un beau soir d'éte'*
> *Parfait de foie gras en gelée au paprika doux
>   à la Hongroise*

The meal was awash in red with splashes of gold and the occasional dash of black, from caviar to wine to vegetables. The dining area was also turned red – with red floodlights, red chairs and menus and red rose petals. It was an extravaganza for the turn of the century. An excess of style, of colour and of drama, but not an excess of dishes or garnishes. It was, like all good meals, a composed moment.

THE VANGUARD OF CREATIVITY IN THE KITCHEN

> 3DS with ras-el-hanout and lemon basil shoots
> Cantonese *músico*
> Mango and black olive discs
> Five pepper melon-CRU/melon-LYO with
>   fresh herbs and green almonds
> Pumpkin oil sweet
> Thai nymph
> Melon with ham 2005
> Spherical-I mozzarella
> Samphire tempura with saffron and
>   oyster cream
> Steamed brioche with rose-scented mozzarella[11]

This is just the first 'act' of a four-part meal at the restaurant elBulli in 2005. elBulli heralded and shaped many of the trends in current high-end dining across the globe. The restaurant, founded in 1964, was located 160 kilometres (100 mi.) north of Barcelona, on the coast, just below the French border. Beginning in the 1990s, under the leadership of chef Ferran Adrià, it became the birthplace of what is often called molecular gastronomy – a label for a myriad of new cooking techniques.

If you do not know what you would be served based on the list of dishes above, that is understandable. Sometimes the ingredients are evident (melon and ham, mango and black olive) and sometimes the technique is recognizable (tempura, cream, steamed); however, the names of most of these dishes create more of a sense of mystery than clarity. What will the 'Thai nymph' be? Insect or seductress? (For the record, it is a Thai salad filling in candy floss, like a kind of crazy *gỏi cuốn* or summer roll. A note from its recipe says, 'This snack is only served when the atmospheric humidity is below 65%.') One could imagine ending this chapter on the ways chefs have shaped restaurants, through kitchen and cuisine innovation, with a litany of different executive chefs, but Adrià is perhaps the most fitting. Like Soyer, like Escoffier, he is interested in the very new, in the way that the dining and cooking experience can be transformed by a restaurant. And if the movement from Soyer to Escoffier is from Romantic painting to modernism, then it is fitting that writers have proclaimed Adrià to be the movement to Surrealism, the Picasso or Dalí of haute cuisine.[12]

Dalí and Adrià were both born in the Catalan region of Spain, though 58 years apart. In his cookbook *Les dîners de Gala*, Dalí says,

> I only like to eat what has a clear and intelligible form. If I hate that detestable degrading vegetable called spinach it is because it is shapeless, like Liberty. I attribute capital esthetic and moral values to food in general, and to spinach in particular. The opposite of shapeless spinach, is armor. I love eating suits of arms, in fact I love all shell fish . . . food that only a battle to peel makes it vulnerable to the conquest of our palate.[13]

To Adrià, this would likely be both a challenge and a claim about what food is, about what it can be, about how we experience it. (We imagine he would make a kind of spinach armour.)

In 1987 Adrià became the head chef at elBulli. That year, at a gathering of chefs, Adrià also heard a maxim from a chef named Jacques Maximin that would transform his work: 'Creativity means not copying.' He and his team took this claim to the extreme. Instead of working to innovate incrementally, they invested in radical new approaches, ways of making ingredients entirely new. Much of their work came to be classified as molecular gastronomy.

At that time, elBulli closed for winter, primarily because it was located in a resort area and there were many fewer customers during the off season (demand changed dramatically after 2000; at one point elBulli had more than a million requests for dinner in a single year). However, beginning in the late 1980s, the kitchen staff used those months (three, then five, then six months) to explore new ways of making food, not simply exploring the recipes of those who came before, but trying to rethink and transform practices of cooking and ingredients. They would explore a hundred ways to freeze and serve a strawberry. They would decide they wanted to make a solid cocktail – and pressed at it from the point of flavour, technique, aesthetics and engineering until they produced the unexpected drink worth serving. During the winter development months, Adrià and his team would also work, like Soyer and Enshū, with designers and manufacturers to make new servingware and new kitchen tools for the specific foods they were creating. Instead of regional cuisine or international French, they opted for avant garde – they wanted to 'codify . . . cooking from a theoretical point of view'.[14] In 1994 what had been part of the kitchen's emerging practice was indeed codified: Adrià decided to devote the restaurant's work to what he termed 'concept-technique' cuisine.

In 2000 elBulli began a catalogue of all of the dishes it created, recording and categorizing them as a way of tracking and even analysing the new techniques and concepts for cuisine that the team devised. In 2006 they set out a manifesto of the restaurant's principles. It included points about cooking, such as:

> Cooking is a language through which all the following properties may be expressed: harmony, creativity, happiness, beauty, poetry, complexity, magic, humour, provocation and culture.
> . . .

Spanish Cook Ferran Adrià, seen in the kitchen of his restaurant elBulli on 16 June 2007 in Roses, Spain.

As has occurred in most fields of human evolution down the ages, new technologies are a resource for the progress of cooking.

The family of stocks is being extended. Together with the classic ones, lighter stocks performing an identical function are now being used (waters, broths, consommés, clarified vegetable juses, nut milk, etc.).

But it also covered service and the experience of dining, such as 'A new way of serving food is being promoted. The dishes are finished in the dining room by the serving staff. In other cases the diners themselves participate in this process', or 'Decontextualisation, irony, spectacle, performance are completely legitimate, as long as they are not superficial but respond to, or are closely bound up with, a process of gastronomic reflection.'[15]

Adrià's deep commitment to eating as an act that 'engages the senses, emotions, and intellect of the participant', which sometimes involves huffing orange-flavoured air from a balloon while you eat sorbet, may seem – like the other eating experiences in this chapter – a far cry from what happens at your neighbourhood restaurant (unless you live in a quite affluent area). However, these acts – thinking through ingredients; adopting technologies that help one to cook better, more safely and more easily; considering the customer and pantry in making a meal – are part of every restaurant kitchen, no matter the price point.

5
THE MAÎTRE D' AND THE WAITRESS

In 2012 Tokyo-based Shin Miyazaki won the international competition for the best maître d'. To do so he had to expertly pair wines with dishes, flambé a pineapple and instil confidence and a sense of ease in his guests – in addition to a battery of other tasks and expectations in the nine-round tournament. One hundred years before that, Oscar Tschirky was providing equally exquisite service for the Egyptian ruler Mehmed Ali Pasha and the American aristocrat Andrew Carnegie at the Waldorf-Astoria Hotel in New York. And two hundred years ago, in Paris, diners were receiving exquisite service at Véry's. But before the first French restaurant, three hundred years ago in Tokyo, teahouses were providing elaborate dining experiences in the establishments that would become some of the finest restaurants in the world.

The 'front of the house' is a distinctive feature of the restaurant. Someone seats you at a table. Someone takes your order. Someone serves you your food. They may do this with aplomb, or it may be an ordeal of slights and judgements. The history of waiters, and waitresses, is hardly linear and even.

It is a profession defined by images of snobby men and sharp women, of warm women and dexterous men. The idea of what a good waiter or waitress should be stays fairly constant across cultures and times, but the lives of the people who take these jobs and their cultural reputation varies. In this chapter, we will look at both expectations and experiences of the front of the house from the customer's perspective as well as delving into the lives of the people who wait tables.

OF SERVANTS, SERVICE AND SERVERS

For most people, for most of history, dinner was served by those who made it, and those they served it to and ate it with were family. However, in this chapter, we are going to explore food served by *others*, a story that begins with servants and strangers.

The early history of waiting tables sits somewhere between entrepreneurship and servitude. These two paths to get food from the kitchen to the person dining are intertwined – and shed light on complicated relationships between waiters and customers and the contentious practice of tipping.

Servants were the first people to provide table service. In royal households, this work involved elaborate traditions and codes even in ancient times. Outside of wealthy households and feasting culture, early table service throughout the world was provided by people labouring in inns and taverns. In the ancient, medieval and early modern worlds, as today, there were travellers: people who were far enough away from home that they could have dinner with neither family nor friends. The world's major religions, including Hinduism, Islam, Judaism, Christianity and Buddhism, have scripture and traditions that present an imperative to offer provisions to strangers. While this is religiously

framed in the context of altruism, at some point the same situation also drove a new kind of business. Invite someone in, but have them barter or pay for food and lodging. Over time, these home and religious businesses shifted. One place where this shift is documented was along the Camino de Santiago, a Christian pilgrimage route in Spain that traces its origins to the tenth century. As people continually travelled the path, it transformed. Initially travellers were fed by occasional abbeys, funded by churchgoers (both local and abroad). However, as more pilgrims took to the route, the roads came to be lined with all sorts of purveyors of foods and other forms of hospitality appropriate for the travelling pious who ranged from the poor to the well-heeled aristocracy. There was even a guidebook

Philipp Kester, *Portrait of the 'Oscar' from the Waldorf-Astoria Hotel, c.* 1904, photograph.

George Boldt,
*A Portion of the
Kitchen at the
Waldorf Astoria,*
1903, photograph.

George Boldt,
*Restaurant at the
Waldorf Hotel,*
1903, photograph.

Suzuki Harunobu, *The Watchers and the Watched*, 1764–72, polychrome woodblock print, ink and colour on paper.

in the twelfth century that published the best places to eat and sleep along the route.[1] While there are still restaurants across the world that evoke a feeling of entering one's home (often because you are literally entering someone's home), other spaces adapted to become more and more codified in their service practices, and expanded to be able to host more than one party. They became inns, taverns and boarding houses. They are places where strangers serve food to other strangers, at a cost.

WAITRESSES IN EDO

Economies that served travellers sprung up along pilgrimage routes to Mecca and to Jerusalem, along

Kazumasa Ogawa, *Mousmée in Country Teahouse*, 1897, hand-coloured albumen silver print.

the 53 stations of the *Tōkaidō* in Japan, and along Incan roads. As discussed in Chapters One and Two, many of these places were not like contemporary restaurants; however, inn or restaurant, they did often have people whose job it was to bring food to the table.

The roads of the Edo period (1603–1868) in Japan are a good example of how food service was part of a complex travellers' economy. The *Gokaidō* (Five Routes) were built to improve communication and commerce across Japan, particularly between Kyoto and Edo. At each stop were inns that came to employ a particular kind of waiter: *meshimori onna*, translated as either meal-serving women or, more vividly, rice-piling women.

The women, who were waitresses in these *Gokaidō* inns, were also a type of prostitute. The businesses along the route were allowed by law to employ only two *meshimori onna*. They were neither geisha (hostesses and entertainers not employed by a restaurant or teahouse and not in the sex trade) nor were they courtesans (higher-class women who worked in the sex trade, usually employed by particular men or social groups). These women were employed by the inn itself and acted as both waitresses and sex workers. They were forbidden by law from wearing anything but cotton, so that they would not be confused with higher-class courtesans in silks.[2]

The images we have of them, from Ukiyo-e prints and early photographs, present them as beautiful and often well dressed. These images, which in English usually are captioned with the term 'waitress', often illustrate the dual position of these women – they hold teapots or trays of rice and pickle bowls, while bedding sits in the background. For example, Utagawa Hiroshige shows these women in his Akasaka print from *The Fifty-three Stations of the Tōkaidō Highway*. A waitress serves

Utagawa Hiroshige, *Akasaka, Ryosha Sho-fu*, c. 1834, polychrome woodblock print, ink and colour on paper.

Utagawa Hiroshige, *Mariko; Meibutsu Chaya*, c. 1834, polychrome woodblock print, ink and colour on paper.

Ernst Ludwig Kirchner, *Head Waiter in Café*, 1904, polychrome woodcut print, ink and colour on paper.

of Naniwa-ya Okita, waitress of the Naniwa-ya teahouse located on the east side of Asakusa Temple, includes this poem:

> While relaxing at a teahouse in Naniwacho,
> No one can fail to stop in here
> as they pass by the leggy weeds of Naniwa's straits
> whatever his reason for coming.[3]

There were also women who were waitresses along these routes who had no other role. Hiroshige depicts one of these in his Mariko print from the same set. The woman who is serving the meal is holding a child on her back and is not rendered in elegant clothing. She is simply serving food at a roadside restaurant.[4] Many years later, these two figurations of the waitress – as sexualized objects and as working women – informed how businesses hired at a moment of social conflict in the early twentieth century.

By the nineteenth century, charming and deft Japanese waitresses were turning up across literature. In a scene in the sentimental novel *Spring Colour Plum Calendar* (1833), former lovers meet up at a restaurant, where the waitress demonstrates an intuitive knowledge of what they need and when.

a customer dinner, while elsewhere other waitresses use mirrors to get made up for work. The bedding that just peeks around the corner signals the other work these women might do, as do the postures and expressions of the men. Women working in teahouses, in and out of cities in Edo-period Japan, became the focus of poetry and stories, which lauded their work and their beauty, a move that may either be a reflection of genuinely good food service or innuendo (or both). For example, the late eighteenth-century Kitagawa Utamaro print

> Just then the waitress brought up some tea.
> 'What'll you have?' she asked.
> 'Yeah, well, grill us three plates of medium-size ones,' Tanjiro said.
> 'What about some saké?'
> 'No,' said Tanjiro. 'We'll stick to food. Good old food. Or, Ocho, what do you say to having a little to drink?'
> 'No thanks,' Ocho said, grinning.
> The waitress, sensing something between them, picked up a small standing screen leaning against

Waiters' Race: An original race between waiters held in Berlin, September 1930, photograph. The route was over 100 metres, and required participants to transport a filled coffee service undamaged to its destination.

the stairs railing and stood it near them to give them some privacy. Then she went down the stairs noisily.

The waitress returns at just the right moment to bring them eel and rice, leaves them promptly, and is ready at the moment they need their bill. These might seem like silly details; however, in terms of 'good service', this unnamed character clearly reflects things that have been central to understanding waiters and waitresses: the expectation of pleasure in interaction, of intuition and attention. While this early Japanese history is highly gendered and often sexualized, the early European version of the perfect waiter is also gendered – but male –

and occupies an interstitial space between adviser and servant.

FRENCH WAITERS AND MAÎTRE D'S

Nineteenth-century Europe is dotted with men who worked their way up from waiting tables to running restaurant empires. While the role of server might seem like it should be subordinate, in many ways, waiters become managers and, especially in early European restaurants, waiters manage their customers.

Stories of snobby French waiters often ring of stereotype. Yet French waiters in the nineteenth century occupied an unusual social place in terms

César Ritz and
Marie-Louise
Ritz in 1888,
photograph.

of their knowledge. Despite being in a position of service, waiters were regularly in a position of power. This would begin with a simple process at the door: the head waiter would decide where patrons were to be seated, sorting them by class and social standing. For people unfamiliar with restaurant cuisine, waiters were more well versed than them with the menu and the customs of dining out. For people who frequented restaurants, waiters often became familiar with their lives, desires, foibles and quibbles. Moreover, male waiters were trained to exude a sense of control, even when they were not in control of a situation (including the basic things, like getting food out of the kitchen).

In his *Paris á table* (1846), Eugéne Briffault described the features of French waiters this way:

> The restaurant waiter should be nimble, alert, quick to respond, clean, charming, a little bit of a picaresque and of Frontinus [an analytic Roman senator known for his hydraulics expertise] . . . The waiter is especially admirable during his rush hours; he is everywhere, serving twenty tables at once; he carries stacks of dishes with the skill of the most accomplished tight-rope walker, without breaking a thing; he forgets nothing, knows how to fix and manage everything.[5]

In the late nineteenth century, the dexterity of waiters, which gave rise to a number of film scenes and cartoons, was celebrated in events called waiters' races. Dressed in uniform the waiters would race each other while balancing trays of plates and glasses. While all in good fun, the contests reflected the physical prowess a waiter was expected to have. At some restaurants, waiters were drilled as if in military regiments. Beyond physical prowess, social interaction – the ability to remember, improvise and manage a room full of expectant customers – was (and is) one of the key skills required of a waiter. A small poem from 1901 spells this out:

Pick out some first-class waiter,
I'll tell you what you'll find,
A man of keen perception,
One with an active mind,
Who reads a guest like magic,
And tells quick as a flash
If he will call for sweetbreads
Or make his order 'hash.'[6]

While France has a long and much fawned-over tradition of waiters who occupy the position for an entire lifetime, some waiters in the nineteenth century moved up the chain of management. Two of the most famous – in Europe and in the United States – became maître d'hôtels.

César Ritz began his career in the 1860s by hopping between a series of jobs (and losing a few) as a waiter, first in his home country of Switzerland then in Paris, at hotels, cafés and working-class restaurants. He was likely never the winner of the waiters' races: he lost one job for breaking too many dishes. However, he clearly had the managerial mind of a waiter (able to keep track of customers' requests, quickly read people, and organize and intuit the room) as well as a commitment to customers. He became a restaurant manager in Paris and then moved on to being the maître d' at various grand hotels across Europe. (During this time, he met and began working with Escoffier.) Eventually, he opened his own set of hotels. Ritz was an ideal fine restaurant manager because he loved two things: happy rich people and what came to be called – after him and his establishments – ritzy experiences. He was as likely to spend time without guests – preparing spaces, making the right hires, discussing menus and decor – as he was to spend it with them.

In the United States, in 1883, a boy named Oscar Tschirky arrived in New York from Switzerland and immediately got a job as a busboy, a young worker whose job it was to clear the tables. Within four months, he was a waiter. His next move was to Delmonico's. There he learned how to work with well-heeled clients, like the Astors and Lillian Russell. An immigrant from a poor family, he spoke three languages and was enamoured with New York's elite. Over time, the feeling grew to be mutual. When the Waldorf Hotel opened in 1893, Tschirky (who generally went by his first name, Oscar) was given the position of maitre d'hotel. Over his career, he became almost synonymous with the hotel. There was a sense that he was in charge of what happened. If one held a special event, he coordinated it; if one just came for dinner, he had coordinated it. People felt he knew everyone, which was in some respects true. Not only did he become familiar, even friends, with a litany of wealthy and famous people, he had an army of contacts to rely on for the best parsley, the best music and the best linens. Tschirky, and other maître d's of the time, created a sense of value by making a patron feel that things were just as they wanted; however, at the same time, their goal was not to make everyone welcome. Fine-dining establishments, especially those at the very top, thrived not on friendliness (which would come to be a desired hallmark of middle-class establishments) but on gatekeeping. By being selectively welcoming, these places created prestige and demand. Tschirky and Ritz built the power of their dining rooms by creating barriers to some and coddling others. This aspect of judgement in service is yet another way that the front of house manages the restaurant, selecting customers as the kitchen selects food.

WAITING TABLES IN THE NINETEENTH CENTURY

In mid-nineteenth century America, service defined – and graded – restaurants. In his book *New York in Slices* (1849), the American journalist George G. Foster says:

> There are three distinct classes of eating-houses, and each has its model or type. Linnæus would probably classify them as Sweenyorum, Browniverous, and Delmonican. The Sweenyorum is but an extension downward of the Browniverous . . . The chief difference to be noted between the two is, that while at Brown's the waiters actually do pass by you within hail now and then, at Sweeney's no such phenomenon ever by *any possibility occurs.*

While Sweeny's or Brown's and eateries of their ilk (the six-penny eating houses described in more detail below) are very much restaurants in the sense of having menus, servers and bills, for Foster, there is only one *restaurant* (italicized by Foster, either because it is still a foreign word or for emphasis): Delmonico's. And its glory is framed by both its cuisine and its service.

Foster was not alone in his fascination with the service at Delmonico's. The restaurant was renowned for its gracious atmosphere and attentive waiting staff. Even when it was just a café, its service and decor separated it from other establishments. It sported richly coloured curtains and mirrors. By the late nineteenth century, its service had competition from places like the Waldorf-Astoria and the Ritz, but initially Delmonico's version of service was unparalleled. The waiters were known for remembering customers' names, providing excellent dish suggestions and serving the meal seamlessly. Like the waitress in *Spring Colour Plum Calendar*, Foster said of the waiters at Delmonico's, 'Without seeming to observe you, [they] are always at your elbow at the moment when you are beginning to think about wishing for something. They listen to you with grave attention which assures you that you are to receive exactly what you have ordered in the shortest possible time.'[7]

Twenty years later, in *Last Days of Knicker-bocker Life in New York*, Abram C. Dayton was still impressed by the discreet service: 'On entering from Fourteenth Street, one cannot fail to be impressed by the absence of bustle and confusion; no boisterous commands are heard, and the waiters glide about as noiselessly as ghosts. An air of luxury surrounds you as the attentive garçon stands motionless before you and respectfully awaits your wishes.'[8]

However, most people could not afford Delmonico's. This did not mean they did not experience eating out while being waited on by servers. If they lived in cities, they went to the predecessors of much of restaurant dining today: of cafeterias, diners and quick-food franchises. In New York City, as well as other major cities around the world, many people ate at inexpensive eating houses. In Manhattan, these low-end places sprang up in the 1830s and 1840s. In this time, business and housing districts in New York were becoming more distinct;

Uniformed Waitresses, Oslo, c. 1899–1930, photograph.

especially after the fire of 1836, many working people were not close enough to go home for lunch (and not rich enough to go to Delmonico's). They were looking for sustenance that would not take too much out of their pay or too much time out of their day. The places they went to were the predecessors of diners, and offered what would come to be called in the United States 'short-order' cooking. In the eating houses with the least service (and often the lowest prices), diners called their orders to waiters who stood at the end of an aisle. These waiters then shouted the order to the kitchen. The menu was limited, and so the dishes were usually ready to serve almost instantly. These places served many people, almost entirely men, during lunch hours in the cities.

An upper-class writer in *Harper's Weekly* in March 1857 described the places this way:

Outside the door was hung a large white placard, on which were inscribed the various dishes to be had within. A small steak was sixpence. A cup of coffee was three cents. The rest of the dishes in like proportion. Dimes shuddered as he beheld the interior. It was a long, low room, filled with about twenty little tables, on which were spread blotched table-cloths that seemed to be afflicted with the disease of chronic mustard-stains. A fatty vapor filled the saloon, through which waiters, with sleeves rolled up and slippers in the last stages of decay, went up and down, performing feats of jugglery with plates and knives. Here and there a few guests were scattered . . . They were all eating, with a strange, savage earnestness, and in silence.

Dimes sank, quite overcome, into a chair, and a tattered, greasy boy shuffled up to us, and took my orders. In a very short time, during which period Dimes's gaze wandered vaguely over the table appointments, the boy returned with two chipped plates, on each of which lay a section of a black, elastic substance, known as a small steak.

These eating establishments were important for urban workers. They provided a place for them to get sustenance in locations where access to their homes and to kitchens was scarce. This new class of people eating out, and new class of dining options, gave rise to new types of service as well. While the historical Foster and the fictional Dimes might have derided the service at these restaurants, it reflected a new trend, taking cues from taverns and takeaway establishments but mixing in the potential for individual choices – the marker of restaurants.

THE RISE OF WAITRESSES

While waitresses would not become a subject of public debate until the early twentieth century, women have been serving food to customers for ages. In family-run businesses, especially inns and boarding houses, women were often in charge of preparing and presenting food. A waitress, however, has a slightly different role: like a waiter, her job is to interact with customers as well as presenting them food.

Through most of the nineteenth century, men dominated the waiting scene in Europe, the United States and China; however, the twentieth century saw a significant change. The workforce altered as the categories of restaurants expanded. Women were most often found working in mid-to-low-priced restaurants – cafés, diners and lunchrooms. In the

Womens Social Political Union Waitresses at Women's Exhibition, London, 1909, photograph.

United States in 1900, women made up 40 per cent of the waiting staff (41,178); by 1940 they made up 68 per cent (356,036 – the industry itself also grew exponentially).[9] In Sweden, in the early twentieth century, 83 per cent of restaurant industry workers were women. Of these, 96 per cent were unwed, and most had recently moved from the country to the city.[10] By 1936 there were 100,000 waitresses in Japan.

With the rise of female servers came debates around women's role in the economy and society across the globe as well as a new cultural icon, alternately beloved and chastised: the waitress. Cowboy poet E. A. Brininstool's 1903 poem 'The Restaurant Girl' is a prime example of the cultural perception of waitresses:

We have heard from time immortal of the man
    behind the gun,
And we are told in song and story of the many
    deeds he's done;
And in other life vocations man has won our
    lasting praise,
And we've heard his valor mentioned in a thou-
    sand different ways.
And fair woman – bless her picture! – we would
    save a little room
To relate about the woman who is perched
    behind the broom;
There are others whom I'd mention, but the
    praises now I chant
Of the girl behind the counter in the smoky
    restaurant.

Ah, the girl behind the counter! She is filled
    with go and dash,
And there's magic in her manners as she
    sweetly murmurs, 'Hash!'
And she flies around like sixty, and she hits

the floor in spots,
When a voice yells from the kitchen, 'Take
    away a plate o' hots!'
Note her wild gymnastic motions when you've
    placed your order, and
She comes tearing back with dishes loaded down
    in either hand!
And 'Draw one,' she carols sweetly as she orders
    coffee up,
And she asks you, 'Cakes or sinkers?' when she
    brings the steaming cup.

There she stands behind the counter, while
    around her are displayed
Slabs of pie, doughnuts and sinkers – deadly
    emblems of her trade.
What a picture for an artist as around the place
    she flies!
Note the grace with which she ladles out the
    soup and slashes pies!
'Shipwrecks flopped – on toast,' she carols. Ah,
    the magic she'll display,
As she balances so deftly on her palm a loaded
    tray.
And there's method in her madness, as she
    shrieks while on the run:
'Send me six links o' cable down here with a
    brown-stone front – well done.'

You can praise a wartime hero, and a model of
    him make.
But the girl behind the counter is the one who
    takes the cake.
Eulogize your earthly idol; sound his praises
    down the line –
But the girl behind the counter in the restaurant
    is mine!
Aye, give me the little maiden when she's work-
    ing at her best,

And I'll leave to you the heroes and the idols
    and the rest.
You can laud them to the heavens if you want to,
    but I'll chant
Of the girl behind the counter in the smoky
    restaurant![11]

People were captivated by waitresses. Restaurateurs also began designing waitresses to captivate. For many years, women who waited tables wore outfits that were similar to household servers (and to their male counterparts – male waiters often wore dark coats, white shirts and trousers, not unlike the livery one would see in aristocratic houses). The waitress would be clothed in a dark dress, with an apron and maybe a bonnet. However, in the late nineteenth and early twentieth century, staff uniforms transformed into eye-catching costumes (at least for women).

In 1895 a Manhattan restaurateur decided his waitresses should wear bloomers. The outfit did gain attention. The *New York Times* reported on it, and said that the one waitress who agreed to wear the bloomers did 'draw a larger crowd, which filled both sides of Nassau Street and attempted to get into the restaurants, but only part of the crowd could be accommodated'. However, most of the waitresses refused the new costumes and threatened to strike (and were supported in this by the waiters who worked with them).[12] This story exemplifies tensions that arose around waitresses, and particularly about working conditions and the sexualization of these jobs. This was not a phenomenon only in America or in the West.

In Japan, café waitresses, called *jokyu*, continued from the tradition of eroticized food service of the *meshimori onna*. Further, in the entertainment districts in cities in Japan, women had long worked in a mix of service professions, from geisha, who provided company and entertainment, to waitresses to women in the sex trade. However, during the Meiji period (1868–1912), Japan began a sustained engagement with countries outside of Asia. Along with a national interest in Western practices and politics, much of the population became fascinated by Western culture. This led to an explosion of different kinds of aesthetics and businesses, including the Paris café. Café waitresses came from a wider range of backgrounds, were working in what was seen as a modern context and engaged with a wider range of women and men than would have gone to the entertainment districts of Japan's cities. For these reasons, the conversation around this work was more fraught. Western cafés became popular in Japan beginning in the 1910s.

The dramatic increase in the number of waitresses was both a product of the popularity of cafés and the shifting expectations of waitresses in cafés. These women were often engaged not only in serving food, but in emotional labour. They listened and talked to clientele, spent time with them and flirted. By the 1930s the customer–waitress interaction became the key aspect of their jobs; to compete, cafés began hiring waitresses at a ratio to customers of almost 1:1 and introducing practices that make those 1895 bloomers seem quaint. For example, one place in Ginza had the women carry small keyboards on which they would play a note and sing based on where a customer touched them. As one can imagine, these kinds of practices led to a wave of discourse in magazines and from social critics.

The waitresses were typified as 'modern girls' (a moniker one sees across the world for women at that point). They were the focus of magazines, in photography and cartoons, in essays and novels. For example, Tanizaki Jun'ichirō's early twentieth-century novel *Naomi* tells the story of a young waitress. One of her customers is captivated by her

A photograph of Harvey Girls gathered in the dining room of the Atchison, Topeka & Santa Fe Railway Company's Fred Harvey House at the Bisonte Hotel, Hutchinson, KS, c. 1920–29.

and decides to take her as his Eliza Doolittle. He educates and marries her. However, modern girl that she is, she eventually controls this man's life.[13]

Many of these women did come to be independent in ways that were new. They did decide with whom they would spend their time, including men. Also, given the poor pay and poor treatment, they learned to organize. Like waitresses across the world, they unionized for better treatment and fairer pay.[14]

In China in the 1930s, the story was similar – but with a very different ending. Chinese literature,

film and magazines sighed, in lust or anxiousness, over the 'modern girl', short-haired, self-possessed and out for pleasure (a similar discourse to that in Europe, the United States and Japan).[15] Waitresses were generally hired for their youth and good looks, they were expected to flirt, and they were often part of the advertising strategy of restaurateurs. The salary of these waitresses was quite low, but they were also tipped, which could provide significantly more income.

However, waiters got the political upper hand by taking a moralizing tone towards waitresses.

As women began waitressing in Chinese cities, they changed the available work for men – competing for jobs and driving down waiters' wages – because of a mix of women's subordinate social position and their eroticization. Just as the novelty of women servers drew crowds in the West, it did so too in the East. The women who took these jobs also trod the same lines between making a good living and being respectable. Employers liked waitresses because they often came at lower wages and increased customer demand; however, in China, the pressure for respectability came not only from outside sources, but from employers themselves. Waitresses were often the victims of sexual harassment, but were blamed for their situation. Relying on and propagating stories of morally corrupt and abused women (playing both sides of the coin), the major guild of waiters successfully lobbied the government to pass regulations outlawing women from working as waitresses. While the guise of the law was for the protection of women, its outcome was to put many of them out of work, eliminating their livelihoods.[16]

WAITRESSING AND RESPECTABILITY

One of the most interesting moments in the history of waitressing comes at the end of the nineteenth century in the Harvey House chain of restaurants. The Harvey House waitresses were touted as a different kind of waitress: nice, middle-class women. As we will see, this claim, true or not, was based on the hiring practices, and contracts and terms, of the restaurants. This Harvey House vision of a waitress came to be idealized in a whole range of middle-American restaurants, which rapidly expanded in the twentieth century. Changes in the image of female workers in these establishments helped waitresses (specifically white waitresses) rather than waiters (white men or men of colour) become the norm.

The Harvey Houses, developed by Fred Harvey, were a chain of restaurants at train stations across the American West. It was not Fred Harvey who invented the idea of hiring women for his restaurants. In restaurants that were situated in more western locales, he initially encouraged his managers to hire black men. However, one of his managers, Tom Raton, thought that it would be easier to control white female waitresses and thought that they might also help reduce the number of violent incidents at his location in New Mexico.[17] The waitresses he and Harvey hired came to be presented as a transformative population in the western United States.

'Harvey Girls' was the moniker given to the Harvey House waitresses, a tradition of branded waitresses that seemed to die out in the 1960s, just as Playboy Bunnies emerged. Harvey Girls were not Playboy Bunnies. Single women earning a wage outside the home were considered morally suspect in the late nineteenth century, and waitresses even more so because they were in constant and seemingly intimate engagement with men. However, waitresses that worked for the Harvey Houses lived in company housing, with matrons who monitored their behaviour and kept strict hours, with strict rules about what types of clothing to wear at what times. Their uniform was plain, long-sleeved with an Elsie collar, black shoes and stockings, and a white apron – the uniform of an actual nineteenth-century French maid. (This particular aesthetic costume of servitude informed many waitress uniforms and depictions over the next century.) Harvey Girls were to wear the uniform for all shifts, generally twelve hours a day, six days a week, and when trains arrived in the night. On Friday night, they were allowed to wear their own clothes to events that the eating house held.[18] For all the regimentation, these women were paid well; given travel, room and board (which included anything in the Harvey House kitchens except for fruit in season); and had the chance to move up socio-economically, either through promotion within the Harvey House system or through marriage (which was the more common outcome).

For some of the Harvey House waitresses, marriage and wealth was not the goal. Two women who provide a sense of the wider opportunities that the Harvey Houses offered are Janet Ferrier and Alice Stackhouse. The historian Lesley Poling-Kempes collected the story of these adventurous friends. Ferrier was a Scottish woman who was told by a London doctor that she would be blind by the time she reached middle-age. Her response was to see the world. She came to America and while working in a Florida resort met Stackhouse, who was committed to the same goal. These adventuring waitresses decided to go west as Harvey House girls. The company preferred women who signed up together, and would assign them to the same location and have them be roommates. This absolutely worked out for Ferrier and Stackhouse. For forty years, they would work for a while, then quit and travel for a few months – visiting a laundry list of countries in four continents. After each trip, they would return to the Harvey House and work until they had saved up enough to travel again. Ferrier never lost her sight.[19]

Becoming a Harvey House waitress was not a simple feat. Women were required to be educated (with at least a u.s. eighth-grade education, equivalent to year nine in the uk, in the 1880s), have excellent speech and manners, and be able and willing to leave almost at once for training and then an assignment at a destination west of the Mississippi for at least six months of work. The company had thousands of applicants.[20] The women who became Harvey Girls were often referred to in the press and in anecdotes as 'smart', in all senses of the word. The system and the company rewarded this smartness. Women who continued in their employment at the Harvey Houses could move up into the position of manager, with equal duties and pay to their male counterparts.[21] (Harvey House kitchens were a different story. The women and people of colour, men and women, who staffed, cooked and cleaned in these houses were often stuck in the lowest-paying jobs and had little room for mobility. Occasionally, men of colour moved up in the system; however, their opportunities were not equal even to those of white women working at Harvey Houses. In this way, Harvey Houses were like many other restaurants in the United States and Europe in the nineteenth, twentieth and twenty-first centuries.[22])

The Harvey House rules for their waitresses were strict in part in order to attract and maintain good staff. The sexualized vision of waitresses was one shared across the globe, and so, to attract and keep the kinds of people they wanted, the Harvey Houses were fighting common perceptions. Moreover, Harvey House waitresses headed west into territory that was considered even more dangerous and ripe with immorality. This reputation, at least as it related to waitresses, was unfounded. In the west, prostitution and waitressing were quite separate occupations (according to one study conducted at the time, only one in 230 women sex workers in California in 1888 had experience as a waitress). However, hand-wringing moralists are rarely persuaded by facts, and the social stigma of being a waitress could be a real liability. In her research in the 1980s, historian Poling-Kempes found that some women who had been Harvey Girls were still unwilling to be interviewed because they did not want their families to know they had waitressed.

There are many stories, in popular culture and oral histories, of successful Harvey House waitresses. Edna Ferber's short story 'Our Very Best People' (1924), originally published in *Cosmopolitan*, tells the story of Hannah, a woman whose father loses her inheritance to gambling. She becomes a Harvey House waitress and marries a brakeman who goes on to become a division superintendent. In 1946 Harvey House waitresses became the centre of another mythologized story of love and success, in *The Harvey Girls*, a musical film starring Judy Garland and Angela Lansbury (based on a 1942 novel). These somewhat cloying stories reflect the hopes and carefully maintained corporate image of Harvey Girls. When the women were hired, they agreed not to get married for a year; if they did, half their salary was forfeited. As waitresses with a reputation for being fastidious and smart in a part of America where men still outnumbered women, the marriage rate for these women was high; however, marriage did not guarantee financial well-being or happiness. The character Hannah in Ferber's story is representative of a group of real women who married well and used their experiences at the Harvey House as a launching pad for a respectable and fulfilling life in the western United States.

GETTING A TABLE

Who does and does not get service in a restaurant is often at the heart of the cultural cachet restaurant workers can bestow or withhold. There are more cartoons and columns about being seated in a bad part of a restaurant than one can count. The frame for these stories is often prejudice – who looks important, wealthy or beautiful.

In fact, most restaurants have a person whose main job is to figure out which seat a person should be in. In high-end dining, this person is the maître d'. With people like Oscar Tschirky, the position

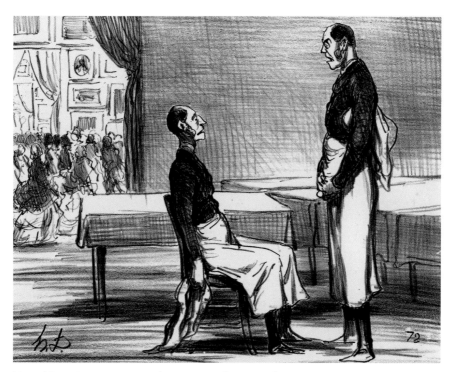

Honoré Daumier, *Le Restaurant de L'Exposition*, from 'Le Salon de 1857', *Le Charivari*, 1 July 1857, lithograph on newsprint.

African American students sit-in – waiting for service and demonstrating against segregation – at a Woolworth's counter in Little Rock, Arkansas, 1963, photograph.

flourished in the nineteenth century and early twentieth century, along with grand hotels. It is still of particular importance in high-end dining. However, at mid-range restaurants, this person is often known as the host or hostess (taking their language from inns and taverns rather than restaurants). At the heart of the position is making sure that customers are seated in a space where there is a waitress or waiter to attend to them. The work of this position is as much about time management of the workers in the restaurant as about placement in a room (though, of course, most hosts and hostesses aim to put people in the more pleasant places first).

Being seated is an experience most diners take for granted; however, in the United States, who could eat where was a pressing issue for more than one hundred years. African Americans were routinely denied service at many eating establishments. During the American Civil Rights Movement of the mid-twentieth century, restaurant service was a key issue and restaurants were a common site for sit-ins, a form of non-violent protest that illustrated – for all to see – the inequality that black Americans regularly faced. On 1 February 1960, four black students sat down at a Woolworth's lunch counter in Greensboro, North Carolina, designated for 'whites only'. The management and staff refused to serve them. The protesters left at the end of the day, but returned everyday afterwards, joined by increasingly more people for the next six months. During that time, sit-ins spread to lunch counters and restaurants across the southeastern United States. Citizens peacefully demanding equal rights were often subject to vile and violent abuse by white management, staff and fellow citizens. On 25 July 1960, three black people – Woolworth's employees – were finally served at the Greensboro lunch counter. Some other restaurants followed suit, but others refused – as they were allowed to do by law until 1964, and as many places continued to do (illegally) after that.

The sit-ins are some of the most well-known stories in the demand for equal access to restaurants; however, they are part of a longer story of African American strategies for attaining access and recognition, including passing and orchestrating boycotts. The historian Audrey Russek tells the story of another dramatic intervention and awareness-raising act centred on restaurants that happened in Maryland in 1961.

In the 1960s African nations were gaining their independence and were sending black African diplomats to the United States. This presented a problem for the State Department. While the United States wanted to show its support for these new nations (especially during the Cold War), the representatives of these countries were subjected to the United States' racial caste system, which was most commonly apparent to visitors in the moments when they were refused service at restaurants. In response to this, the State Department considered creating a hybrid of a Green Book (a guidebook that presented places where black people were welcome as they travelled across the country) and the Michelin Guide (the standard-bearer of restaurant guides across the world). While this idea did not get off the ground, another did: the State Department would reach out to restaurant owners and managers in the Washington, DC, area and encourage them to extend service, not to American blacks, but to African blacks. Further, they would provide training for workers to recognize (that is, profile) Africans and African Americans.

After this programme was underway, a group of black journalists from the *Baltimore AfroAmerican* newspaper created a plan for an undercover investigation, to demonstrate the state of restaurant service for blacks, African and not, and to document how local restaurants responded to African diplomats.[23] To do so, they decided to pose as a group of African dignitaries. Herb Mangrum, who would play the finance minister of a false nation, rented elaborate traditional African clothing, including a turban with a leopard-print crown; fellow journalists Rufus Wells and George Collins wore formal coats with tails and top hats. The group hired a limousine and assumed fake names and accents. They toured five restaurants in the Baltimore area. At each one, they would see if they were to be seated and served – and what that service was like.

On 22 August 1961 they began their tour. The outcomes ranged widely. At the first place, the staff was so taken by the story of the African entourage that the waitress asked for an autograph. At the next, they were seated; however, the service was cold and actively sceptical and hostile. The manager told them, 'We don't serve Negroes. Africans, yes, because President Kennedy told us so.' This was a direct reflection of the State Department's work, although the spoken sentiment and poor treatment undercut the purpose of the training. Their reception at yet another restaurant also supported the clarity, but poor implementation, of the State Department plan. The host initially refused to serve the party, but a manager later did seat them because he was worried about the repercussions from the State Department. Two other restaurants refused the party entirely. One claimed to be serving no one at the time (a common anti-integration strategy); the other simply turned them away.

While the Civil Right Acts of 1964 changed the American restaurant scene, prejudice around service – from waiters to customers and customers to waiters – of minorities continues to be a problem in restaurants. Continued studies – qualitative and quantitative – of the experiences of black diners demonstrate that racial profiling and racism still affect what table people are given and the quality of their service.

TIPS

Restaurants are places with complex power dynamics. This can manifest in single interactions or in the relationships that form between customers and waiting staff over repeated visits. However, one of the most fraught moments in this interaction is when the waiter or waitress brings the bill. How people pay the bill – and tip – varies between cultures. In Germany, for example, parties often split the bill quite exactly, whereas in the United States, a variety of different ways of splitting the bill, or not, are adopted. In many places, the bill is still delivered to the men in the party, despite the fact that a woman might be just as likely to pay for the meal. The greatest diversity however is probably in tipping.

The question of tipping for service in restaurants is, historically, a Western concern. Tipping originally began as a medieval vail – payment given to a servant for exceptional service or, more often, to a servant by a guest staying at the house. When one would visit a great home, one would give a small payment to the staff – footmen, valets, other Downton-Abbey-type professionals – for the work they did while the guest was there. This custom morphed into tipping servers at restaurants, likely through the path of coffeehouses or taverns.

One of the most charming, though apocryphal, stories of tipping is that the word itself comes from an acronym: 'To Insure Promptitude'. In one version from around the 1760s, the creator of the first English dictionary (*A Dictionary of the English Language*) Samuel Johnson and his friends frequented a coffeehouse which had on the table a bowl engraved with the words 'To Insure Promptitude', which were shortened to T.I.P. While such a vessel almost certainly existed, the *Oxford English Dictionary* refutes this as the origin of the word. It was in regular usage for servants by the 1750s. In Germany and France, the terms for tipping – *Trinkgeld* and *pourboire* – promote the health and happiness of the server, translating loosely as 'drinking money', with the simultaneous suggestion of a toast and a bit of cash with which to imbibe. The term is originally German, and was adopted into French.

Tipping, a custom that began with servants, moved into places with public servers; however, these people were not servants. It is that complicated experience of tipping – where it is no longer part of a formal master servant relationship, but is still tied to service – that makes for a different kind of relationship. Restaurants, among other service industry establishments, turn tips from a vail into a marketplace exchange, fraught with debate.

Tipping bubbles up to the surface the complicated dynamics of restaurants: having a relationship around food that is explicitly not commensal, which is defined by a market relationship. As long as tipping has been around, it has been debated. In the early twentieth century in America, several states passed laws prohibiting tipping. In South Carolina, Tennessee and Washington state, for example, tipping and taking tips was against the law; however, because the laws were so ineffective and difficult to enforce, they were repealed within a decade. In Europe, tipping was transformed by service charges in the mid-twentieth century. In 1943 the UK Catering Wages Act established a minimum wage for servers, changing the economic incentives and structures around tipping. In 1955 France passed a law that required a service charge on each tab.

Through changes in law, custom and business practice, tipping transformed across the world into the patchwork that we see today, where travelling often necessitates learning what is expected. The United States has the highest expectations for tipping – around 20 per cent of the bill. In Central and South America, you can generally tip 10 per cent: in Guatemala and Chile, that is expected on top of any service charge, while in Ecuador, it is not. In Costa Rica, tipping is generally not expected at all. While in Japan, Korea, Thailand, Vietnam, and outside of cities in China, people do not expect a tip, and may even consider giving one impolite; in India, Hong Kong and the Philippines, and urban areas of China, a tip (around 10 per cent) is expected. Most countries in the Middle East do not have tipping customs, but Israel and Saudi Arabia do. Most African nations also have tipping customs. While it seems that places that were occupied by European countries for a significant amount of time are more likely to tip, places like New Zealand, where one is not expected to tip, undermine that premise. Europe itself demonstrates a staggering diversity of expectation, from the Swiss and German tradition of simply rounding up, to 10 per cent on top of service charges just across the border in Austria. The diversity, in Europe and across the globe, reflects both cultural mores – how cash is viewed, the wide variation in concepts of gifts, bribes and fees (none of which are tips, but all of which affect the concept of a tip) – and economic conditions (the wage system within the local economy or the relationship to tourism). Further, travel experts do not even agree on the expectations in different places. The good, or bad, news is that people have been debating these local and cultural differences since tipping began.

While tipping behaviour can be predicted, to a certain extent, by sociological and psychological studies and by waiters and waitresses, it is a phenomenon that is fairly complex. Some people have argued that tipping lowers the status of the person doing the service, reinforcing the power of the customer. Others argue that tips function more like gifts, creating bonds or potential bonds between the server and the customer. At this point, tipping may also be part of the ritual experience of the restaurant, something symbolic rather than instrumental. However, tipping does appear to be used by customers as, and understood by waiting staff to be, part of a social discourse to signify myriad things: to signal solidarity, to signal bad service, to signal the diner's own sense of generosity, to make clear a recognition of a good job or someone else's bad time. It is a performance of a relationship.[24]

Anthropologists have classified two waiting staff paradigms: the waiter or waitress as 'non-person' and the waiter or waitress as interactive service worker.[25] While some literature separates these two categories based on the type of establishment, often the realities of waiting tables are more nebulous. The job requires enough interaction to welcome and satisfy the guest, but not so much that the customer feels burdened by engaging with a stranger. Seasoned waiting staff, from high-end dining to diners, often pride themselves on being able to identify and correctly interact with a given party. Over the course of the history of the restaurant, waiters and waitresses have navigated the position – and the culture of restaurants has made a wide range of behaviours acceptable, including the replacement of the waiter or waitress with the diner's own labour in the twentieth century, as we will explore in later chapters.

'Grosser Kurfürst', Ladies' Cabin, North German Lloyd, Royal Mail Steamers, c. 1890–1900, photomechanical print.

6
ROAD FOOD

While many of the historic developments in restaurants happened in cities, restaurants have also been transformed along the city's opposite: the road. From the inns along pilgrimage routes to the boarding houses and hotels thriving in cities, the history of restaurants is never far from the history of travel. In the nineteenth and twentieth centuries, changing forms of transit – ocean liners, trains, cars, highways and motorways – transformed the dining scene. As we discussed in earlier chapters, the density of cities helped the development and spread of the restaurant across the globe; however, it is the sparseness of the road – with its smaller concentration of people and places – that creates the conditions for it to shape aspects of the restaurant.

Travel raises the question of how people get food in places that are unfamiliar. Innovation on roads, rail lines and passages has been largely driven by the desire to create eating experiences that are familiar and also safe. To some extent, eating on the road is eating whatever happens to be there; however, the restaurant innovations that emerge on travel routes are about making people feel less uncertain about what they are putting into their mouths.

The origins of restaurants on roads are found along the trade and pilgrimage routes of ancient times. These routes were important spaces through which large numbers of strangers regularly moved and in which they had to make arrangements to eat. In addition to the long-distance Christian pilgrimage routes of Europe and the Middle East and the vast trade routes in Asia (from which we get Marco Polo's representations of Chinese restaurants), individual and isolated countries like Japan were establishing routes, often including paved and graded roads, by the middle of the first millennium CE. Along these roads, locally owned and government-regulated eating establishments thrived, picking up pieces of restaurant culture such as menus and private tables as time went on. However, in the early decades of the nineteenth century, the road, which had been the domain of animated living beings (people walking, horseback riders, donkey-drawn carts, oxen-team wagons) was transformed by travelling machines, marking

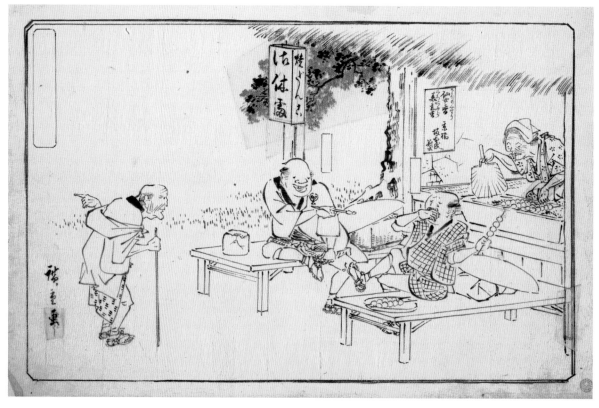

Utagawa Hiroshige, *The Famous Practical Jokers Yajirobei at a Wayside Restaurant*, c. 1840, monochrome woodblock print, ink on paper.

a seismic shift that continued into the twentieth century. The changes that these machines – trains and eventually cars – made to the experience of travel in turn transformed restaurants.

STEAM TRAINS AND SEPULCHRAL SANDWICHES

The first steam trains were established in the 1820s in England. Faster than horses, but fixed in their paths, they revolutionized the speed and route of travel. They often cut travel time in half; however, people still had to eat on long journeys, and the system of inns and taverns that had developed around the carriage roads was not accessible to rail travellers because the train line was often located away from this existing infrastructure. Instead, train passengers often coped by eating before they headed out on a journey and then again when they arrived at their destination. Some packed food to consume on the train. There also developed an entire industry of on-the-train and on-the-platform food sales. Newsboys would sell apples and other small bites. In the United States, enterprising African American women who called themselves 'waiter carriers' would sell fried chicken and other foods to passengers on trains that came through town.[1]

Passengers also ate at establishments at stations or towns when the train would stop to get more water (a necessity of steam power). These stops were short, so depot dining spots cropped up. Station

Gustav Kalhammer, *National Railway Station Restaurant, Vienna X, Josef Pohl*, 1911, colour lithograph.

Edouard Manet, *The Railway Restaurant*, c. 1879, pen and ink on wove paper.

tearooms in Great Britain provided simple meals (soup, sandwiches, savoury and sweet pies, and cakes). While many travellers railed, in diaries, news columns and other literature, against the railway food, the novelist Anthony Trollope in 1869 provided perhaps the most poetically rich description of the poor food that these stops served: he described his rail station sandwich as a 'whited sepulchre, fair enough outside, but so meagre, poor, and spiritless within'.[2]

In India the food had a better reputation. Station restaurants offered both Indian and British food, which, rather than being the tasteless or disgusting food and poor service typical of Great Britain and the United States, was often spoken of with joy: attentive and copious staff, 'delicious aromas' and variety, features that would be repeated at scale later in the American Harvey Houses. France also fared fairly well, with train depot restaurants that came to be destinations in their own right. As more people began to travel by train, and as trains fed tourism, hotels cropped up along train routes as well.

Around the world, destination hotels were built along train lines. In North America, with their low population densities and large expanses, these resorts were created as the appeal of train lines. In the United States, these resorts ran down the Florida coast to the Keys with the Flagler line; they cropped up in western states like Arizona and New Mexico, driving southwestern Native American art crazes. However some of the most stunning examples are Canada's grand hotels, built at massive scale along the railways. The first, the Windsor Hotel in Montreal, was opened in 1878, followed by more across the 1880s. The idea was to provide amazing settings and hospitality to drive visitors from abroad to ride the Canadian rails. The hotels echoed successful ones in Europe like the Ritz or the Vier Jahreszeiten in Hamburg.

DINING ON THE TRAIN

While destination dining became a grand business, dining in motion was not far behind. In 1868 George Pullman debuted the dining car. Dining cars were added to the Union Pacific, Baltimore and Ohio (B&O), Chicago, Burlington and Quincy (CB&Q) and Pennsylvania lines and were named after famous spaces of commercial hospitality: Delmonico, Southern and Tremont. The menu, seven pages in French and English, reinforced this notion by serving multi-course meals. One might begin with the consommé, followed by a turbot, then have an entrée of roast duck with tomato salad and braised celery, topped with charlotte russe for dessert. The cars were decked out in finery fit for the original Delmonico's: chandeliers, rich woods, plush upholstery, carpets; fine china, white linens and silver. Customers were waited upon. The Delmonico car had two cooks and four waiters.

Usually dining cars had their own branded china and silver. Many rail lines had simple patterns (white plates with a coloured design on the edge and their logo); however, there was also a range of florals and patterns with images that played up the scenery of a particular train route. The B&O had a pattern called Centenary that featured full blue-and-white images of their trains in picturesque views. The Santa Fe's Mimbreno pattern was conceived and designed by the railroad's architect and designer Mary Colter, who based it on motifs from the Mimbres, a Native American group in New Mexico and Arizona. The silver on the cars was generally engraved with the name of the rail line.

Dining cars spread across the train-faring world. In 1870 the first dining car aboard the train system in India was put into service. The car had an à la carte menu, a fully stocked bar, trained waiters and a chef. It served both Indian and British cuisine,

Photograph featuring Badrutt's Palace Hotel in the background, 1938.

Fairmount Hotel Vier Jahreszeiten, Hamburg, 2014.

William Notman & Son, *Dining Room, Windsor Hotel, Montreal, Canada*, 1916, photograph.

from roast chicken to madras mutton curry and biryani. Because many of the people who travelled on the railway, which was owned by a colonial company, were of British origin, the flavours of the Indian dishes were muted; at the same time many of the British dishes were prepared in the style of Indian cuisine and included some Indian spices.[3] Across the world trains offered riders their choice of foods with service while they were ferried from one place to another. On-the-train dining took off and was a touted feature of train travel well into the twentieth century.[4]

KITCHENS ON TRAINS

How does one make elegant meals on a train? By working in and with small spaces. The typical kitchen would have been 2.4 metres × 2.4 metres (8 ft × 8 ft), the size of a small home kitchen. It served up to 48 customers who ate at the tables of the dining car one at a time. The kitchen had a sink, stove, prep counter and pantry, and cold items were kept in an adjacent cold-storage unit that could be drawn from at stops.[5] The menus of the dining cars were somewhat regularized. The dining car staff,

Strobridge & Co., *Pullman Compartment Cars and Through Trains: Interior of Dining Cars on the Cincinnati, Hamilton and Dayton R.R.*, 1894, colour lithograph.

George H. Mead, *The New 'Chicago Great Western Limited' Daily Between Chicago-Dubuque-St. Paul-Minneapolis-Des Moines-St Joseph-Kansas City, c.* 1899, photograph.

to some extent, controlled their own cars. For example, according to an 1893 operating manual, the head of the dining car could order supplies as needed along the route as long as their purchase was made from the dining car's sales.

The service staff on Pullman train cars was famously all African American. The cooks, meanwhile, were both white and black. The people in these positions were sometimes unionized and sometimes not. One of the most famous chefs on the dining cars was James Copper, an African American who worked for the Pullman company for more than 25 years before reaching mandatory retirement age. On the occasion of his retirement in 1925, he was written about in the *New York Times*. While his association with the famous Polish pianist (and prime minister) Ignacy Jan Paderewski was the main focus of the article, the editorial gives a good sense of the kind of work Copper did. Pullman and the rail lines often emphasized the subservience of

Detroit Publishing Co., *Dining Car on a Deluxe Overland Limited Train*, c. 1910–20, photograph.

Geo. R. Lawrence Co., *Entire Dining Car Interior*, c. 1905, photograph.

rail workers in service positions and fought against their rights as workers; however, as the experience of Pullman porters demonstrates, these jobs could also be ways to ascend into the middle class and to garner social, political and cultural power. The *New York Times* article suggests a few ways that chefs may have become empowered through their roles; in it there is a report of an exchange between Paderewski and Copper that paints a more complex relationship between staff and customer: "'Please tell Mr Copper that the meat was excellent, the salad marvelous and the pastry better than ever.' The waiter delivered the message and returned. 'Mr Copper,' announced the waiter, 'said for me to thank Mr Paderewski and tell him the soup was good, too.'"

The *New York Times* story also complicated chains of command, proclaiming that Copper recommended James Davis, a young African American chef from Chicago, to the Pullman company to succeed him in his dining car.[6] In the small space of the dining-car kitchen, chefs took on the role of ordering supplies, managing materials as well as meals, and – in the best of circumstances – forming relationships with customers, forging pathways for protégés to build equally strong careers moving across expanses in the confines of the kitchen.

Postcard featuring Pennsylvania Railroad chefs working in a dining car kitchen, pre-1907.

HARVEY HOUSE STANDARDS

While Pullman dining cars were popular on the East Coast lines where places were close together and trains stopped frequently, they were impractical on the long, sparsely populated western lines because people could not move between cars (until the invention of connecting vestibules).[7] At stops people ate what was available quickly since trains would often depart after only about thirty minutes. This fare included items sold pre-made by people on the platform. The meals were better in the east and derided as terrible in the west, probably owing to more competition among food-sellers within the more highly populous eastern states and their better access to quality ingredients. Restaurants at train stations in the western United States were infamously bad, known for tough, greasy meat, rancid fats, dense bread and poorly made old coffee. The service, too, left much room for improvement. Often people ordered and paid for food that they never saw, because they had to board the train again. It happened with a frequency that made people believe it was a deliberate way to increase profits, though in many cases it may have only been due to inefficient waiters and kitchen staff.[8]

Fred Harvey had eaten (and left uneaten) his fair share of poor train food. He began his working life as a busboy in a place frequented by new immigrants in New York, but made his way westwards working for train companies. Harvey saw the need for a good place to eat at the train depots. He initially went into business with a partner, Jasper Rice, and worked with the Kansas Pacific railroad to operate three eating houses. Rice didn't like the restaurant business, and Harvey didn't like that the Kansas Pacific was nickel-and-diming him – that is, upping his business costs with accumulating hidden fees – on shipping supplies. So they quickly decided to fold the restaurants.

In 1875 Harvey tried again. He set out on a new path with the upstart Atchison, Topeka and Santa Fe rail line. This burgeoning and often bullish company agreed to provide Harvey with the space, utilities, kitchen equipment and free transportation for supplies and employees; Harvey would provide the food and the materials for the front of the house (such as dishes and furniture) and he would take any profits.[9] While it might seem like a ludicrous deal on the railroad's part, it turned out to be a winning investment. Over the course of its financial success, Harvey Houses brought into being many of the features of road food in the twentieth century, foregrounding standardization of operations and offerings, playing up cleanliness and taste, and see-ing the restaurant business as a series of calculations about customers.

In a landscape of greasy spoons and saloons, the luxe interior decor of the Harvey Houses was crucial to their success. The first review of the first location in the *Leavenworth Times* in 1876 made this clear, describing the Harvey House as: 'The neatest,

cleanest dining hall in the State, everything bran [*sic*] new. The crockery, cutlery, and silver-ware of the choicest patterns, and the table supplied in the best of style. It was a luxury to set down to such a table.' While this might seem overblown, Harvey's attention to table-setting cannot be undersold. He bought custom silverware from Sheffield, England, oversized linen napkins and 220-centimetre (87-in.) tablecloths – not the 180-centimetre (71-in.) ones that were often used – as well as porcelain from Limoges.[10] His goal for Harvey Houses was not simply to be a place where one could eat during a journey, but a place where one could dine.

Providing travellers on the rail lines of the American West with a clean place to eat and a good waiting staff was an undoubtedly welcome move, but this was not the heart of Harvey's contribution to the history of restaurants. His most important contribution came in how the Harvey Houses were run. He built a chain – that is, a company that centrally administers a series of local outlets. Chains were a relatively new phenomenon in the late nineteenth century, but they were not unheard of; chains existed in Europe and Asia as well as in the United States, where department stores, banks and other industries had pioneered many of the basic business principles. The scale of Harvey's chain was impressive, but it was his organizational decisions in the operation of this large chain that reverberated in the succeeding decades and in the contemporary dining scene.

Take, for example, how the restaurant procured its beef. Before Fred Harvey served a steak, trains and ships had already transformed beef. Part of the financing from the transcontinental railroad came from England to facilitate beef shipment (think of all those beefsteak societies). British demand also drove innovation in refrigeration compartments, initially on ships (shipping live cattle was very resource intensive) and feeding into rail shipment as well. Refrigerated train cars in the 1870s made it so that fresh beef became a greater part of the American diet, too.[11]

When the Harvey Houses opened, despite the coordinated transit and processing of beef, beef sales to restaurants were almost always local, or at least piecemeal. Restaurant managers or cooks ordered beef from a particular purveyor for a particular restaurant. Harvey changed that. Given that he operated at so many locations, Harvey realized that instead of having the Leavenworth manager order beef from one place and the Santa Fe manager order from another, he could cut costs and standardize quality by ordering all his beef, for the entire chain of restaurants, from a single purveyor. He made a deal with Slavens & Oburn, a Kansas City meat-packing outfit, to buy at least 540 kilograms (1,200 lbs) of meat a week for 12.5 cents a pound. He empowered his managers to cut similar deals – if there was a good deal on beans or delicious jam at a sweet price, they were to buy not only for the local outlet, but for the entire chain. It was a system that harvested discount and uniformity at volume. And of course, the swiftness of the train (and for Harvey, its lack of shipping cost) made the system successful and profitable: food was simply moved down the line, from one stop to another, so every kitchen got what it needed – and also what every other kitchen got. A side effect of Harvey's deal to procure beef was to change the experience of eating beef for many people. Steaks at Harvey Houses were served still pink, a new and alarming prospect for customers who were used to well-cooked (and therefore less likely to be dangerous to eat) meat.[12]

The standardization of food was not just about sourcing. The Harvey Houses eventually had a single chain-wide chef who devised new recipes and then sent those recipes out to the separate locations to be followed to the letter. Regulations abounded: from when the staff had to be back in their Harvey House dorms (11 p.m.), to how thick a slice of bread should be (three-eighths of an inch).[13] Brewing coffee was described in a multiple-page process. Harvey Houses kept meticulous records, which were sent to the main office. These records included information about sales and inventory (how many eggs were sold, how many pounds of butter were in stock, how many were used) and also about employees (who was doing their job well, who should be groomed for promotion and who was problematic).[14]

The Harvey Houses workers and managers also developed and documented replicable systems of service. The most famous example of this is the cup code. Instead of writing down a customer's beverage order, the waitress would position the cup in a particular way that signalled to her co-worker, a beverage server, what to pour: coffee, a cup in its saucer; milk, a cup flipped and put on the table; ice tea, a cup flipped and leaning against the saucer; hot tea, a cup flipped and placed on the saucer, with the handle direction indicating the type of tea the customer wanted. Systems like this were important because of the brevity of station stops – every minute counted in order to get customers happily fed before their train took off again.[15]

Serving a complete meal to a whole train of people in thirty minutes required planning and precision. The cup code is one example of how this worked; however, it is just the tip of the iceberg. Before the train arrived, the restaurant would receive a telegram that would tell the staff the number of passengers to expect and how many would be headed to the lunchroom and how many to the dining room. The dining room served more expensive and elaborate cuisine at a higher price; until the 1920s, to be seated in the dining room one also required a jacket (which could be borrowed from the restaurant).[16]

The coordination was not just for timing; it was also part of improving the customer's experience. For example, the menu at the Harvey House stops along the same route was varied so that diners would not eat the same chicken over and over. The different locations changed their menus simultaneously every four days, rotating the approved recipes from the company's head chef.[17]

Though the setting would move from tracks to asphalt, the frameworks of scale and uniformity that Harvey Houses initiated would prevail in roadside restaurants. Among them was a practice that would come to define middle-American dining: Harvey Houses were known for significant portions. They served mammoth steaks. Instead of six or eight slices, they cut a pie into quarters. For all his measuring and managing, Fred Harvey's (apocryphal) last words were, 'Don't cut the ham too thin.'[18]

WAGONS, CARS AND THE 'DINER'

Automobiles drove the next dramatic change in dining across the world. The car fostered a type of restaurant food – fast food – which typifies wide swathes of contemporary dining today. We will take up fast food in Chapter Eight, but here we want to look at the foundations of eating on byways and highways.

The story of American road restaurants begins with lunch wagons. The first lunch wagons, typified by Walter Scott's Pioneer Lunch, were the food trucks of the 1870s. They came to locations where large shifts of workers would leave a plant or factory at the same time. The trucks would quickly serve fresh food (sandwiches mostly) to the clientele through a window in the wagon. By the 1880s lunch-wagon owners began to deck out and expand their

conveyances. Samuel Jones added a small standing counter; Charles Palmer did him one better: adding stools. In 1897 Thomas Buckley rolled out the grand lunch wagon: its interior had lamps, tile mosaics and nickel-plated coffee urns. It resembled a typical diner in many ways, except that people could buy an already outfitted wagon and drive it to the locations where they wanted to do business.

The next innovation in lunch wagons was, in fact, the dawn of the diner. At the turn of the twentieth century, Patrick Tierney began manufacturing and distributing an even grander lunch wagon: one that could be fixed in a spot for a while; that had modern amenities like electric light, booths and smooth, manufactured surfaces; and which even contained indoor bathrooms. To advertise his overhauled and upgraded lunch wagon, Tierney christened it with a new name: the diner.

The interplay between mobility and fixedness was important for these new restaurants: they were dealing with the changing patterns of a business, paying new property taxes and subject to new zoning laws, particularly around roving food sales. The restaurants were an investment, but they were also affordable to buy and maintain. Furthermore, the company offered payment options (a relatively new financial practice). By the early 1930s there were at least 4,000 of these diners.[19]

Roadside dining, especially along highways, often seemed as transient as the travellers. In the 1920s roadside stands were popular. These were usually one-storey buildings with a service window and a counter. They could be closed when driving season ended, when it became too cold to be whizzing around in an open automobile (which may explain why states like California, Texas and Florida were the birthplaces of drive-ins and fast food). Usually built by their owners, roadside stands did not require a huge financial investment for set-up

Arthur Rothstein, *Lunch Wagon for Bean Pickers. Belle Glade, Florida*, 1937, photograph.

A. H. Closson, 'Night Lunch Wagon', United States patent drawing, patented 17 January 1905.

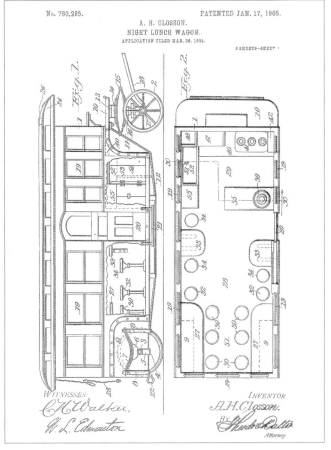

costs, and they were thereby economically viable even when only used for part of each year. Many of these stands also offered kerbside service, the predecessor to drive-throughs. In 1921 the first drive-ins opened in Dallas, Texas – part of the movement of quick in-car dining focused on barbecue. The drive-in made its mark initially in the western United States (where expansive settings matched new forms of transportation and sparked new ways of dining in them). The Pig Stand – 'America's Motor Lunch' – set the pattern for drive-ins.[20] You would drive up, a person would take your order and then they would bring the food to your car. However, you would not drive away – instead, the servers would clamp a specially designed tray to your door, making a restaurant table out of your automobile.

These places often had large signs but little aesthetic appeal. For train-oriented restaurants or restaurants along earlier pilgrimage routes, a regular supply of customers could be expected to be in the same places over time. Because driving changed how people experienced their surroundings, the need to draw the attention of drivers was paramount. In some cases, the buildings became their own outlandish billboards. The most stunning examples of these are found on highways across the United States: restaurants shaped like dogs, owls, coffee pots, ice-cream cartons, oranges and giant chickens. Since being attention-grabbing and economical was at the heart of most roadside restaurants, their facilities often did not include parking lots, effective trash systems or what the historians John A. Jakle and Keith A. Sculle call the 'gentry impulse' of 'good design'.[21]

In response to the state of many roadside eateries, a group formed an organization called the National Standowners' Association, which aimed to 'make a war on temporary, ugly shacks'.[22] From reports in local newspapers across the United States,

it appears that the organization had a three-pronged approach. First, it created a system of certification. However, it seems that this certification in many places did not exactly work as the association owners wished. Articles from the Midwest report people being defrauded of their $5 fee, for which they were supposed to receive signs that certified their restaurants' cleanliness. In other regions, the association was better regarded (perhaps people received their certification signs), and newspapers ran articles from the organization about the growth of roadside businesses and about changes in the industry (including a popular article about the decline of the hotdog and the rise of the barbecue sandwich,

Walter Evans, *Lunch Wagon Detail, New York*, 1931, gelatin silver print.

John Margolies, *Collin's Diner, Route 7, Canaan, Connecticut*, 1977, photograph.

which was in fact McDonald's first offering). While the National Standowners' Association may not have transformed roadside dining, the changes in expectation that it championed did. Over time, stands became less prevalent, and clean, service-oriented restaurants that conformed more to café or diner frameworks began to dominate roadside dining.

FAMILY DINING

Just as restaurant dining had expanded thanks to women's participation in the last part of the nineteenth and early decades of the twentieth century, so women changed dining on the road. The rise of cars, the middle class and the expansion of leisure consumption and holiday trips in the United States in the twentieth century, especially in the post-war period, led to an increase in families on the road. Attracting these customers – families – became the impetus behind much of the advertising, menu choices and decor for roadside restaurants of the period, especially along the growing standardized highway system. This is the moment that gives us kids' menus, large booths, air conditioning and more thoughtful interior design.[23] This transition to family dining is apparent in the rise of places like Howard Johnson's.

In 1935 Howard Johnson was certainly not looking at an empty stretch of motorway on the way to Cape Cod, a popular holiday spot. However, he did

Carol M. Highsmith, *Neon Sign Outside Theo's Drive-in Restaurant in Grand Prairie, Texas*, 2014, photograph.

see an opportunity that was being missed by the chains, like White Castle, in cities and towns across America. These roads had many of the problems Fred Harvey had seen along the railroads. When people travelled, they did not already know the terrain, and America had so much bad food and so many uninviting establishments, especially for families.

Johnson, with the cooperation of a franchiser, built a restaurant along a popular route to Cape Cod in 1935; before the tourist season of 1936, he built four more. Each of them sported the same colonial-style building with turquoise cupola and orange roof. They all also carried food distributed from Howard Johnson's central offices. In this way, they built on the distribution systems of chains, which Fred Harvey had put in motion fifty years earlier. By 1937 there were 39 restaurants in the franchised chain. Though they eventually cropped up in cities, including New York, Howard Johnson's were made for highways – and he got in on the ground floor. When the Pennsylvania Turnpike was opened in 1940, it featured an identical Howard Johnson's every 80 kilometres (50 mi.).

Howard Johnson's were not, in either the pre-war or post-war era, the height of dining. They were, however, recognizable and replicable. Food-distribution systems and common architecture were the features of America's highway franchising, and they made Johnson's chain successful. The

John Margolies, *Coffee Pot Restaurant, Lexington, Virginia*, 1982, photograph.

centralized system required less initial energy to expand to new locations (one did not have to develop a menu, design a building or find a kitchen supplier, for example). Howard Johnson's also developed customer loyalty, not only because there the sense of gustatory surprise (and perhaps disgust) of an unknown restaurant could be avoided, but because one knew the familiar surroundings and amenities would be there, wherever you drove, within a particular area. In the northeastern United States, on many a highway in the late 1930s and early '40s, you could be guaranteed fried clams, french-fried potatoes, rolls and butter; or a club sandwich with cream cheese, guava jam, walnuts, peanut butter and crisp lettuce – the same rolls and the same peanut butter – at whichever of the two hundred Howard Johnson's you entered. And you would know that a HoJo was on the horizon from its turquoise and orange palette.

Howard Johnson's, c. 1930–45, postcard.

MICHELIN STARS AND YELP REVIEWS

Assessing chefs and restaurants is a pastime as old as the chefs and restaurants themselves. Restaurant recommendations for travellers extend back to the ancient world. In some ways, the tradition of critics can seem almost changeless. Grimod's unnamed Jury Dégustateur (a group who taste-tested and ranked food for his gastronomic journal) sounds not unlike the culinary elites that comprise the Diners Club World's Fifty Best Restaurants Academy. However, the history of reviews is deeply intertwined with that of travel. As travel became more accessible to a larger group of people, so too did the guidebook industry. There was not a lack of restaurant reviews in the nineteenth century;

however, the guides that we use today are all twentieth-century inventions. The century saw the rise of an industry of road guides that began with Michelin, but took off in myriad directions.

The Michelin Guide was started in 1900 by the French tyre company, in order to encourage people to take more driving trips. The red book debuted at the World's Fair in Paris (along with conveyor belts, talking films, escalators, X-ray machines and Campbell's soup). At the time, France led the world in car ownership; however, the automobile was still a relatively new form of transit and an even more novel site of leisure. The guide was designed to encourage people to travel to places across the country, giving them dining and lodging information. It was made at a loss to the company, but over the

Cover to the Michelin Guide information booklet, 1900.

course of the following century, achieved its goal, encouraging travel and linking the company's name with pleasant associations.

The book's editors were always committed to good meals. In the first edition they said, 'we promise to strike from this book without pity all hotels reported to us as having poor food, inadequate rooms or toilets, deficient service.' However, it was not until 1926 that they introduced the star system to identify good places to visit. (From 1923–5, the stars were used to identify status and price rather than as an evaluative grade.) Michelin stars were as difficult to attain in the 1920s as they are today. Before the Second World War, only about a dozen restaurants

had three stars. Even today, under a global Michelin Guide regime, only around 120 restaurants have three Michelin stars. They are hard to get and equally hard to keep.[24]

The guide was initially put together by a team of Michelin travel representatives in collaboration with groups of local councils, friends and entrepreneurs. Professional positions were eventually created for evaluating restaurants and writing the guide. The inspectors (as they are referred to often by the press and never by the company) are as undercover as spies – even their families cannot know their line of work. In recent years, Michelin has divulged more information about who these people are and what

Duncan Hines,
*Adventures in
Good Eating*
(1945).

their jobs are like: they are degree-holding professionals (in cooking or hospitality); they eat many meals out a year (between two and three hundred) and eat every course a restaurant offers; they are paid and expensed by Michelin; they are trained in both an official programme and an apprenticeship to look for and reward certain aspects of ingredients, complexity and service.[25]

In the United States, the year 1936 marks the emergence of two guides worth examining in greater detail: Duncan Hines's *Adventures in Good Eating* and *The Negro Motorist Green Book*.

Duncan Hines's *Adventures in Good Eating* (1936) was one of the first American road-dining guides. Duncan Hines (who went on to be the face of a boxed-cake empire) was a travelling salesman and an avid leisure traveller during the 1930s. While the publication is frequently credited to Duncan and he is named as the author, it was a joint project with his wife Florence, who often travelled with him. He recalls in his 1955 memoir, 'We began jotting down notes about our favorite eating places: the general quality of the food, the sanitation (most important of all), the service, and "specialties" of the house.'[26] For Christmas 1935 Mr and Mrs Hines compiled a list of their favourite places – 167 of them – along with information about each and had it printed for their friends instead of Christmas cards. Much to

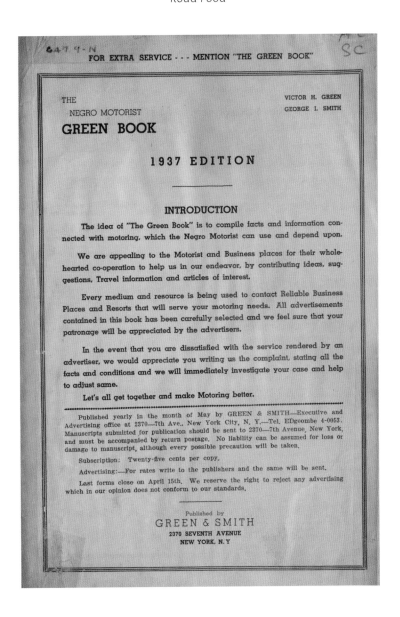

FOR EXTRA SERVICE - - - MENTION "THE GREEN BOOK"

THE
NEGRO MOTORIST
GREEN BOOK

VICTOR H. GREEN
GEORGE I. SMITH

1937 EDITION

INTRODUCTION

The idea of "The Green Book" is to compile facts and information connected with motoring, which the Negro Motorist can use and depend upon.

We are appealing to the Motorist and Business places for their wholehearted co-operation to help us in our endeavor, by contributing ideas, suggestions, Travel information and articles of interest.

Every medium and resource is being used to contact Reliable Business Places and Resorts that will serve your motoring needs. All advertisements contained in this book has been carefully selected and we feel sure that your patronage will be appreciated by the advertisers.

In the event that you are dissatisfied with the service rendered by an advertiser, we would appreciate you writing us the complaint, stating all the facts and conditions and we will immediately investigate your case and help to adjust same.

Let's all get together and make Motoring better.

Published yearly in the month of May by GREEN & SMITH—Executive and Advertising office at 2370—7th Ave., New York City, N. Y.—Tel. EDgecombe 4-0053. Manuscripts submitted for publication should be sent to 2370—7th Avenue, New York, and must be accompanied by return postage. No liability can be assumed for loss or damage to manuscript, although every possible precaution will be taken.

Subscription: Twenty-five cents per copy.

Advertising:—For rates write to the publishers and the same will be sent.

Last forms close on April 15th. We reserve the right to reject any advertising which in our opinion does not conform to our standards.

Published by
GREEN & SMITH
2370 SEVENTH AVENUE
NEW YORK, N. Y.

their pleasure and surprise, people loved it. Several of the friends who received the list asked if they could get copies for their friends, and through word of mouth the list and its critical apparatus spread. In 1936 the Hineses', having realized that there was clearly a demand for a guidebook that was not influenced by advertisers and which was aimed towards an audience of motorists, published the guide and sold it by mail order.

The guide provided only the names of places that were recommended – those spots that met the Hineses' standards of cleanliness, service and good food. For such locations, the guide often included short notes. The range of restaurants that made it into the guide was pretty wide – from formal restaurants to cafeterias, chains (Harvey Houses abound) and local gems, places set for tourist kitsch (the North Pole-themed Christmas Tree Inn in

Arizona) and those that simply provided good food along the way. Florence died in 1938, but Duncan Hines continued the guidebook, which grew in popularity with a growing car-owner class. In fact, it was Hines's fame from the guidebook that led to him being the face of cake mixes (and pickles and a plethora of other food goods). *Adventures in Eating* was published regularly until 1962, eventually employing an additional editor and with people who would canvas the restaurants to make sure they still met the Duncan Hines standard. There was never any advertising. Hines vowed that he did not accept any food, money or other goods or services from the people who ran the restaurants he recommended;

however, he did sell his seal of approval for them to display (once they were in the book) and used his recommended restaurants as book distributors. He also formed relationships with restaurateurs on his lists – sometimes called the Duncan Hines Family – that may have led to him receiving gifts from these people. He was always both a salesman and a businessman as well as a man who became synonymous with assessment and helping people – in particular white families and women – find good places to eat on the road.

At the same time that white Americans were enjoying Hines's recommendations, the guides put out by all kinds of commerce bureaus, and reviews

Russell Lee, *The Bar at Palm Tavern: Negro Restaurant on 47th Street, Chicago, Illinois, April 1941*, photograph.

and travel spreads in magazines, African Americans were creating a counter-public. African Americans were unable to access most of the restaurants lauded in white publications. In fact, travel was fraught with danger if they did not exercise caution and journey prepared. *The Green Book,* as it came to be called, was meant to make safe and welcoming travel somewhat easier. Like Hines's text, it was a list of recommendations. Likewise, it was mostly addresses and names of restaurants (as well as inns, petrol stations and other vital services). However, the criterion for inclusion was first and foremost that black customers were welcome. *The Green Book* was published over a similar span of years as Hines's *Adventures*: 1936–66.

Victor H. Green, the book's creator and editor, was a postman. Unlike Hines, he was not constantly on the road; however, he had access to a network of postmen, and he also believed in the knowledge base of his readership. To gather intelligence for the book, he solicited information from other postmen, from readers and from people in the African American tourism and business trades. He paid contributors, both for recommendations and for stories, and he funded the book in part with advertising money. While Michelin was looking for exquisite cuisine and Hines was looking for sanitary conditions and good food, *The Green Book*, as the civil rights activist Julian Bond said, 'was a guidebook that told you not where the best places were to eat, but where there was any place'.[27] Both its authors and publishers hoped that progress towards civil rights would obviate the need for its continued publication, and *The Green Book* did cease publication soon after the passage of the 1964 Civil Rights Acts that legally desegregated restaurants in the United States; de facto segregation, however, remains an American reality.

While road-oriented guides have continued to flourish, restaurant rating systems with a new focus emerged in the latter half of the twentieth century. The road guides aimed to make dining along the road a pleasant experience; however, their rating systems transformed restaurants into the destination or reason for travel. Furthermore, professional reviewers have today been usurped by surveys and amateur reviewers. While this has expanded exponentially with online reviewing, from blogs to Yelp, this crowdsourced and lay reviewing, which is not unlike *The Green Book* or Hines's guides, was innovated by the Zagat Survey. In 1979, when the survey began, it was not unlike the first Michelin Guides. The initial guide was based on a survey of Tim and Nina Zagat's friends and friends of friends. They were looking to get a sense of the best places to eat in New York City, for people who lived and travelled there. While Michelin moved towards employing anonymous reviewers over the course of its guidebook, the Zagats expanded the reach of their survey until it included hundreds of thousands of reviewers. It was a more democratic guide that 'lay no claim to a norm by which all the restaurants are judged'.[28] Instead, Zagat also relies on collective averaging, punctuated by reviewers' remarks. This format has led the way to the much-used and much-maligned Yelp review site (which is simply the poster-child for a whole range of online reviewing forums).

Yelp reviews are on a starred scale, but there is no given criteria for assessment. Zagat at least has categories for food, service and decor. On Yelp, the criteria are sometimes given by the reviewer in their discussion of the place but are sometimes fully absent. What Yelp substitutes are narratives: people give detailed accounts of their experiences, sometimes with photographs, often with a rundown of their meal and significant interactions with the staff. People are generally more likely to review restaurants when they have had an outlier experience (very good or very bad) – and are even more likely to review a location when the experience has been negative. This is in some ways a real substantial difference between the guide system and systems like Yelp. Guides remove the bad reviews – they are there to steer people towards the good rather than away from the bad. Yelp, then, is a hybrid of the journalist restaurant reviewer, known for writing negative estimations as well as recommendations, and the guide reviewer, who is there, like a paper concierge, to recommend.

While it seems miles apart, what Yelp does for readers is not unlike what the Harvey Houses were trying to do over a century ago: to provide a person with the ability to know something about where they are going to eat, to feel sure that this restaurant will be good and clean and safe, and to create familiarity in the gustatory unknown. The familiar and the fast continued to be central aspects of restaurants' evolution in the twentieth century with the rise of automation, which we discuss in the next chapter, and fast food – our focus in Chapter Eight.

7

THE MACHINE
IN THE RESTAURANT

The 'Freestyle', a touchscreen drink machine that dispenses more than one hundred flavours in any consumer-created combination from a single tap, was introduced by the Coca-Cola Company in 2009, but represents only one of the latest in a long history of machines in restaurants. By the seventeenth century we have records of fanciful, yet quite real contraptions for serving food and beverages. Henry van Etten described in 1633 an elaborate beverage dispenser he had designed. The design was picked up and modified by Henry Wistanly in the 1690s into a machine called the 'Magic Barrel'. In addition to entertaining people with a show of shooting and cascading water and fire, the customer could, as if by magic, choose from a range of different drinks – coffee, wine, beer, milk or water – which flowed from a single tap. By 1710 the Black Horse tavern in London sported a similar machine, dubbed the 'new Mathematical Fountain'.[1]

In this chapter, we discuss how central technological breakthroughs in cooking and the related work of acquiring, inventorying and serving food have been to the development of restaurants. We will look at examples of technology in and from restaurants, from automats and conveyor-belt sushi to flash freezing and sous-vide cooking, from the business computer to the cafeteria tray. One would expect gas stoves and refrigerators and copper pots to transform the food business, but restaurants arose in the West in conjunction with the Industrial Revolution. The evolution of the restaurant was bound up in the wider cultural and scientific shifts in how people used machines, such as mechanical looms, to do things and to understand things, such as human motion. These innovations subsequently mechanized human behaviour (as seen in the work of an assembly line). Thus many of the most important technologies in restaurants are about labour: who is doing what and how.

MACHINE SERVICE

The Magic Barrel and the Parisian Café Mécanique are some of the earliest examples of people's delight at having machines provide food. They also demonstrate how that delight can make money.

These kinds of mechanical servers were novelties until the end of the nineteenth century, when restaurant service was transformed by technology in more large-scale ways.

By the mid-1890s people across the world were regularly going to quick-service chain restaurants. The customers of such establishments ranged from the in-and-out (and sometimes down-and-out) clientele of sixpenny houses, to the smartly dressed working women at lunchrooms, to the travelling customers of the Harvey Houses. However, all of these places had staff who served the food. The emergence of two technologies – for self-service and for more wide-scale machine service – transformed the physical layout of restaurants and altered the work of serving food.

The cafeteria – a restaurant that forced customers to serve themselves – developed a suite of new technologies that reshaped restaurants in this period. In outline, the cafeteria was based on quite an old food-service technology: the buffet. The buffet is an arrangement used across the world. It was quite popular for entertaining (at parties and feasts) in the eighteenth century. It was also how most European pubs, taverns and other drinking establishments served food. In updating the idea of the buffet, the cafeteria both applied old technology to new problems (enabling people to eat quickly had not previously been the role of the buffet) and also generated new technologies like the cafeteria tray. (Yes, a cafeteria tray is a particular technology and it had to be invented – by William and Samuel Childs in 1898, as they built their small empire of cafeterias, one of the early successful restaurant chains.)

While most of these early buffets were casual, cafeterias required moving through 'geometrically arranged assortments of provender', where one would either serve one's self or be served, and then move on to the drink and finally the

payment counter.[2] In the United States in 1893 John Kruger displayed his 'cafeteria' at the Columbian Exposition. His version was a self-service restaurant based on the *smörgåsbord*, a popular kind of restaurant for the Swedish community in Chicago. Kruger's name for his creation was a play on the word 'café' and the Spanish suffix for shop, *-teria*. He was not alone in his invention (and perhaps not even in his nomenclature). The cafeteria was an idea whose time had come. In the late nineteenth and early twentieth centuries, self-service became a new way of operating, in restaurants as well as shops. Self-service was efficient, reflecting the need to reduce the cost of labour and to feed more people more quickly. In 1885 a self-service restaurant called

A Coca-Cola Freestyle machine, installed at a Wendy's in Irving, Texas, 2010.

Esther Bubley, *Washington, DC: A Cafeteria*, 1943, photograph.

The Lunch Counter: a waitress stands in the middle of the counters during lunch time at the Exchange Buffet in New York City, c. 1920, photograph.

The Platinachrome Company, *A Childs' Place in Philadelphia,* PA, 1908, postcard.

the Exchange Buffet opened in New York. By 1894 a 'cafeteria' was enough of a well-known concept that the *Chicago Tribune* used it as an analogy for a street peddler who sells pencils that you pay for and to which you 'help yourself' – and they also included two articles about how people were stealing from these kinds of restaurants.[3]

However, self-service eating was far from glamorous. It harkened back to non-restaurant spaces: the boarding house, the saloon, even the home dinner table. It was machines that managed to bring excitement to self-service. The best example of this was the automat, a class of restaurant that displayed various food choices in glass cases, which one could purchase by putting a coin into the slot of the chosen case. The coin unlocked the glass door and allowed the patron to take the food.

The features that make the automat part of the history of restaurants (and not just that of

technology) remind us of the defining qualities of restaurants and show the various ways they evolved. The automat was not a takeaway place – people were expected to eat in the restaurant. The space had mirrors and marble-topped tables. It aimed to be an inviting place to partake of a meal, alone or with friends. Customers chose from a range of options for their meal. The automat presented food the way it would be encountered if ordered from a human server. The food was plated and visible; the automat was not simply a collection of vending machines.

INVENTING THE AUTOMAT

The automat was the product of intercultural borrowing and exchange. The first vending machine (for holy water) was likely invented in first-century Greece, and for centuries people sporadically used

Berenice Abbott, *Automat, 877 Eighth Avenue, Manhattan*, 1936, photograph.

'Serve Yourself!' automated restaurant in Stockholm, 1905, photograph.

these kinds of machines to dispense everything from tobacco to books. However, in 1867, when an Englishman patented his coin-operated dispenser, it led to a revolution in mechanical vending. By the 1880s coin-operated vending machines were being used for everything from chocolate to perfume. Paris, home of the Café Mécanique, had the first vending machine bar: the Bar Automatique, which was established in 1891. Five years later the bar's founder Philippe Leoni teamed up with a German engineer, Max Sielaff, who worked for a company that developed and marketed vending machines. Leoni and Sielaff had the idea of taking the Bar Automatique to the next level: they developed an entire restaurant that was automated, which they debuted at the Berlin Trade Exhibition in 1896. It was a hit, and within three months, they opened the first version of this restaurant to the public.[4] They named it Automat, which, like Xerox, Band-Aid and Kleenex, became the generic identifying name for this creation: the automat.

Despite its positive reception at the trade fair, the first German automat did not stay open very long. Both Leoni and Sielaff returned to the business of manufacturing machines (where they had both started) rather than restaurants. They turned their idea into Automat G.m.b.H. Unlike restaurant chains which began to emerge around this time,

An automat for sausages and meat in front of a butcher's shop, Berlin, Germany, 1935.

French chef Pierre Charlot, surprised as he gets two sandwiches for his money, one cream cheese and one hand, at an automat on 5 March 1969. Charlot, who was touring New York City with a group of 55 French chefs, was visiting the automat when the manager hand-delivered the sandwich through the coin-operated 'window' used to dispense food to customers.

Automat G.m.b.H sold the equipment to create the automats. New European automats were independently owned. Because they were made from kits that included everything from the vending cases and counters to coffee dispensers and signage, they often looked and worked very similarly and aimed for the same population of diners. The food, however, was not standardized, and despite appearances, automats did not have a shared advertising strategy. In some places there were even changes and updates to the machinery. For example, in the Netherlands automats developed heated hatches, from which they sold hot foods like croquettes, French fries and sausages. These heated hatches eventually became a universal automat feature.

The automat restaurant was a successful business for both Automat G.m.b.H and many entrepreneurs across Europe, including in London, Manchester, Copenhagen and Paris. By 1913 the American guidebook *The Economical European Guide* included thirty automats with addresses:

'Automat' lunch houses (where you help yourself) are good in both Germany and Switzerland; they are in almost every city. They are only at Milan in Italy. All kinds of foods and drinks (beers, wines, coffee, etc.) . . . The price is generally from 70 Pf. to 1 Mk. All automats have retiring rooms for ladies and gentlemen, usually very nicely appointed. Vienna, Austria, has many large automats.[5]

By the time that the guidebook's author Carl Wilson wrote this, America had its own automats.

In 1902 the first American automat was constructed. Joseph Horn, who had opened a cafeteria in Philadelphia with his counterpart John Hardart, saw the automat while in Germany. Whether he was directly invited for a tour by Max Sielaff or whether he simply ran into the concept while visiting his homeland is debatable. What is certain is that Horn saw the automat and knew that it was ripe for an American audience. He ordered the kit for a large automat to be installed in Philadelphia. The first shipment of the equipment sank in a shipwreck; the second arrived and was assembled under Sielaff's supervision. Horn and Hardart's trial was a success, and over time they opened Horn & Hardart's Automats in New York and became a leader in the restaurant chain industry. By 1941 they had 147 restaurants in the northeastern United States.

THE MODERN APPEAL OF THE AUTOMAT

The appeal of automats, in Europe and the Americas, was multilayered. Much of it had to do with the very thing that made these places unique: how the machines repositioned human bodies within the space of the restaurant. With food dispensers instead of waiters, the automat could

Horn & Hardart Automat, Times Square, New York City, c. 1930–40, postcard.

Edward Hopper, *Automat*, 1927, oil on canvas.

be fast. It did not rely on a chain of human interaction. Rather, the diners determined their own
pace. They could linger in choosing their food or
decide immediately. They did not have to wait for
the kitchen to prepare their order or the waiter to
bring it – as soon as the decision was made and
the coin inserted, there was the food, waiting to be
slipped from the case. Customers could eat and
dash (having already paid) or 'for one lousy dime
sit all night'.[6]

For the expanding group of urban men and
women working in the city, this speed was helpful.
One could have a decent meal quickly and then get
back to work. Furthermore, the position of human
bodies made the negotiation of payment easier
(just slip a coin in the slot) and could make the cost
lower. There was no waiter (or crowd of fellow diners) to judge the cost of your meal and no tip to pay.

This vision of speed, thrift and egalitarianism
made automats a place that writers and artists
mined repeatedly. Irving Berlin and Moss Hart's
Depression-era musical satire Face the Music (1932)
included two automat songs. The opening number
lampooned American aristocrats (the Rockefellers,
Astors, Hearsts, Vanderbilts and Whitneys) who
were forced by the Depression to eat sandwiches
and beans at an automat. The second song, 'Let's
Have Another Cup of Coffee', continued the story
though with a more hopeful, chin-up (or head-
in-the-sand) optimism and soon became a classic.
In 1934 this same Depression-era frame was taken
up in a grimmer register in the film Sadie McKee.
Down-on-her-luck Sadie McKee, played by Joan
Crawford, gets her coffee and looks longingly at the
pie of another customer. The 1937 film Easy Living
uses the automat to a similar effect: a poor woman
finds a fur coat and ends up being fed by an automat
worker (who is actually a wealthy man). This kind
of juxtaposition and lack of clarity about who is rich

and who is poor in the automat was in fact part
of its charm.

Automats were also responsible in part for a
change in social behaviour in restaurants. One
of the most striking depictions of the automat is
Edward Hopper's painting Automat (1927). Like his
famous Nighthawks, the scene strikingly juxtaposes
the bright interior of a restaurant with the dark
exterior of the city at night. However, Automat
places the viewer inside the restaurant, with a single
patron. The woman in Automat is, as the restaurant
intended and advertised, alone. She is also, as the
restaurant intended and advertised, a well-dressed
woman in (to steal from Hemingway) a clean,
well-lighted place. That these restaurants were
appropriate for women from all walks of life was
another important feature.

In Sweden, the automat was one of the first
restaurants for women. In Stockholm, by 1912, the
main clientele of the automat were women 'from the
spinning industry' and 'whose small incomes do not
allow for luxury, but who do not wish to abandon
themselves to the foul dishes of the guesthouses'.
While it eventually came to be associated with those
down on their luck, like the American automat, the
restaurants began in the fashionable business parts
of town and then moved into working-class areas as
well. A single automat would serve upper-class and
lower-class people simultaneously at a time when all
other Swedish restaurants were intensely segregated
by class.[7]

The automat was, from its inception, a place
that allowed people to play with anonymity and the
kind of intersections that such a facade allows. This
was true of the first restaurants in Paris, where one
could eat out alone in public. The restaurant is a
cultural form that allows for a wider range of people
to take on, as customers, a wider range of social
positions. The automat intensified this aspect of

the experience by getting rid of waiting staff. Thereby, it created a world where Patti Smith could meet Allen Ginsberg. In her memoir, Smith wrote,

> One drizzly afternoon I had a hankering for one of those cheese-and-lettuce sandwiches. I got my tray and slipped in my coins but the window wouldn't open. I tried again without luck and then I noticed the price had gone up to sixty-five cents. I was disappointed to say the least, when I heard a voice say, 'Can I help?' I turned around and it was Allen Ginsberg . . . Allen added the extra dime and also stood me to a cup of coffee. I wordlessly followed him to his table, and then plowed into the sandwich. Allen introduced himself. He was talking about Walt Whitman and I mentioned I was raised near Camden, where Whitman was buried, when he leaned forward and looked at me intently.
>   'Are you a girl?' he asked.
>   'Yeah', I said. 'Is that a problem?'
>   He just laughed. 'I'm sorry. I took you for a very pretty boy.'
>   I got the picture immediately.[8]

The automat, with its lack of staff and affordability, made it possible for people to help each other, a trope we see in films as well. It was a place where strangers could meet, creating spaces for people with differences in age, class, sexuality and gender to intermingle – and spaces for unexpected delight.

UNTOUCHED FOOD AND AUTOMAT ASSUMPTIONS

The aesthetics of the automat touted its modernity. The original automats were manufactured in a then-popular Art Nouveau style. They included elaborate glass and woodwork and dolphin-shaped taps for the coffee urns. By the 1920s automats began to take on a more modern Art Deco look: sleek with straight lines and shinier surfaces. However, the most notable features of the automat's aesthetic were always the rows of symmetrical, glass-fronted boxes sporting picture-perfect, untouched food within.

With the food in glass-fronted boxes and no restaurant workers in sight (save those bussing tables), the automat gave a sense of cleanliness. In the last few decades of the nineteenth century, people began crusading for safer food. In 1896 Germany instituted a food chemist training programme to enforce its 1879 Food and Commodities Law; in 1906 the United States passed the Pure Food and Drug Act.[9] That chain restaurants like Horn & Hardart's Automats had uniform, regulated food added to their 'trustworthiness'. (This was also a moment where brand-name foods became more popular for the same reasons.) The image of the automat was that it was appropriately antiseptic. The food was behind glass, neither touched nor exposed. Building upon this idea of safe food, the automats also often advertised their freshness. Horn and Hardart proclaimed that they did not sell any food not made that day. (They had separate restaurant outlets in lower-income areas where they explicitly sold day-old foods). The aesthetics of modernity, the touting of freshness and the person-free, isolated food boxes added to the notion that Horn & Hardart's Automats were safe and clean.

Despite this, the Horn & Hardart Company's key role in food safety history was as a defendant in a case that established a precedent about how much we can expect our food to be touched or adulterated. On 12 May 1926, a plaintiff from Pennsylvania was eating strawberries at a Horn & Hardart restaurant when a tack, residing in said strawberries, punctured her gums. She brought a case of negligence against the restaurant. However, her claim was ultimately denied. In part, this was based on the Horn & Hardart chain-mandated way of preparing strawberries: '[Berries were] placed in a colander, washed under pressure of city water, individually hulled, patted in a towel, and placed in individual dishes for serving.' So, in theory, the restaurant had done everything right. The judge's ruling reflected changing standards and experiences of food's provenance and consumer's risk management in the early twentieth century:

> Now the presence at times of some foreign substance in food, viands poisonous and impure, the infectious character of meat and drink, are things which, in the ordinary experiences of life, as we know, happen both in homes and public eating places. Foods are assembled from distant places; they pass through different ownerships and handlings, all of which in the nature of things may have contributed to the food or drink not being absolutely pure or safe. Therefore it seems to us the fact that the plaintiff got this tack in her jaw when eating the strawberries, which at this season of the year, May, must have come from a distance, would not in and of itself be evidence of negligence on the part of the defendant.[10]

The ruling implied that sometimes, in this modern world, we have to expect a tack. The clean and rational process of preparing strawberries at the automat is the very thing that allows a tack to be justifiably in one's food. Furthermore, the restaurant has no liability for presenting strawberries as seemingly untouched and picture-perfect behind glass. It is the consumer's misplaced faith in the food system, according to this ruling (which continues to be cited in U.S. cases) that makes eating strawberries dangerous.[11] We will turn back to this vision of food, but first a quick look around, away from the pies behind glass and fountains of coffee and chocolate milk.

THE WORKERS IN THE AUTOMAT

The fantasy of the automat as worker-free is demonstrated in the following quotes from a customer's description of the opening of the first Stockholm automat:

> The serving is automatic without waitressing. Almost as if the different courses were to walk up to you at the table . . . The machine seeks to be a stop on the way to the happy time when, without effort, one simply receives services, as the machine works by itself. Instead of waitressing, dishes, and so on, the machine only has three large cases with shining mirrored glass, and other fine details.

> I regarded the Automats as a miracle of technology . . . For the longest time, I refused to believe there were humans inside the machine. I wanted to believe they were purely 'automatic'. I imagined that, behind the nickel-plated wall with its hatches, the work simply handled itself. Up until the day a red, sweaty face poked up from inside the half-moon hatch in the wall, asking whether my forty pennies meant sausage or rice pudding . . . I was shocked. The machine had not understood me clearly. The human had to intervene.[12]

Invisable labour was part of the magical experience of the automat. Of course, as with most disappearing acts, the question is where we look to see how the trick is done. The illusion of the automat works by asking customers (and every subsequent cultural observer) to keep their eyes on the food in the box. In the automat, the labour went two places, both important in their own ways.

The most obvious place that labour manifests in the automat is by dint of the customers: self-service is the word we often use for this practice. Self-service food – a relative of the takeaway – has existed for millennia. It is exactly what was happening at the taverns in Pompeii. However, the idea of dining on food and drink that one served oneself is, in some ways, novel. Bars, saloons, taverns, coffee- and teahouses may have long asked people to serve themselves food, but the drink was generally served by a bartender. Even diners and hash houses had people to derisively sling food, plated, at the customer. Contrary to the previous quote, the kind of self-service found in automats is a far cry from a structure where 'one simply receives services'. The rebranding, in automats and cafeterias, of this kind of customer-as-worker labour structure as 'self-service' made possible the later rise of fast-food restaurants.

Not only did automats transfer labour to the customer, which reduced the cost to companies of hiring workers, but the automats framed the experience of self-service as a good in itself. Signs around the restaurants proclaiming things like 'Help yourself' were part-instruction, part-advertising campaign: these messages showed up in newspapers, in magazines and on postcards. The notion, spoken and implied, was that as a customer without a waiter or waitress, one could be quick; one could be private; no one else touched one's food and one did not have to tip. The transfer of power was presented as (and perhaps in experience was) worth the value of doing one's own table service.

However, automats did have employees. There were people behind the boxes at automats, and sometimes people in the restaurant itself – preparing food and cleaning up. Horn & Hardart's managers' manuals illustrate this, spelling out the labour these unseen people did. Hiding kitchen labour was not new to restaurants. The point of the back-of-house staff, in general, is to stay in the back. In the twentieth century, when kitchens moved into the open (which we discuss in later chapters), the gesture towards transparency was transformative. Still, the automats foregrounded the absence of workers to a high degree. Like the women who digitize books for Google, the image of the automat worker came to be a disembodied hand.

Coffee preparation is one place where one sees the monumental amount of labour these restaurants hid out of sight. Coffee shows up in almost every popular representation of Horn & Hardart – and it is not just because the coffee was cheap. Horn & Hardart transformed American coffee. Their machines, originally of European origin, introduced drip coffee to the United States. Coffee was often a selling point of restaurants because there was *so much bad coffee*. In the early twentieth century, the move from what would today be described as almost undrinkable coffee to drinkable coffee was an important marker of differentiation. (Good coffee is still an important aspect of a restaurant: the fast-food restaurants McDonald's and Dunkin' Donuts both decided to invest in it in the 2000s.) Along train routes Harvey Houses had touted freshly made coffee; Hardart & Horn's automats made a similar claim. To achieve this, both organizations included rules that described exactly how and when to make coffee. Horn & Hardart even roasted their own beans. The *Managers' Instruction Book* of 1942 demonstrates what was expected of the automat workers:

The proper preparation and care of coffee is the most important feature of our business.

To secure coffee of uniformly good quality, the following rules must be strictly adhered to:

Use two gallons boiling water to each pound of coffee.

Water must be boiling before adding to coffee, as must also the water in the coffee urn jacket (i.e., the heated water used to keep the coffee dispenser itself hot).

1. Put one pound dry Coffee into new allegheny bucket.
2. Fill gallon measure with boiling water, and pour over dry coffee.
3. Refill gallon measure with boiling water and add to Coffee.
4. Take coffee paddle, and move from side to side to break up lumps. Do not stir.
5. Pour into heated urn through coffee bag. (Never allow urn containing coffee to remain uncovered.)
6. Repour one gallon of the brewed coffee. This process, once begun by the Coffeeman, must be followed by the same man through to the end, in its proper sequence, and without interruption or delay.

Let finished coffee and bag remain ten minutes in making urn before transferring to dispensing urn, or before putting on sale. Immediately after making Coffee refill hot water urn.

Be especially careful in the early morning of making coffee properly.

Flush urns out with clear water after each making, and dry with cheesecloth which is to be kept in pan of water with coffee bag.

Horn & Hardart relied not only on the technological innovation of the automat itself, but on a rising form of management. As a large chain, it promoted a 'scientific eating experience', where standardization was of the utmost importance. At Horn & Hardart, the goal (and its manifestation) was that each restaurant had the same food plated in the same way. The baked beans always had a 1×1 inch square of bacon on them. In Europe, one would see a variety of different foods behind the glass. However, the labour involved in producing visually attractive food was the same. Cooks prepared the meals with more attention to their presentation than one would see in an average café because food was chosen based on how it looked. Appealing to the eye rather than just taste was an important aspect of the business model. The shift to the visual experience of food as the predominant mode of advertising and appeal took hold in many types of quick-food places.

This highly regulated system shaped labour as well as food. In it, automat workers became interchangeable. In the United States, the workers at automats were likely to be new immigrants or people of colour, especially women. Groups of labourers with depressed wages were economical for the owners and managers of automats, and because they were not seen or heard, their identities did not shape perceptions of the restaurant.[13] In Europe, most automat workers were also women working at very low wages. They often worked 92 hours a week.[14] Kitchens of automats were surprisingly un-automatic.

By the mid-1920s, Horn & Hardart began including cafeteria-style dining in their automats, but customers continued to buy macaroni and cheese from glass boxes into the 1990s. What people who dined at or even heard of the automat took away was pure delight at the mechanical – a box of pie, just for you, opened with a coin. However, what the restaurant industry took away was the increasingly mechanical experience of production

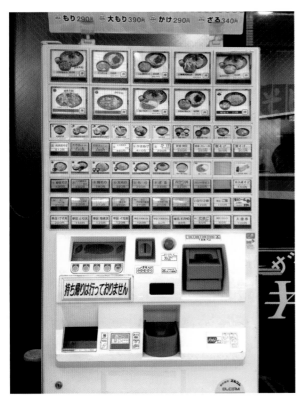

Vending Machine Restaurant in Tokyo, Japan: purchase a ticket for the meal outside the restaurant and get your food at a counter inside, 2014.

(by humans in the automat and its successors) and a low-human-interaction experience of dining. Leoni and Sielaff's automats and Horn & Hardart's Automat ushered in new forms of dining. While the fully mechanized restaurant has remained as a novelty, many pieces and practices of the automat live on, in clever ways and in ways so prosaic that they likely go unnoticed.

INHERITORS OF THE AUTOMAT

In Japan, an almost fully automated automat operates today. Jihanki Shokudo is a machine-only noodle and sandwich restaurant in Isesaki City, northwest of Tokyo. It uses vintage food-vending

machines to offer up cheap ramen, curry burgers, tempura udon and Italian toasted sandwiches. It has no staff other than the owner, who stocks the machines and comes to take out the rubbish a few times a day. Patrons are expected to clear their tables themselves in addition to getting their food. It is a delightful novelty, aimed at creating a unique experience as much as a meal.[15] The last Horn & Hardart Automat was basically a novelty restaurant for years before it closed, and the New York Public Library revived it as an exhibit (distributing recipes from the restaurant rather than food) in 2012. One can even buy a vintage automat machine from online purveyors. However, the legacy of automats is more vibrant than nostalgia stops imply.

Eatsa is a growing chain of automats in the United States. One enters Eatsa, a quick, fresh bowl-based restaurant, and orders on a tablet. The customer then waits for the food to show up in a glass-fronted cubbie. Just like the automat, without ever seeing a person, the customers take their food and find seats at a fashionable modern table or standing bar (just like the automats of old). The atmosphere is a cross between fast-casual (wood and metal) and futuristic (neon, with a wall of boxes on which one's name is projected when his or her food is ready). Notably, like the automats of old, the restaurant only *seems* workerless. Five to six people still prepare food behind the wall unseen.[16]

The latest manifestation of this technology, which began in Japan and is making its way across the globe, is the electronic menu (which is one aspect of Eatsa). Like the automat, electronic menus allow customers to see what is on offer, to choose their selection and in some cases to pay. The electronic menu, which is basically a touchscreen tablet, always includes images of the dishes on offer. The food is delivered by a server, and servers are on offer for those who do not want to use the electronic menu. Like the automat, the main point of restaurants that use these menus is not a service-oriented atmosphere, but a quick, convenient and often affordable restaurant.[17]

CONVEYOR BELTS IN THE RESTAURANT

While some restaurant technology – like the automat food dispenser – was invented just for food, much of our food technology migrated from other sectors of the economy. The factory is one of those sites. Factories transformed the restaurant in multiple ways. They changed the foodstuffs available through the standardized, mass manufacture of everything from flour to Vienna sausages. They

created another class of people able to patronize restaurants, ushering in places like diners, as we saw in Chapters Three and Six. Yet perhaps one of the most important changes restaurants inherited from the factory was not in people and foods, but philosophies and configurations. We see this in the managerial systems of the automat, Lyons (see later in this chapter) and the Harvey Houses in the early twentieth century as well as in later fast-food chains. We also see this in the many ways that restaurants bring the machinery of the factory into the dining space itself. The conveyor belt provides a prime example.

Conveyor belts began far away from the food industry. Thomas Robbins invented them at the

Digital cubbies at Eatsa in San Francisco, 2018.

YO! Sushi Bar at Bluewater, 2007.

very end of the nineteenth century. They were initially employed mainly in mining industries, such as coal. In 1913 Henry Ford repurposed the conveyor belt into a key part of his assembly-line production of automobiles. By the mid-twentieth century, conveyor belts were being used across the world in industrial settings, including in the growing field of industrially produced food. Conveyor belts moved beer bottles, Swiss rolls and even eggs across factory floors, preparing them for markets – and for consumption in restaurants. However, in the 1950s restaurateurs in Japan and America brought the conveyor belt into the restaurant itself.

In 1954 Insta-Burger franchisers James McLamore and David R. Edgerton were displeased with the existing Insta-Broiler method of making burgers. They thought the Insta-Broiler method, the namesake of the restaurant, was too messy, dangerous and slow. They approached General Restaurant Equipment, the company which made popular Sani-Serv and Sani-Freeze ice-cream and shake machines, to see if they could come up with a better solution. In response, the brothers who ran General Restaurant Equipment, Frank and Donald Thomas, designed the flame broiler. It used a conveyor belt to move burgers between gas flames, delivering a cooked burger at the other end. The new machine transformed burger-making at Insta-Burger so dramatically that McLamore and Edgerton ended up buying out the rest of the franchise within four years and rechristening it Burger King, 'home of the flame-broiled burger'. The Thomas brothers were also impressed with their technology and with the ever-expanding franchise fast-food market, so they decided to join it, creating the Burger Chef, a now-defunct chain that had 1,000 locations in the 1970s. The flame-broiler machine made making burgers quicker, safer and less reliant on skilled labour (even if that skill was knowing when to flip a burger). The operator simply put raw patties in, retrieved cooked ones from the other end, and sometimes cleaned out the grease-collecting channels (which had been designed to reduce fires).[18]

Meanwhile in Osaka, a major industrial hub, Yoshiaki Shiraishi, a sushi purveyor, was also having a difficult time with his restaurant. Sushi, the restaurant's speciality, needed to be delivered fresh; however, labour was costly. Adding more waiting staff to serve more customers would require him to raise prices. Sushi was already considered a costly food, something that the mostly factory-employed citizens of his town could rarely, if ever, afford. His business was in peril and needed to reduce costs, but the food it was preparing required prompt delivery.

In 1954 Shiraishi visited a brewery, and seeing the beer bottles move along the conveyor belt, he realized that he might be able to employ the same technology in his restaurant. While the flame broiler was a notable development, cooking food on conveyor belts was not unheard of; having a conveyor belt replace your waiter was. Shiraishi thought it was worth trying and so developed his own conveyor belt, made of stainless steel, so that it could stand up to being washed regularly. After four years, he

opened his small restaurant with its conveyor-belt method of serving.

The customer, who stood at the dining counter that surrounded the chef's workstation, put in an order; when the chef completed the order, he would put it on the belt, and the customer simply picked up their sushi as it passed by. Because of the reduced labour costs, Shiraishi could serve sushi for two-thirds the original price. The conveyor belt was a success and led to a 240-restaurant chain, simultaneously transforming sushi into a common and then a global food.[19]

Like many of the technological innovations that transformed the restaurant scene (including the automat), conveyor-belt sushi had its coming out at an international exposition. After the 1970 World Exposition in Japan, there was greater national and international attention and adoption of the patented conveyor-belt system. Over time, such systems were altered in a number of ways. Sit-down counters were installed. Rather than making particular orders, the chef would simply make an array of sushi, which people would pick up from the moving conveyor belt as they desired. The plates, which were colour-coded, would be counted up at the end of the meal to calculate the cost (this is also done in some Spanish tapas bars). Belts snaked out from a single central bar to allow for booth seating. These features added to the cost savings that allowed sushi to be re-envisioned as an everyday food, as it is now across the world.

MATERIAL SCIENCE AND THE RESTAURANT

The technologies of heating and cooling have long affected restaurants: how one can cook and keep foods cool changes cuisines entirely. Major developments in kitchen technology – gas stoves, copper pots and refrigeration – transformed the industry.

John Margolies, *Hojo Restaurant, Niantic, Connecticut*, 1978, photograph.

In the 1880s artificial refrigeration and freezing were developed, but they destroyed the texture and flavour of meat. These new technologies allowed beef to be imported to Europe at much greater quantities from Argentina and Australia. However, this beef would not be served in fine restaurants. Much of it went into home and institutional (schools, military, hospitals) dining, though some made its way into not-so-appetizing meals at restaurants. The same is true of canned vegetables. From the 1810s on, canned vegetables were readily available, but they were generally mushy and not flavourful.

However, scientists continued to perfect methods of preservation. Clarence Birdseye's quick-freezing method, created in 1929, fixed the texture and flavour of frozen food and transformed restaurant dining. With the invention of the convection oven in the 1940s, it became possible to reheat frozen food more easily and with less damage to the product. In 1947 the first microwaves came onto the market – as big as a fridge and as expensive as a car – and were used in commercial kitchens for decades before they moved into people's homes (a trend that emerged in the 1970s and exploded in the 1980s). The latest in this trajectory of food-preservation technologies is 'modified atmosphere' packaging, which uses certain combinations of air (for example, to vary the amounts of different component gases) in order to keep materials fresher longer without freezing or drying.[20]

Perhaps the most famous examples of how these technologies affected the development of restaurants is Jacques Pépin's work with Howard Johnson's.

After working at the famous French restaurant Le Pavillon, Pépin took a job at Howard Johnson's. While he initially worked in New York, at a Queens location of the restaurant chain, his real contribution was creating gourmet food – at an industrial scale, for large-scale distribution. It was a job that required him to begin by making meals for twelve and then figure out how to make them for 2,500. For the dishes that could be scaled, the next question was making sure that these items could be prepared (sometimes even pre-cooked), frozen and reheated properly by the many cooks across the United States in Howard Johnson restaurants. A classically trained, top-notch French chef, Pépin also learned to be a food scientist: 'My vocabulary increased with my understanding of terms such as *bacteria and coliform counts, the specific gravity of sauces, emulsion,* and *total solids,* and I learned what could and could not be frozen and how to freeze and defrost foods properly so as to retain maximum flavor and texture,' he wrote. His aim was to change mass dining, which he did, leading the way for Red Lobster and TGI Fridays and generally improving expectations of middle-class American restaurant food.[21]

Sometimes new cooking techniques come not from scientists or food corporations, but from independent restaurants. Sous vide is one such example. People have cooked in leaves, husks and bladders for centuries, probably millennia, in order to keep food moist and protected. Pouch cooking is not at all new. Yet sous vide, cooking in a plastic pouch, has a clear and recent birth date: 1974. It is a great example of how and why restaurants both employ and transform traditional cooking techniques (which then often make their way back into home kitchens). Sous vide was the solution to a problem of product and profits that faced Troisgros, a three-Michelin-starred restaurant in Roanne, France,

in 1973. Troisgros was struggling with its much-celebrated foie gras. Customers were clamouring for it, but meeting this demand was causing the restaurant to lose profits. When it was cooked, the foie gras was losing 30 to 50 per cent of its mass. The chef Pierre Troisgros turned to one of his colleagues, the chef at a nearby hotel restaurant, Georges Pralus.

Pralus had always liked to tinker and readily took on the challenge. Pralus thought that if he encased the foie gras before cooking it in a lower temperature water bath, it would retain its moisture and flavour. To do so, he turned not to traditional forms of casing, like pig bladders or parchment, but to plastics. Perhaps he had seen the work being done with food preservation and plastic – the initial development of the cryovac in the 1960s. His first trial, with a single layer of plastic, left an expensive mess. However, by triple-wrapping the foie gras and forcing out all air, the product only lost 5 per cent of its mass and, perhaps more importantly, tasted rich and delicious. The method was a triumph not only for Troisgros, which is still open and still holds three Michelin stars, but for Georges Pralus, who went on to teach and popularize the method in restaurant kitchens across the world.[22]

TRACKING DINNER

At elBulli, the high-end avant-garde restaurant led by chef Ferran Adrià, the staff had a system that tracked what every guest had eaten. It was consulted so that guests always had a completely new menu; it also included information about guest needs and preferences. This system digitized the work of great restaurateurs and maître d's like Beauvilliers and Tschirky. In the twenty-first century, at a restaurant that used all kinds of machines to make avant-garde food experiences, this is, frankly, unsurprising. Nor is it particularly surprising that most restaurants

The exterior of a Lyons teashop along Piccadilly, London, 2 July 1953.

use computers to track orders, calculate bills, order ingredients and issue pay cheques. What may be more surprising is that a restaurant invented the computers that do this.

Established in 1894 in England, Lyons was one of the first successful chains. It was part of the rise of restaurants whose clientele were mainly women (and whose employees and managers also were often women). Lyons teashops were part of an enterprise that stretched across Great Britain. Lyons was initially an importer of teas, then it started opening shops that served tea and light meals, the first in 1894. There were 37 shops by 1910.[23] These became part of both the working-women luncheon circuit and the shopping-and-leisure circuit. Quick, nicely appointed and not-too-expensive, these were not elegant hotel tearooms, nor were they working-class cafés. They filled a space that expanded as women entered the middle-class workforce in England. (Women have almost always been part of the labouring class.) While there were independently owned teashops, Lyons was a chain. Its stores touted the freshness of their baked goods as well as the efficiency and cleanliness of their staff. Lyons had a strong central management system, which included centralized baking and distribution as well as a

A busy scene at Lyons Corner House Brasserie, Coventry Street, London, 1942.

centralized recruitment and training programme. The managers of Lyons often came from the ranks, working their way up from positions as waitresses or doormen (and because of this, the company had many women in shop management).

In 1923 John Simmons, a mathematician from the University of Cambridge, joined the staff of Lyons, ostensibly to lead the accounting department. However, he was forward thinking and instead interpreted his job as information management and logistics. Simmons was invested in making sure people had the information they needed to make decisions and even changes throughout the organization, in order to improve the business. Geographically dispersed, but with so many central-ized processes, Lyons presented wonderful logistics

problems for Simmons: 1. Baked goods from the bakeries needed to be distributed; 2. Orders from each store had to be placed based on their needs; 3. The bakery needed to produce the right amount of goods. Further, the company needed to be making money from selling the baked goods, and the managers needed to be empowered and invested enough to do their work well.

After the Second World War, this was a particularly pressing and problematic issue. Sales were down, in part because of the wartime bombing of over 250 Lyons locations, shortages in the ingredients for cakes and a more general shift in culture. Already the company had removed its beloved Nippies (the name of Lyons' waitresses) and replaced them with self-service.[24]

At that time, the managers (often called manageresses in Lyons literature and writing about the company) would fill out forms each morning about the baked goods they sold and the baked goods they needed to order. As customers ate through that day's delivery of cakes and ices, the forms would move through the Lyons system – to inventory clerks at the main office, to the bakery, to the delivery personnel – and the next morning, the required amount of freshly baked goods would arrive and the paperwork would begin its journey again.[25]

For the managers of the teashops, the seemingly worst thing that could happen, given the tight profit margins they operated on, was to have too much inventory and for cakes to go unsold; therefore, the majority of them under-ordered by just a little. This meant that many stores lacked goods to sell by the end of the day and forfeited a small amount of possible profit.

OF CAKES AND COMPUTERS

Simmons was interested in finding a logistical solution to his supply-chain question, and he was quite amenable to using new technology to do so. Lyons was a company that embraced systems and technology. A 1935 issue of *Refrigeration Engineering* (a riveting read), contained an article titled 'A New Ice Cream Installation: England's Leading Restaurateur Finds Many Uses for Refrigeration', reads: 'It appears that the restaurateur is one of the most versatile of refrigeration users today, and Lyons has been a leader for several years. Problems concerning ice cream, beverage cooling, milk, wine, drinking water, truck refrigeration, bakery and candy conditioning – these and other uses have popularized refrigeration in England.'

In addition to these food uses, the article discusses a new Lyons establishment that boasted central air conditioning.[26] In 1947 several Lyons employees from Simmons' team went to America. There they were introduced to ENIAC, one of the first computers, built for military calculations during the Second World War. While the kinds of calculations this computer produced were not what Lyons needed, the team still saw the possibilities for a different kind of computing. It was clear that the order and supply chain for baked goods to the restaurants was an area where the digital computer might be able to help. This kind of computing – focused not on single complex problems, but on many simple ones – was the foundation for their proposal to build another kind of computer. The company, which specialized in tea and cakes, hired a team of engineers and mathematicians who could build this machine to its needs and specifications.

However, deciding to use a computer added its own piece to the logistics puzzle: data entry. The LEO (Lyons Electronic Office) team knew that they could reuse the data for the cakes and breads in each stage of the process – for ordering, for manufacture, for delivery and for calculating expenses – but the amount of ordering data was still staggering. They ended up streamlining it by calculating a baseline for each shop. For example, the customers of the Piccadilly location usually ate the same number of Swiss rolls each day. The company instructed managers to change their orders, by calling into the Lyons data entry centre if eating patterns changed.[27] Customers had their morning and afternoon buns, teashop managers had more time to tend to their staff and stores, and profit increased (though one must acknowledge that the moment for the teashop was waning; Lyons replaced most of its locations with Wimpy burger joints). Moreover, for the rest of the restaurant industry, a computerized system of payroll, ordering, inventory control and sales analysis was born.

We started on this journey in the history of restaurants by pointing out that we now believe that what allowed us to evolve into human beings was a technological breakthrough that allowed us to spend less time chewing than other hominins. We learned to pound and slice root vegetables and fresh meat. This allowed us to evolve into the humans we are today. Over the thousands of years of human cooking, there has been a march of technological breakthroughs: roasting, broiling, boiling, steaming, smoking, curing, pickling and freezing. Technological transformation continues to be the motor of change in the world of restaurants, driven by cost and new forms of demand coupled with the imaginative instincts of humans. These changes often shift labour to tools and machines; however, the machines in turn facilitate shifts in social relationships, in the structure of places and experiences. In the next chapter, as we turn to fast food, we see how this functions at a global scale.

8
CHAINS AND LOCAL GEMS

Restaurants currently operate on a wide range of scales, from one-person owner-as-cook/server/accountant operations to mega-corporations like Yum! Brands (43,617 restaurants in 135 countries). Giant global businesses can seem to be built on the premise of existing out of time and place, while unique establishments, from American 'mom-and-pop' diners to tiny tasting-menu-only restaurants, seem to thrive on the specific cultures and geographies to which they are tied. However, the story of the places where people eat – chains and independent businesses – is often more complex. In part, this is because all restaurants balance the need for efficiency, and therefore economy, with the desires of their specific clientele. In this chapter, we examine just a few businesses out of millions: at one end of the spectrum, McDonald's, and at the other, Scott's Bar-B-Que and the *shojin ryori* restaurant Gesshinkyo.

TIME AND RESTAURANTS

Innovation in machinery, from autos to automats, is an important part of the history of restaurants.

Changes in the management of time and space are an even more influential force. Nineteenth-century production-management techniques transformed time management – by speeding up processes in the kitchen, and with that, reducing the customer's waiting time for food, so they could go on to the next part of their day. While this trend began in places like the Harvey Houses, Lyons and automats in Europe and the U.S., it received yet another boost from fast-food restaurants.

All twenty-first-century restaurants rely, in some way, on innovations from the fast-food economy. This is because such time-saving innovations made being profitable simpler for places serving food. However, restaurants differ in their commitment to fast food as an ethos. While scale is one part of the equation, another is time. McDonald's has honed, proliferated and exported an ethos of 'fast'; the other two places we explore make their money from systematic slowness, even though eating a meal at these restaurants may take no longer than it does at McDonald's. A cultural pushback to fast food has consisted of ideas of 'slow food', focusing on small-scale food production and local ingredients and preparations. The organization Slow Food was an early and strong player in the food culture critique of large-scale, industrial food production in the late twentieth and early twenty-first century. It has a vivid anti-McDonald's history: it began in 1986 to fight against the establishment of a McDonald's at the Spanish Steps in Rome. However, the slowness that this chapter examines both is and is not the slowness of the Slow Food movement. Rodney Scott and Toshio Tanahashi are independent businesspeople and are dedicated to local food traditions; however, their commitment is not as much about changing agricultural systems and consumer visions, as promoting an ethos of a lifelong commitment to food and hard-earned preparation: barbecue for Scott and vegetables for Tanahashi.

THE MCDONALDIZATION OF MCDONALD'S

There are many chains, and chains on many different scales. In 2016 five hundred chains accounted for half of all restaurant sales in the United States ($491 billion), and chains have been growing rapidly in other parts of the world for the past two decades. One of the most well-known chains across the world is McDonald's. McDonald's has almost 37,000 restaurants serving 68 million customers per day. As of 2017 McDonald's has faced a few years of decreased profits; however, for the previous five decades it was a business powerhouse.

The story of McDonald's is often told as a specific history beginning in 1955 when Ray Kroc opened an Illinois franchise of the McDonald brothers' eponymous Pasadena, California, burger joint. However, let us begin, instead, with some now-ubiquitous scholarship. In 1993 the sociologist George Ritzer published a book that explored a phenomenon in capitalist globalization that he coined

'McDonaldization'. For Ritzer, McDonald's was the perfect example – not only because people had come to apply the 'Mc' prefix to everything from doctors to mansions, but because of the practices and experiences of McDonald's itself. He defined McDonaldization this way: 'The process by which the principles of the fast-food restaurant are coming to dominate more and more sectors of American society as well as the rest of the world.' Ritzer argued that the McDonald's model is based on four principles: efficiency, predictability, easily quantifiable food and service, and control.[1]

If these concepts seem to echo Harvey Houses and Horn & Hardart's Automat, there is a reason. McDonald's is another step in the rationalized and standardized restaurant, a movement to which Soyer and Escoffier contributed as well. This is a movement that gained steam at the turn of the century (the nineteenth to the twentieth century): investments in scientific management, which is sometimes called Taylorism, named after Frederick Taylor. The precursor of Ford's assembly line, Taylorism was a management technique that believed one could turn a better profit by honing every element of the process (though the key words were 'efficiency' and 'precision'). Taylor's systems aimed to reduce variation through technologies that relied on a combination of time-keeping, environmental control and mechanization.

In some respects, scientific management yielded delicious results. The food and coffee at Harvey Houses and automats was lauded in comparison to that of their competitors. And fast food is engineered to taste and feel good. However, achieving these effects depends not just on food science, but on a kind of business practice, which, for the sake of brevity, we will call 'fast food', and which is built on specific systems of employment, design, management and ownership.

A picture of a southern town: life in wartime Reading, Berkshire, England, 1945: men and women photographed enjoying a spot of lunch at the self-service Lyons Cafe.

MAKING MCDONALD'S

Even McDonald's did not start out as McDonald's. To return to our narrative: the first McDonald's mainly sold barbecue – or aimed to mainly sell barbecue. In 1937 brothers Mac and Dick McDonald joined the vast sea of entrepreneurs who opened carhops in California. In the 1930s in the United States, this new kind of restaurant, the carhop drive-in, became popular, especially with teenagers. These restaurants replaced the dining room with a car (and often some outdoor tables). Named after their serving staff, who served between vehicles, carhops as a type of restaurant rapidly evolved through a series of innovations that made service speedier: replacing the shoes of waiters and waitresses with roller skates and adding speaker-phones at each parking spot for people to place orders.[2] The McDonald brothers also aimed to cash in on another popular trend: the barbecue sandwich. Hot dogs, which had been America's most popular quick food, were being rapidly displaced by hot sandwiches. The McDonalds did offer hamburgers, but they were committed to their barbecue, advertising their pork and importing hickory from Arkansas for their smokehouse.

However, by 1948 they were earning much more from hamburgers than barbecue sandwiches: 80 per cent of their sales. Because they were a little bored and had already generated enough wealth to live comfortably for the rest of their lives, they decided to reformat their business to sell burgers, lots of

The original McDonald's restaurant, featuring a ten-item menu built around a 15-cent hamburger, San Bernardino, California, c. 1955, photograph.

Betty Whittington, a carhop, serves motorists stopping at Prince's Drive-in, Houston Texas, 1945.

burgers: 'Our whole concept was based on speed, lower prices, and volume.' The McDonalds' contribution to the history of restaurants was to strip away many of what had come to be restaurants' defining features. They fired their waiting staff (twenty carhops), they replaced the china and flatware with paper cups and wrappers, and they reduced their menu from 25 offerings to nine. They even added a penalty for asking for specific condiments. Everyone got two pickles, ketchup, mustard and onions on their burger; anything other than that would mean waiting significantly longer.[3] So if the brothers transformed the restaurant so significantly, why not say that McDonald's simply became a takeaway brand? How were they different from the thermopolium in Pompeii, which provided a choice of a

few quick foods and a spot to alight and eat them if one wanted?

As unlikely as it may sound, children may be the answer. Carhops, the first drive-ins, were teenage meccas. Because of this, they were not considered family restaurants. Apart from a few diners that adopted kids' menus after the Second World War, restaurants in general did not cater to children.[4] When the McDonalds got rid of their carhops and the car park hang-out culture that accompanied this manifestation of the drive-in, their restaurants had greater appeal to families.

Other elements of the physical plant of the original McDonald's restaurant heightened this appeal. The first McDonald's, by coincidence rather than design, had an open kitchen. Customers could see the food being prepared because of large windows that made up most of the exterior.[5] (Open kitchens were not common, though again, some diners in the post-war years had adopted them and promoted them as a way for customers to know that the food was hygienically prepared.) The large glass windows did two things for McDonald's that propelled them headlong into family dining. First, it allowed parents to feel like the food preparation was safe and careful. The McDonalds prided themselves on how clean their kitchen was, especially its two gleaming 2-metre (6-ft) grills. Second, it turned out that children enjoyed seeing food being made. Because of the large windows (and lack of teenagers), parents would send their children into the shop to pick up dinner. The children enjoyed the independence and seeing the cooks in addition to enjoying the simple foods (fries, shakes and burgers) built on sugar and fat. To their credit, the McDonalds recognized the importance of this demographic – and the chain continued to cultivate its relationship with children as customers.[6]

Changes to the kitchen as well as to the dining experience also reveal ways in which McDonald's maintained a restaurant lineage and, at the same time, began to revolutionize it. Mac and Dick McDonald created a modified *brigade de cuisine* for burgers, shakes and fries. Just as Escoffier had his grillardin, the McDonalds had their grill men. They also had shake men, fry men and dressers (the station that put on condiments).[7] The kitchen could move more quickly because everyone had and knew their specific job.

The McDonald brothers further transformed the kitchen by outfitting it with a variety of new machines and tools. They worked with a small manufacturer named Ed Toman. Their relationship was not unlike that between Soyer and his manufacturing partners. The McDonalds would come with

ideas or needs for the kitchen. With Toman, they would develop the new piece of kitchenware – from those large griddles to stronger spatulas to burger-dressing lazy Susans. Toman's most significant invention is familiar to many people today: the ketchup dispenser. Press the pump and a pre-measured amount of ketchup is dispensed.[8] Machines like this – enabling single-movement tasks and making it possible to use precise quantities of ingredients – are at the heart of fast-food restaurants. Over time, the ketchup dispenser would be joined by an army of pre-made food products, specialized fryers, ticketing formats and proprietary ice-cream systems.

A small but telling example of how the McDonalds invested in ways to streamline food preparation is their work on the hamburger bun. In the 1950s hamburger buns were distributed to McDonald's restaurants partially connected to each other and only partially sliced (buns at many places are sold this way now). The buns were delivered in cardboard boxes. This required workers to unbox the buns, separate and slice each one, then dispose of the box as rubbish. It might not sound like much, but McDonald's, like all systems of maximized standardization, was based on streamlining even the smallest things. So the company changed how buns came to the restaurant: they made them fully separated, fully sliced and in reusable boxes (which were initially more expensive but over time became significantly cost-efficient).[9]

MAKING A FRANCHISE: STANDARDS, EFFICIENCY AND GROWTH

The McDonald brothers were doing swift and profitable business by 1952, when they opened their first franchise, with businessman Neil Fox in Phoenix, Arizona. For the shop, they designed the building from scratch, with an eye to it being the prototype for many more franchise locations. The design included now-familiar elements: lots of glass; a low, red slanted roof and golden arches. Ironically, the first architect, who designed much of the McDonald's look, hated the arches so much that he would not complete the project. A sign-maker-cum-architect, who loved them, not only finished the building but illuminated the arches.

The architecture of restaurants has always been an important part of their function and appeal. The first restaurants in China and France transformed eating by providing individual tables. Self-service restaurants like cafeterias and automats changed how customers moved in restaurants, retrieving their own food and choosing their seats. Diners and other short-order restaurants put the kitchen in the dining space. Dining cars and drive-ins brought the menu and food to people on the go. It is not a surprise then that a big part of what fast-food restaurants brought about was a change in the layout of the restaurant. They move customers through space in ways that are constant and fairly simple: queue to order; get napkins, ketchup in little paper cups and maybe your own drink at the self-service counter; sit at stationary tables; walk your rubbish to the provided rubbish bins at the door. These spaces make visual cues for behaviour apparent (the availability of napkins and bins, the ropes or bannisters of the ordering line) and, like the automat, train customers in how to be their own waiters and busboys.

John Margolies, *McDonald's Restaurant Sign, Alfran Street, Green Bay, Wisconsin*, 1992, photograph.

Fred Turner and Ray Kroc, the executive leaders of McDonald's Corporation, looking at blueprints of a future restaurant, c. 1975.

Despite their investment in the design for the first franchisee, the McDonald brothers were not focused on franchising: they priced their system pretty low and did not expect McDonald's to be a cohesive empire. In fact, they expected the Phoenix location to be 'Fox's' – it was their local partner Neil Fox who wanted it to be a McDonald's. They weren't interested in building a chain, even with offers from others, like the food company Carnation, to fund the expansion. They regularly gave out information about how they ran their business, even to people who did not pay to franchise (including Glen Bell, who went on to found Taco Bell).[10]

It was an ice-cream system that brought the McDonalds in contact with the man who would make the restaurant into an international power-house. In 1954 a milkshake-mixer salesman (and accomplished pianist) named Ray Kroc visited McDonald's. He saw their ten mixing machines, which had been altered to mix in a paper cup instead of the stainless-steel cup with which they had been sold. (Mixing directly in a paper cup provided enough speed to get the restaurant's many orders filled in a more timely manner.) He saw the long lines of people. He saw the other restaurants copying the McDonald's model. Kroc's first instinct was to open up his own franchise of McDonald's. At that time the McDonald brothers were looking for a new franchising agent, so he told them to contact him when they found one, so he could buy into the business. However, Kroc changed his mind, calling them a week later to see if they wanted to hire *him* as the new franchising agent.[11] The way Kroc franchised McDonald's, more than all the increased productivity and low-cost burgers in the world, is what made it into an empire – and made restaurant franchising a successful business proposition, leading to the explosion of chains we see today.

Chain restaurants have existed since the nineteenth century, but franchise restaurants are a twentieth-century creation. A franchise differs from a chain in that a franchised business does not have a single centralized operator; instead, multiple owner-operators buy into the bigger company. The company gets a fee and then often a cut of the profits. In return, the franchisee gets the systems of that business. This selling of secret knowledge is not unlike the systems of education and knowledge distribution in seventeenth-century Japanese schools of cooking. The first restaurant franchise was likely A&W Root Beer in the 1930s, though several franchise restaurants emerged at the time, and invention is, as we have seen with gas lighting and vending machines, often a simultaneous manifestation of culminating social and technological conditions. In the American post-war boom, franchises exploded, and by the 1950s a franchise was a common thing. Most of these franchises ran on two separate revenue streams: one, the owners of restaurants would receive their profits from the business they managed and operated; and two, influenced by the rise of advertising and managerial culture, these owners would have a second business that sold their ideas, practices, designs and supply chains in a digestible, repeatable form for a fairly high price.[12] Whether these franchised businesses succeeded or failed was often not central to the success of the franchiser.

Kroc saw the possibility of another path. Instead of the signing of the franchise agreement being the moment at which the company profited, Kroc shifted the paradigm so that the moment of the franchise agreement was the beginning of a relationship and of continued store profits. He set up McDonald's franchises differently from other models. There was a low buy-in fee, but the company got a percentage (1.9 per cent) of the sales from every store. If the stores did well, the company did well. McDonald's, the company, was invested not only in making more franchises, but in making more successful franchisees.

Like Fred Harvey, Kroc created a system where the company had many specific operations and procedures – it had tomes on how to make coffee or pour a drink of Coke. Each McDonald's location was expected to follow the rules of McDonald's to the letter. However, like Harvey House, McDonald's also incorporated the innovation of individual restaurant owners. In 1972, when it came to the attention of the McDonald's corporate chiefs that one of their franchisees was opening early and selling breakfast, the owner of that franchise location, Herb Peterson, was reprimanded. (Other franchisees were also experimenting with breakfast at the time, but none of these were sanctioned by McDonald's corporate division.) However, instead of falling into line, Peterson believed in the potential of breakfast and of a specific breakfast food he had developed. He was given an audience with Kroc to pitch his breakfast sandwich, the Egg McMuffin. While he had prepared for a profits and margins discussion, the company lore says that as soon as Kroc tasted the sandwich, he was convinced. That year, McDonald's became the first major fast-food chain to serve a breakfast menu; it included the Egg McMuffin.[13] As a franchise company, McDonald's has long worked in dynamic tension between owner-operators that know their customer base on one side and the need for standards, standardization, products and practices, which can be standardized across each of their restaurants, on the other side.

EXPERIENCING MCDONALD'S

Over time restaurants have become more and more democratic in terms of whom they cater to and serve. The international chain fast-food business opened up yet another demographic: children. While restaurants that cater only to children are still rare (think Chuck E. Cheese or the now-defunct Showbiz Pizza in the U.S.), many fast-food restaurants see children as an important part of their customer base.

McDonald's has been, since it was revamped in 1948, a restaurant *experience* as much as a purveyor of food. This is, in part, what makes fast-food restaurants: they are places with a specifically cultivated ambiance. That ambiance is made for child consumers and their caregivers, rather than just adult customers. The furniture is fastened to the ground. It is plastic. There are built-in playgrounds. There is no expectation of reasonable conversation. There is no sense of needing to wait.

As such, McDonald's has possessed built-in appeal for families and children since the 1940s, but it has also worked to cultivate this type of customer. Beginning in 1969, McDonald's built its advertising around ideas of fun and experience rather than just the food alone (which could be bought in many places). In a set of advertisements released that year, a butler picks up McDonald's in a Rolls-Royce and delivers the meal to his boss along with cash change; McDonald's employees dance and sing the company's jingle while they clean the restaurant; a father sprints from his car to get McDonald's for the family while they wait for a train to pass. These adverts framed McDonald's as the place to go for a good time – as well as for value, speed and cleanliness.

In the 1960s McDonald's also came out with their child-targeted mascot, Ronald McDonald. Originally played on regional television in 1963 by Willard Scott (who would become an American television icon as a weather presenter on early morning national television), Ronald made his national debut in 1969 along with newly invented characters from McDonaldland: the Hamburglar, Mayor McCheese and Grimace. Shortly thereafter these characters were featured in McDonald's playgrounds with the memorable prisons of Officer Big Mac and the cage-like Grimace bouncey platform.[14] In 1977 a franchiser in Kansas City created another child-focused promotion, the 'Happy Meal', which included a hamburger, fries and a fizzy drink in a circus-train-shaped box. It was quite popular, and in 1979 the Happy Meal was introduced nationally.

GLOBAL YET NOT GLOBALIZED MCDONALD'S

Sometimes globalization is presented as homogenization. This seems to fit in the case of McDonald's – which has introduced architecture, decor and flavours that are now standardized across the globe. However, this is far from the whole story. Going global actually involved recognizing the desires of the local clientele and adapting pieces – the right pieces – of a theoretically uniform restaurant system.

McDonald's decided to go global in 1970. At the time, there were no universal low-cost restaurants. Places like the Ritz had chains that extended across the world, but they targeted high-end travellers. And most countries already had forms of quick dining out – noodle shops, pizzerias, cafés. However, what McDonald's was attempting was new and difficult. In the late 1960s McDonald's experienced its first failure in an attempt to expand into the Caribbean through Puerto Rico. Then they tried Canada and initially failed. In 1970 they tried the

Opening the First McDonald's Restaurant, Beijing, China,
23 April 1992.

with which he was engaged. He did not change the menu of McDonald's at all, but he did change its pitch – presenting the hamburger as an innovation, changing the pronunciation of McDonald's (Ma-ku-do-na-ru-do) and advertising in ways that appealed particularly to Japanese youth. Across the world, the expansion of the McDonald's market continued to rely heavily on children and their parents.[15]

When McDonald's moved into other international markets, it made sure to adapt but not to change too much: its cachet, after all, is in being McDonald's. However, the company has modified its menus to accommodate dietary restrictions – removing cheese from Big Macs in Israel, serving Vegetable McNuggets and the mutton Maharaja Mac in India – and occasionally catered to local taste by serving beer in Germany or McSpaghetti in the Philippines.

Because the architecture of McDonald's is so iconic, and because its layout is designed for its function (fast food relies on certain spatial relationships for ordering, seating, tidying and so on), the physical building of a McDonald's is one aspect that is rarely changed across different settings. However, even with this standardization, cultures navigate spaces in different ways. Lines are part of how a McDonald's, and much of self-service in general, works. In Hong Kong in the 1970s, introducing McDonald's meant providing a certain amount of instruction in queueing (which customers did take to). Conversely, in Leiden, the Netherlands, people do not normally queue – locals continued to just clump together and order according to their time of arrival. In France and Russia, there is a mix of using and not using queues at McDonald's locations.[16]

McDonald's also varied its advertising and aesthetics to target different cultures. While McDonaldization and McDonald's are often decried for their homogenization of the world,

Netherlands – and bent their system far enough to include chicken croquettes and apple sauce on the menu. Again, they failed. While the restaurants in these locales didn't close, they sustained losses for years. Finally in Canada, in 1971, McDonald's cut prices dramatically, increased clientele and in a few years turned a profit (and then returned to regular prices).

It was in Japan, in 1971, that McDonald's first succeeded in becoming an international business. It franchised to a successful Japanese retailer who understood the market and the marketing strategies anthropologists have pushed back against this story. A clear and elegant example of this comes from Indonesia, where the company began to operate in 1991. The various uses of Ronald McDonald across the country interrupt a one-way or homogeneous narrative about McDonald's as a global enterprise. In Jakarta, at the largest McDonald's there, there is a statue of Ronald McDonald. This is a common trope at McDonald's restaurants from Tulsa, Oklahoma, to Shanghai. However, instead of standing and waving or sitting on a bench (the two most common forms of these Ronald statues), the Ronald in Jakarta is seated in an Islamic meditation pose. He is sometimes called 'Ronald Bertapa'. Tapa, a Javanese meditation practice, is used as a traditional way to cultivate power. Another statue of Ronald, this time in Bali, is fashioned in the form of a Balinese temple figure. Both of these statues refigure Ronald in the form of Indonesian religious iconography. One could interpret these as adaptations no different from the McSpaghetti and Maharaja Mac; however, the final depiction of Ronald in Indonesia signals something different. The anthropologist A. Lukens-Bull calls this version 'Freedom Fighter Ronald'. The image was posted in Indonesian McDonald's to celebrate the fiftieth anniversary of Indonesian independence from the Dutch. Celebrating victory, Ronald, the Hamburglar, Grimace and Birdie the Early Bird ride on a tank towards a barbed-wire fence. During the same period that these banners were posted, the McDonald's workers wore red berets. Each of these features, as well as certain menu changes in Indonesia, were led by the original owner of the McDonald's franchises in the country, Bambang Rachmadi. His goal, which was successful, was to create a McDonald's that was both American and Indonesian, that spoke to the customer base looking for a global experience imbued with a sense of local power. This kind of local framing contests notions that McDonald's is a once-and-always American restaurant. As the anthropologist James L. Watson has written, 'McDonald's has become a saturated symbol, so laden with contradictory associations and meanings that the company stands for something greater than the sum of its corporate parts.'[17] We will see in the next chapter that global foodscapes are always layered – and always working at intersections of customer desire, cost margins, cooks' experiences, cultural positioning and local custom.

LOCAL GEMS

Despite various incarnations, at the heart of what makes a successful chain is its homogeneity – in food, in architecture and in experience. The local gem is the chain restaurant's antithesis. These are places that become important because they are unique. What is the place of the one-off in the history of restaurants? Such restaurants, and the discourse around them, become increasingly important in the late twentieth and early twenty-first century. They are places that have been deemed 'authentic'. Within an inherently commercialized industry, it is worth exploring what diners and critics mean by 'authentic' and what makes restaurants who earn this label valuable.

Local gems are usually initially crowned by the people who live nearby. In some places, warm service makes a local gem; in others it is the edgy or disaffected service. At a Bolivian restaurant in Madrid, the staff and customers form bonds based on knowing each other as individuals and respecting each other's privacy. Meanwhile, 'hons', competent waitresses with saucy attitudes, make a small collection of Baltimore, Maryland, diners local gems. While local specialities – like Delta tamales from Mississippi – can be the hallmark of a local gem, sometimes the food is just standard fare, like the *tonkatsu* in Hirakata, Japan. What these places do have in common is that they serve a local clientele in a way that fulfils their specific needs and desires: the right price, the right atmosphere and the right dishes. Because of this, some such places are inexpensive and quick (lunch for working people), while others are high-end and impressive (special occasion meals). What separates them from their competitors is often a distinct sense of identity, for the restaurant and for diners who patronize it. They are the places that, like McDonald's, have become a brand within and sometimes even beyond their community.

Eating at a local place is a hallmark of a certain idea of 'good' travel. This is a kind of paradox: local places are local because they are fully of that place, because they have a clientele that is local and food that works within the local cuisine (often relying on geographically bound foodstuffs and practices – which gets us to ethnic dining in the next chapter); yet it is those same qualities that make them desirable to visitors as well. To examine how these places function, let us ignore our own favourite local gems and look at two others: Gesshinkyo in Tokyo and Scott's Bar-B-Que in Hemingway, South Carolina.

SCOTT'S SETTING

Scott's Bar-B-Que is one of many barbecue restaurants in the southeastern United States. Barbecue restaurants are rarely fine dining (though the twenty-first century has made almost all foods available as both high- or low-end dining). They generally have counter service or a buffet, with tables at which to dine. They serve meat that has been smoked (most often pork, but sometimes chicken, beef or mutton) and an array of Southern side dishes (collard greens, baked beans, coleslaw, macaroni

and cheese, green beans, fried okra, yams or hash). Barbecue restaurants engender fierce loyalty.

Scott's Bar-B-Que is located in Hemingway, South Carolina, a town of 573 people in a rural, mostly agricultural area. This place has given rise to two different manifestations of the local restaurant phenomenon. The Scott family opened Scott's Bar-B-Que in Hemingway in 1972. Hemingway is also the original home of Sylvia Woods, who moved from South Carolina to New York City, and there ran one of that city's most famous soul food restaurants. The Scott family's paths never crossed with Woods, who opened her eponymous restaurant in 1962 in Harlem. However, aspects of these two restaurant businesses have significant parallels for understanding place, identity and the spectre of authenticity in restaurants.

The restaurant Sylvia's was made successful, in part, based on Woods's ability to establish an

Sylvia's Restaurant in Harlem, November 2008.

inviting space for people to inhabit. She hosted a collection of regulars: people who were happy to have both a food that was familiar from home and a place that felt like theirs. Woods was also good at inviting other kinds of people in, particularly celebrities and tourists, who came for 'authentic' soul food. Sylvia's, like Scott's, thus had a dually constructed authenticity. It served food and cultivated an atmosphere recognized and appreciated by what sociologists would call an 'ingroup', people who share identification – in Sylvia's case, African Americans with roots in the U.S. South. At the same time, it became recognized by outgroups as having laudatory markers of soul food culture.

Scott's Bar-B-Que, like Sylvia's, serves a wide-ranging clientele. However, it is located not in Harlem but in Hemingway, a small town. In terms of competition, Hemingway has one Chinese restaurant, one Mexican restaurant, a couple of Southern food restaurants and a handful of fast-food places. It is not located near a major, or even minor, city. Yet it has steadily increased its business since 1972. There is often a queue of people waiting to order, and regularly this line snakes out of the door of the restaurant. Scott's large customer base is grounded in two sources: frankly incredible barbecue and a tide of publicity that began in the early 2000s and continues to the present day.

Scott's is not a formal place. It began as a grocery shop, and the then-owner Roosevelt Scott started cooking barbecue and selling it in the store. Grocery-restaurants were a common occurrence in the twentieth-century U.S. South, not unlike the ubiquitous pharmacy soda fountain. Having a varied business model was good for shop owners, and customers liked the opportunity to get prepared foods and drinks and to linger for a while. These kinds of establishments often served as community hubs, where news would be exchanged along with

goods and services. Scott's still sells shop goods, both snacks and staples, though most of its business is in barbecue. There are coolers in the back with fizzy drinks and juices, and food staples and snacks near the ordering and payment counter. It also has about eight tables, with vinyl-padded chairs. Food can be eaten in, taken to go or eaten at the few outside tables. The walls of the restaurant are covered with accolades and pictures of various celebrities and dignitaries who have visited. It is a hotchpotch of framed pictures, mounted plaques, and clipped and posted newspaper articles. The blue-and-white painted breeze-block building, with its tin roof, barred windows and standard screen door, is a study in Southern vernacular architecture.

Scott's country aesthetics come not from a consciously branded design but rather from being rooted in its particular geographic and cultural location. Because of this, its lowbrow or low-key design is an asset that reinforces its position as 'authentic' – a local jewel. However, it is not the vision of Scott's but the smell of it that is the most alluring: smoke. It is this smoke – how it is made, what it does to the meats it touches – which makes Scott's a beacon for people of all ages, races and incomes, whether they are from South Carolina or beyond.

TREE TO TABLE

The service at Scott's relies on the labour methods of quick restaurants, including counter service, self-seating and packing orders in disposable containers; however, the procuring and cooking methods are anything but quick. They begin with felling trees and cutting timber. The Scott family has relationships with people who own land with hardwood trees as well as holding 40 hectares (100 ac) of their own land. When a tree is ready to harvest, members of the Scott family head out to cut and collect the wood to use in their barbecue. They do not use a single type of hardwood, but they do use local trees, so the species are somewhat limited. Oak is common; fragrant pecan, an occasional find.

Next they make the charcoal. This involves burning the hardwood in barrels designed by the Scotts in conjunction with a local welder (not unlike the McDonalds' relationship with their kitchen implement maker). Then they begin the process of smoking whole hogs. Because they smoke over charcoal and the threat of fire is real (Scott's smokehouse burned down in 2013), they use lean pigs, which means forming the right relationships with their meat providers. The pigs are cooked butterflied and whole. They begin the process at four in the afternoon and are not done cooking them until four in the morning, at the earliest. As the meat cooks it is basted and then finished with Scott's vinegar-based barbecue sauce, which is tangy and hot with just a hint of sweetness.

SCOTT'S AS A SENSATION

In 2009, after thirty years of regular successful but ordinary business, Scott's Bar-B-Que was written about in the *New York Times* by the food writer John T. Edge. The article was not a food review, but a profile piece. Scott's was the object of cultural interest – with restaurants and restaurateurs being interesting cultural as much as culinary topics. From interviews and observation, Edge described Scott's methods. Aimed at a culinary world interested in slow food and food provenance, the piece focused on Scott's practice and its relationship to time. The result was not only cultural interest but culinary interest.

Much of the discourse around Scott's is about Rodney Scott, the pitmaster, and son of Roosevelt, who opened the store in 1972. Rodney Scott cooked his first whole hog at eleven years old, which makes

sense in a family business. He has remained committed to a way of cooking that is both labour- and time-intensive. Since Edge's write-up of Scott's, there have been a further slew of articles about the restaurant, a film, and many media appearances by Rodney Scott. Scott was inundated with offers to franchise his operation, to sell his sauce and to create a commercial empire. He turned those offers down, while still managing to engage with a national audience, driving business to his location and participating in food-focused events. When Scott's smokehouse burned down in 2013 (a common occurrence for barbecue restaurants), Scott went on a tour, and the FatBack Collective (a group of pitmasters from a variety of restaurants) held fundraising events. From across the United States, people who loved barbecue donated money to help rebuild the smokehouse.

In 2016 Rodney opened a new restaurant, in the city of Charleston, a two-hour drive from Hemingway. It follows similar protocols as the original restaurant, though the wood is not hand-chopped and the menu has a slightly higher price point and the restaurant a fancier interior. The original Scott's Bar-B-Que still does a great deal of business and continues to be run by the Scott family. The location in Hemingway continues to be a unique place, with time-intensive culinary practices, set against the packaging, ordering and condensed menu designed by fast-food restaurants. It has served a local and national clientele and is a site of both cultural imagination and community engagement.

RESPECTING VEGETABLES AND TIME AT GESSHINKYO

Toshio Tanahashi ran a twenty-seat restaurant in an upscale area of Tokyo from 1992 to 2007. It was in most ways nothing at all like Scott's Bar-B-Que. The restaurant, Gesshinkyo, specialized in *shojin ryori*. This is Zen Buddhist vegetarian cuisine, which goes by different names across the world, but is the physical manifestation of shared philosophical tenets: it is made without harming living creatures, so it is without meat or fish; it is made to not interrupt meditation, so without pungent flavours (like garlic); it is made to combat wastefulness, by using all parts of the vegetable, root to leaf; and it is made to express respect for ingredients and their setting – to bring out their own characteristics and use them at their peak ripeness or freshness.

Zen temples and monasteries across Asia have long served food to worshippers and pilgrims, a tradition that led to temple restaurants. Tanahashi was trained, in the 1980s, by the abbess Myodoni Murase, of the temple Gesshinji. A nun in her eighties, Murase was a dedicated Zen practitioner and cook. For example, after being partially paralysed in her thirties, she started waking two hours earlier so that she could still grind her own sesame paste every morning with only one arm. Tanahashi was required to watch her make her sesame paste at 3 a.m. for a year before he could try to do it himself. These exacting timelines were echoed in other parts of his apprenticeship: he could not use a knife for a year, or season a vegetable for two. Attention and discipline were at the heart of his three-year training. Perhaps more germane, Murase is not an outlier in her dedication or practice: Zen abbesses across East Asia are known for their cooking, and have been cooking at temples for hundreds of years. At Sankoin, a temple in Koganei, western Tokyo, they pass their tradition from one nun to another, teaching techniques to draw out the best of the vegetables they use and using them entirely without waste. For example, Abbess Koei Hoshino says, 'When cooking eggplant [aubergine], the stems are usually

discarded as inedible, but we cut them into tiny leaves and put them in soup as a decorative garnish. They are edible, of course.'[18]

In the decade before Tanahashi went to learn the craft of Zen Buddhist cooking from Murase, other women, in South Korea and the United States, were turning out equally stunning vegetarian and Buddhism-rooted cuisine. Outside of Seoul, at the temples of Jinkwansa and Baekyangsa, nuns were making the same kinds of food, serving them in temple meals to the devout and the curious. At Baekyangsa, Jeong Kwan is one of the nuns who leads the kitchen. She joined the monastery at seventeen years old and is now in her sixties. Like Murase, she invests a great deal of time in her cooking. The ingredients that she prepares come from the grounds she tends, which include nutmeg and citrus trees planted before her birth, and from the land she forages around the temple complex and monastery. She and two other nuns also prepare ingredients themselves, fermenting a range of pickles and sauces and caring for these mixtures, sometimes for years.

A similar tradition of collectively owned vegetarian restaurants in the United States sprung from a wider array of philosophical traditions, going through a resurgence in the 1970s. Most came not from Pacific-rim religious practice, but from New England traditions of vegetarianism that trace their roots to movements of the Enlightenment. Their lineage is descended from transcendentalists like Ralph Waldo Emerson, Romantic writers like Mary Shelley, activists and journalists like Margaret Fuller, theologians and reformers like Sylvester Graham, and physicians like William Alcott. These people were vegetarian for a variety of reasons, from feminist political ideologies to critiques against factory meat production, from religious aspirations for clarity to epidemiological goals of disease reduction.

In 1850 Alcott decided to 'call a convention of these scattered friends of vegetarianism' in Philadelphia. The 1850s and 1860s saw the rise of two major vegetarian periodicals and other vegetarian writing across Europe and America. By the late 1880s explicitly vegetarian restaurants had opened across the United States, England and continental Europe, including Hiltl in Switzerland – originally named the 'Vegetarian Home and Abstinence Café' – the longest continually running vegetarian restaurant outside of Asia. From that moment, vegetarian restaurants were part of a niche, often countercultural market that dwelt at the intersection of ethical, political and health concerns. This history includes unlikely stories, like a chain of vegetarian restaurants in Memphis in the 1920s, and expected ones, like the rise of vegetarian restaurants across the United States in the years around the Pure Food and Drug Act (1906), which had been spurred to passage by concerns about the health dangers of mass meat production. With the rise of 1960s counterculture movements, a new generation of these restaurants emerged, which included a successful vegetarian chain called Cranks in England. Cranks was commercially successful, unlike the financially disastrous attempt by the Childs chain, under its vegetarian owner William Childs, to make the chain's menu meatless in the 1920s. However, a common thread in the story of vegetarian restaurants is often that they were quite local, and even community-owned.

Two of these restaurants, which began in the 1970s, are Moosewood and Bloodroot. They are both collectives in the northeastern United States (in Ithaca, New York, and Bridgeport, Connecticut, respectively) that have continued to serve diners and communities into the twenty-first century. Moosewood was run by a collective of nineteen people who were invested in simplicity and back-to-the-land movements, and has, since its inception,

been creating cuisine that is not unlike Zen temple cuisine: vegetarian dishes that are delicious, attentive to their ingredients and produced in ways that are ethical and often local. Moosewood was spearheaded by a woman, Therese Tischler, who asked friends (many also women) to shape a restaurant committed to health and ecological sustainability. Now one of the most famous vegetarian restaurants in the United States, Moosewood has continued to shape how people imagine vegetarian restaurants to be. This image includes a homely aesthetic in addition to a political and philosophical stance towards farming and egalitarian economic models in service of sustainability. Bloodroot is also a small collective, but with a different political driver: it is part of feminist vegetarian movements. It was founded in 1977 by five women who had met at consciousness-raising rap sessions. At these sessions, they would talk about and listen to each other's experiences as women raising children, running homes and living in a patriarchal society. For five of these women, the discussions emboldened them to change their futures. The group wanted to provide a space for other women and a way for them to support themselves – and each other – financially. They established the Bloodroot restaurant and bookshop to nourish political agendas, too: rejecting patriarchal food systems and respecting the earth and animals with local, vegetarian fare. They embraced a collective, consensus-driven governance and work structure, and an ethos of feminist community-building – all customers would be safe and encouraged, but they would also clear their own dishes.

Also in the United States, in San Francisco in the 1970s, Zen Buddhism had taken hold of a cadre of young Americans. Many of them had begun their journey in counterculture movements in Berkeley, California. One, Deborah Madison, started her career at Chez Panisse with Alice Waters. Like

Exterior of Moosewood Restaurant, Ithaca, NY, September 1992.

others who spent time there early in their careers, Madison has carried forward a commitment to seasonal food; however, her commitment to vegetables and vegetarian cuisine, which she used to shape a nation of eaters and chefs, also emerged from her engagement with the San Francisco Zen Center. Unlike the nuns of Jingwansa and Baekyangsa, Madison did not continue her Buddhist practice, but she has continued commitments to sustainable, attentive, vegetarian food practices.

In 1979, while a student of the San Francisco Zen Center (which has a fraught history), she opened Greens Restaurant, which relied on the foods farmed at the centre's farm, Green Gulch, where Madison had also worked. The restaurant was not located at the Zen Center and was not for practioners and visitors, but instead built as a business to support the Zen Center and draw on its students' talents and labour. Like the Green Gulch farm and the temple restaurants, the restaurant was run by devout people who basically made enough money to cover their accommodation and meals.

With a site overlooking the Bay Bridge, Greens Restaurant became, like Chez Panisse in Berkeley,

a place that transformed how people understood fine dining. An early lunch menu included items like Niçoise pizza with capers, olives and fresh herbs, and brochettes described as 'marinated tofu, mushrooms, tomatoes, peppers, and other seasonal vegetables skewered and cooked over mesquite charcoal'. (This was an early use of the now-ubiquitous nomenclature of 'seasonal vegetables'.) Greens Restaurant was a new kind of vegetarian restaurant in the United States, noted for both its audience and formality (high-end, not focused solely on vegetarians). However, while Greens emerged from a different coast and vegetarian tradition, it was also part of the long history of collectively owned American vegetarian restaurants such as Moosewood and Bloodroot, the same counterculture moment of origin as well as some of the same collective, local and Earth-friendly goals. That it relied on Buddhist traditions, via Japan, shifted the food served and the aesthetics of the dishes. Rather than the homespun and often bran-inflected food traditions of the northeast (influenced by famous American vegetarian advocates like John Harvey Kellogg and Sylvester Graham), the food at Greens was in the vein of what would become California cuisine: fresh, often bright and vegetable-forward.

While vegetarian women were transforming ingredients and food scenes across the world, Toshio Tanahashi began his career as a disgruntled office worker. By the late 1980s vegetarian cuisine and Zen Buddhism were moving from counterculture to vogue in the United States (a 1987 *New York Times* article lets us know that 'vegetarians need no longer defend their diet at parties'[19]). In Japan, Tanahashi left his job to pursue his apprenticeship with Murase. Over the following three years, he learned to ferment his own condiments, to make lotus root shine in its own right, to grind sesame paste for hours and to steep flowers in water for seconds.

In 1992 he opened his small restaurant. Gesshinkyo was a one-person show. Tanahashi cooked and served the entire meal – and cleaned the restaurant's 'every nook and cranny' by himself.[20] There he served ten-course meals to a small audience of diners. While the menu was always changing, every dinner began with a sesame tofu, made each day beginning with the meditative and labour-intensive grinding of seeds. Then customers would move on to miso soup before turning to a litany of seasonal delights: for example, rice with lily bulbs, matsutake prepared to perfection, taro with truffles and chrysanthemums, wild mizudama in a salad, aubergine as condiment and stew and pickle. His restaurant, like Greens, was not a temple restaurant. Instead it built 'a cuisine out of the monastic and the modern'.[21]

SLOW FOOD

There is a mass consumption of Rodney Scott and of Toshio Tanahashi as food celebrities, but there is not a mass consumption of their food – because they have not increased production as demand has increased. In fact, part of their excellence is a refusal to make more, a refusal to see their customer rather than the food itself as the driver. This is not inherent to the cuisines they have chosen. Some barbecue and vegetarian fare is mass-produced to serve many people. With the rise of electric smokers, barbecue chains are now ubiquitous.

Instead Gesshinkyo and Scott's Bar-B-Que have invested in methods that are deliberately slow. The people who run them, Tanahashi and the Scotts, are committed to perfecting their trade and to maintaining a faith in traditional methods while still innovating technique: for example, making charcoal from their own wood, but doing it in a personally designed barrel apparatus; or grinding sesame seeds every morning, but teaching cooking workshops during the day to supplement the infrastructure of a high-end, high-rent restaurant; or experimenting with new vegetable preparations. As Tanahashi says, 'I'm always trying new things, because although this style of food has been served at Japan's temples for centuries, traditional need not mean old. We are new people and need to give our senses new experiences.'[22]

In descriptions of these restaurants, people often focus on the labour involved in their culinary practices – and how that labour leads to better food. At the same time, the frame that helps us understand their value is often centred around cultural capital, rather than only food preparation and service. Discourse around Tanahashi always returns to Buddhist religious tradition and practice, even when he is making crème brûlée. At Scott's Bar-B-Que, part of the cultural legacy is the same hard legacy that Sylvia Wood capitalized on – that of being black and Southern in the United States. 'People keep talking about how old-fashioned what we do is. Old-fashioned was working the farm as a boy. I hated those long hours, that hot sun. Compared to that, this is a slow roll,' Roosevelt Scott said of his family's barbecue methods.[23] Scott's comment challenges temporal claims about what is old-fashioned. The idea that places like Scott's and Gesshinkyo demonstrate long-held traditions is an important aspect of how both have been romanticized; the same idea is also a feature that sets them apart from the discourse of fast food, which despite being a movement of the last century, still often stands for a kind of contemporary mentality. Scott also contrasts the 'long hours' of working on the farm with the 'slow roll' of just-as-long hours running his own barbecue place. This juxtaposition says much about what makes local gems significant: they are often run and visited by people who care about them as independent entities, as places that are governed by the rules and visions of a particular place or practice – in direct contrast to the standardized governance and standardized experience of successful fast-food places like McDonald's. In the final chapter, we continue this examination of place as a central aspect of the restaurant by turning to global cuisine.

9
GLOBAL DINING

International dining has long been a worldwide phenomenon. You could get a great Chinese meal in San Francisco in the 1850s. Kyoto was home to a French restaurant in the 1890s. Polynesian food was popular in Mexico in the 1950s. In the 1980s Nairobi had an excellent Brazilian steakhouse. Dining with geographically and culturally specific roots in places outside of the one in which it is being eaten is a phenomenon in which restaurants have played a significant part. The appeal of food that is from 'far away' has roots in the very beginning of restaurants in China. Travelling merchants would go to places that served food from their home provinces, and they would take colleagues and business partners there, sharing southern Chinese cuisine with their northern counterparts.

Whether in Mumbai or Oslo, restaurants that serve food from other places often began as part of migrant culture. From the Del Monicos' Delmonico's in 1827 to today, migrants have often opened restaurants. According to the United States census records, in 1860 around 60 per cent of restaurant workers were foreign-born. The same was true in 1900, in 1950 and in 2000. The country of origin from which these workers came has changed over time, from Scotland, Ireland and Germany to Italy, China and Greece to countries of Central and South America and the former USSR.[1]

The anthropologist Krishnendu Ray explains the social and economic conditions of this pattern, which occurs the world over. Immigrants often end up in the food business because it has low overhead costs and is easily supported by self-exploitation (working long hours and employing the labour of family and friends). Furthermore, because immigrants have what Ray calls 'cultural knowledge about esoteric food', they are able to fulfil the desire of both customers from their own cultures (who desire the food of home) and customers in the dominant culture (who desire novelty). Part of this pattern involves captivating consumers with new food experiences. Immigrant restaurateurs then cultivate these new food experiences in an 'aesthetic transaction' with the majority culture, to use Ray's term. While new foods become rote foods in many cases (for example, salsa), their novelty-by-association with other cultures is a central part of the story of eating globally, locally.[2]

While food writers and scholars often seem to focus on the dynamics of cultural appropriation or on discerning what is 'authentic', the most interesting work on how restaurants transform tastes falls between these two philosophical poles. Such studies chart the realities, loves and power differentials that mark how cultural exchange happens in societies and economies of inherent plurality and inequity. In this chapter, we will take up the multivalenced experience of dining across cultures as well as the role of migrants in cultivating those dining experiences and shifting restaurant landscapes. To do this, we will examine the global reaches of the Chinese restaurant over two centuries, the fêting and fetishization of cosmopolitan dining in a famous German restaurant between 1928 and 1943, as well as the global business success of Nordic dining.

RESTAURANTS OF THE CHINESE DIASPORA IN THE AMERICAS

While the global spread of American fast-food dining in the twentieth century is widely documented, other cuisines have clearly made their way across the globe as well and often with more speed. While French food was international haute cuisine before there was 'haute cuisine' (the term was coined in the twentieth century), Italian and Chinese restaurants are perhaps even more prolific, in part because they moved across borders as food for everyone, beginning as working-class food rather than high-end cuisine.

'Chinese food' is a misnomer, as are all national descriptors for food. Food cultures rarely emerge from nation states, but rather from regions that, in the case of a country like China, are quite different and geographically distinct from one another. It is only when we look through global and nationalist lenses that we develop terms like 'Chinese', 'British', 'French' and 'Belizean' food. The food of immigrants is often tied to nations (Chinese food) rather than regions (Sichuan food) because immigration and migration are experiences where national identity is key (for issues of legal status, often tied to the conditions of migration).

Looking at how Chinese restaurants became a central part of the restaurant scene in the Americas between the 1840s and the 1970s illuminates how ethnic dining functions for the owners, workers and diners of these establishments. We can see how this happens in three countries in the Americas: Peru, Cuba and the United States (ending with a story in England). Each of these manifestations of the Chinese restaurant has its own nuances reflecting the culture of the Chinese immigrants and the dominant culture of the country. Chinese food became a global cuisine thanks to the forces of human migration, colonialism and trade. The proliferation of Chinese restaurants across the Western hemisphere can be told as a story of nation states, a story of migrants or a story of eaters; however, in the nineteenth century, it is perhaps most interestingly a story of Guangdong.

The heart of the Guangdong province is the city of Guangzhou (Canton), which sits at the head of the Pearl River Delta, a major port area in southern China that includes Macau and Hong Kong. The Portuguese settled in Macau in 1557 (after arriving first in 1517 in Guangzhou), and over the course of the nineteenth century many European countries established outposts in the region (by a mixture of treaties and force). Political forces – both incentives from abroad and instability at home – fuelled large-scale migration from the area between 1840 and 1900. This immigration led to the Chinese restaurant in the Americas – and to specific patterns

Utagawa Yoshikazu, *Ijiin Yashiki ryōri no zu* (Inside a Foreign Restaurant), 1860, polychrome woodblock print.

of restaurant dining that continue today. Four stories of people from Guangdong – in Peru, Cuba, California and New York – trace the lineaments of international dining.

THE CREATION OF CHIFA

Chifa, which refers both to a type of cuisine and the restaurant where it is served, has become so popular in Peru that it is integral to the national cuisine (like pizza in the United States). The distinctive and beloved Peruvian dish *lomo saltado* is a chifa dish. It is stir-fried beef marinated in vinegar, soy sauce and spices, with onions, tomatoes, coriander and potatoes, served with rice. Other chifa foods include dishes that are also part of the general Chinese cuisine in other parts of the Americas: *sopa de wonton*, *arroz chaufa* (fried rice) and *tallarin saltado* (fried noodles, like *lo mein*). How did Chinese food come to be Peruvian food?

Chinese labourers picking cotton on irrigated land at the foot of the Andes, Vitarte, Peru, c. 1900, stereograph.

In the nineteenth century, thousands of Cantonese men came to Peru to work as contract labourers on sugar plantations. The men who made up this population were a mixture of forced and voluntary migrants. This migration was partially driven by the Opium Wars and by the end of the transatlantic slave trade, which changed how plantation owners across the Americas sourced their labour. Almost all of the migrants arrived to and worked in oppressive conditions. In 1877 the form of contract labour these Cantonese men experienced was outlawed (in response to Chinese pressure around the starvation, enslavement and other forms of violent exploitation of these migrant workers by plantation owners); however, for more than thirty years Chinese people continued to migrate to Peru, for a variety of reasons: to get away from wars and rebellions in China, to find better economic opportunities or to flee famine.[3]

A key part of the employment contracts between Peruvian employers and Chinese migrants (before and after 1874) was the guarantee of rice. These contracts were usually written and administrated by the Portuguese in Macau, who also governed the transit of the labourers from Guangdong. In order to fulfil the contracts or perhaps mostly to keep the peace – uprisings occurred when the rice supply disappeared – Peruvian employers imported rice and established local rice crops. Cantonese Peruvians were thus able to cook their own food – usually the food of the lower classes in southern China: rice with some vegetables and meat. This was not the high-end sea cucumbers, sharks' fins and swallows' nests of spectacular Chinese cuisine that caught nineteenth-century imaginations inside and outside of China. Instead it was simple fare with rice at the centre. Much of the population was male – and came from a culture where men cooked.

Many of these men married Peruvian women (native Peruvians, Spanish Peruvians and African Peruvians) and these women played a central role in the rise of chifa. They largely came from cultures where women cooked, which meant that the food in these households often retained Cantonese elements as well as adopted Peruvian ones. Between 1850 and 1900, many Cantonese immigrants also began to work in domestic service, extending southern Chinese cooking beyond their own homes. The most significant element in the national rise of chifa was the *fonda*. These were small restaurants, which flourished in nineteenth-century Peru, that served a variety of Chinese dishes, inflected with Peruvian cuisine, based on what ingredients were available and also on the exchange of cooking practices between people of different origins – from Peru and countries in Africa, as well as China. This expansion was possible because the women who Cantonese Peruvians ended up marrying were already small entrepreneurs. They ran local shops or food-service businesses themselves.[4] As studies of migrant restaurant entrepreneurs across the world demonstrate, local in-network financing is a key part of this economic model. The women that immigrants married had some amount of capital, business savvy and independence. This meant that they were poised to work with their husbands to create these new restaurants, often initially within their communities, ultimately expanding outwards.

Chifa *fondas* began, as one might expect, by serving the communities of Chinese and Chinese Peruvians in enclaves established in major cities like Lima as well as small municipalities across the country. As Chinese Peruvians began working in a wider range of more lucrative trades (such as selling furniture and other imported goods), a set of more refined chifas began to crop up, which were also frequented by non-Chinese Peruvians. Furthermore,

as Chinese Peruvians began to open restaurants in a wider range of locations, not simply in the communities where they lived, a broader clientele frequented these places. We will see a similar pattern in San Francisco and New York.

CHINESE CUBANS AND CUBAN CHINESE RESTAURANTS

While Peru and Cuba share a history of Spanish-legislated indentured Chinese sugar plantation workers between the 1840s and 1870s, the restaurant scenes that came out of these communities are not the same. Despite what seem like similar conditions of labour and cultural intersections (African, Spanish, Native American, Chinese), the food culture and restaurant scenes in these places evolved differently. The Cuban Chinese did not have access to rice at the scale that the Peruvian Chinese did. Instead they became known for farming, selling and preparing vegetables. In Havana, by 1858, the Barrio Chino was established in an area between black and white neighbourhoods, anchored by a Chinese restaurant, which served both communities as well as the Chinese one. The barrio continued to grow over the next century. Unlike the symbolism that might be suggested by the barrio's location, and unlike the chifa, the food of Cuba's Chinese restaurants – and later diasporic Cuban Chinese restaurants – is not a fusion cuisine. While clearly both cuisines would be changed by being cooked in the same kitchens by the same people, Cuban Chinese restaurants would often serve Cuban and Chinese food alongside each other: plantains next to *lo mein*, offerings of both pepper steak and *moros*. In this way, Cuban Chinese restaurants as an international phenomenon showcase one of the hallmarks of restaurant dining: the provision of menu choices.

Tao Jin Rong, founder of Restaurant Tien Tan, one of the most popular Chinese Restaurants in Cuba, 2007.

Over time, a second wave of Chinese immigrants arrived, international businessmen who came by way of California. Unlike the very poor indentured labourers of the first wave, these were wealthy Chinese who brought with them tastes and structures of large, formal Chinese restaurants, like those that flourished in nineteenth-century San Francisco. This mixture was evidently successful. By the twentieth century, Cuba had a large Chinese population and a vibrant Chinatown in Havana. However, in the decade after the Cuban Revolution, many Chinese Cubans fled to the United States, in particular to New York. After often initially working

in restaurants and other service industries, they built up capital to open their own places, restaurants whose origins were not in the New York Latino and Chinese communities to which they had moved. Instead they reflected their own already distinctive identity group.

In the 1970s and 1980s, Cuban Chinese restaurants boomed, even leading to places like Asia de Cuba, a chain of high-end restaurants run by (the non-Cuban Chinese) Philadelphian Jeffrey Chodorow. Cuban Chinese restaurants in the United States appealed to a broad intersection of people for different reasons: to Cuban expats looking for a taste of home, to Chinese Cubans themselves, to Latino immigrants looking for foods that reminded them of home (where there would have been a Latino Chinese restaurant) and to other ethnicities of North Americans who were interested in new food mash-ups (especially those made from combining foods from other beloved familiar traditions).[5] Thus the Cuban-Chinese restaurant as a form was shaped not only by initial immigration patterns of Chinese to Cuba, but by movements to and from the United States. It has been shaped by the desires of local populations, by serving people who are not of Chinese descent and by making menus that capitalize on choice.

COMMERCE, CELEBRITY AND CHOP SUEY THROUGH CALIFORNIA AND THE EAST COAST

Just as the food culture in Peru and Cuba came from the distinct class and geographic conditions of the migrants there, so did the structure of restaurants that came with migrants to the United States. People emigrated from China to California, a colony of Spain, beginning in the early nineteenth century; however, with the First Opium War in the early 1840s as well as the gold rush and the need for labour for railways, many more immigrants came to the United States and particularly California. Beginning in the 1840s, large numbers of immigrants from Guangdong arrived in California, bringing with them restaurant traditions of home. Because the migration to California had a longer timeline, and because of the boom-and-bust economy of gold mining, Chinese food in California had a different history of class and expansion than in Central and South America.

In China, through the Qing dynasty (1644–1912), restaurants were often housed in single buildings with different tiers. Combining elaborate banquet dining (continuing a tradition from early Kaifeng restaurants) and the quick and cheap noodle stands that had grown up in the same bustling mercantile city, these restaurants were both large and commonly found throughout China. The Englishman John Henry Gray described them in his *China: A History of the Laws, Manners, and Customs of the People* (1878):

> The restaurants are generally very large establishments, consisting of a public dining-room and several private rooms. Unlike most other buildings, they consist of two or three stories. The kitchen alone occupies the ground floor; the public hall, which is the resort of persons in the humbler walks of life, is on the first floor, and the more select apartments are on the second and third floors. These are, of course, resorted to by the wealthier citizens, but they are open to persons in all classes of society, and it is not unusual to see in them persons of limited means. At the entrance-door there is a table or counter at which the proprietor sits, and where each customer pays for his repast. The public room is immediately at the head of the first staircase, and is resorted to by all who require a cheap meal. It is furnished, like a café, with tables and chairs, a private room having only one table and a few chairs in it.

People eating at dim sum restaurants and tea parlours in Guangdong were sometimes segregated by gender. The bill was totalled by the number of empty dishes, and customers were entertained with music, storytelling, gossip and even songbird competitions.[6]

The kinds of restaurant experiences Gray described, along with the cuisine, were imported along with the migrants. Large Chinese restaurants

The interior of a Chinese restaurant on Dupont Street, Chinatown, California, in 1895, stereograph.

Detroit Publishing Company, *A Chinese Restaurant, San Francisco, California*, 1898, postcard.

in nineteenth-century San Francisco were renowned for their reasonable prices and for their decor. In 1865 at Hong Heong Restaurant, diners passed through the ground-floor kitchen and upstairs into rooms filled with Chinese tables, lamps and screens. They were served Chinese dishes in Chinese dishware with chopsticks, which was standard for Chinese immigrants but something oft commented upon as a difficulty for others, and were often treated to live music and sometimes even recitations.[7]

The food at San Francisco Chinese restaurants was often inexpensive but 'excellent', per the *New York Tribune* among others. For $1, a person could get a substantial meal that included both European food and Chinese food, which was often interpreted as hashes and curries, later as chows or 'chop suey'.[8] The inexpensive food was quite a draw because the boom period in San Francisco drove prices for many things, including food, through the roof. The people who frequented these California Chinese restaurants, both those of Chinese and non-Chinese descent, often worked in gold mining. The wealth in San Francisco itself helped establish highly success-ful Chinese merchants and the gold in California soil led to some Chinese miners striking it rich. This meant that in the case of California there was also a robust market for high-end Chinese food, including imported items like sharks' fins and swallows' nests.[9]

On the East Coast of the United States, Chinese restaurants also flourished, but mostly away from the eyes of white diners. These restaurants catered almost exclusively to their Chinese clientele, from well-to-do importers, laundry owners and mer-chants to the many working-class people who had immigrated in the mid- to late nineteenth century from the Pearl River Delta in Guangdong. While the non-Chinese Americans would mainly order inexpensive meals, the Chinese clientele, when they

had the money, splurged on the costly imported tastes of home. Beginning in the 1870s, we have reports of non-Chinese people, for reasons of curi-osity or connection, who dined in these restaurants – for example, a 'lawyer of decidedly Bohemian tendencies' who takes someone to dine at Mong Sing Wah's in New York, touting the restaurateur as 'a Celestial Delmonico'.[10] By 1902 the *New York Herald* printed a description of these bohemian, exoticism-seeking customers that seems oh-so-current: 'When he chooses a Chinese dinner he must have a restau-rant where no white man has ever before trod, if he can find one. As soon as others begin to frequent it, again he flies.'

'A Chinese Dinner in New York – Enjoying a Meal', from *The American Magazine*, vol. XVII (1884), illustration.

New Years, Chinatown (Port Arthur Chinese Restaurant, New York), undated, photograph.

Most New Yorkers in 1896 were not thinking about having Chinese food for dinner. Then a misreported story fuelled a Chinese food craze for a dish that came to be called 'chop suey'. The Chinese foreign minister Li Hongzhang visited the United States. At a banquet at the Waldorf, he supposedly ate little of the European food served and later enjoyed rice, diced chicken and vegetables. While it is dubious that any of this actually occurred, newspapers across the country, large and small, reran this story; in subsequent weeks, other stories discussing the event and the dishes that were supposedly made for Li Hongzhang graced the pages of papers. At the heart of the craze was a dish dubbed 'chop suey', an

Americanized stir-fry that often included offal and vegetables in small pieces, based on dishes from Taishan, a city in the Pearl River Delta. Chinese food became an overnight sensation, moving from a specialized genre of food for the adventurous to one that attracted flocks of young American men and women. The popularity of Chinese food also changed the food itself and the types of restaurants that served it. Chinese restaurants started popping up in popular entertainment districts outside of Chinatowns. Chop suey became more like the foods with which those new diners were familiar, with less mysterious flavours and ingredients (no more ginger and dried mushrooms) and cooked using more

Westernized techniques – the ingredients cooked into a soft stew rather than being presented stir-fried and still crunchy.[11] The restaurants that capitalized on this boom were usually run and staffed by Chinese people, and continued to be decorated with Chinese art, lanterns and furniture; but they were open late, catering to the people in the area in which they were operating – to theatre goers; to would-be bohemians; to African Americans; to adventurous young ladies, proper ladies and ladies of the night; and to those who were down on their luck. In general, these Chinese restaurants had a reputation for serving a cross-section of people who were staying out late, searching for low-cost, low-stress entertainment.[12]

As in Peru, with the new wave of Chinese immigration to the United States in the 1960s, along with expanding interests in regional cuisines, there was a shift to seeing cuisine through increasingly local rather than national lenses that led to different type of Chinese restaurant. These places marketed themselves as Sichuan and Hunan rather than just Chinese.[13] While the food was still transformed for the local population – made less spicy, often sweeter – it also reflected a growing interest in expanding into new types of Chinese food. This kind of localization and regionalization, in concert with a push for continually newer food experiences, created a restaurant landscape that today includes many forms – from homogenized fast-food shopping mall or food court Chinese and formal Chinese banquet halls, to specialized hand-drawn noodle joints (a dish that originated in northwest China) and high-end restaurants serving Chinese tasting-menus. Along the way, who runs and works at Chinese restaurants in the United States has also changed from Chinese immigrants to a range of ethnicities, particularly Asian ethnicities, working from a menu

and economic model that has seen more than 150 years of success.

CHINESE RESTAURANTS IN ENGLAND

The popularity of the Chinese restaurant in England took a different path. Like elsewhere in the western hemisphere, the first Chinese restaurants were created for and by Chinese immigrants. In England, this notably occurred in Liverpool, where people first immigrated as sailors and then moved into service industries such as laundry. The restaurants in these places, like the very first restaurants in northern China, served people who were looking for the food of home. Unlike in the United States, Cuba and Peru, where members of the dominant culture began going to Chinese restaurants because of cost, location and familiarity with Chinese foods, the Chinese restaurant became popular for white people through an orchestrated 'event' restaurant and news publicity in England. Like the cafeteria, the automat, the Michelin Guide and the sushi conveyor belt, the first Chinese restaurant for white people in Britain was developed and debuted at an international exposition.

The 1884 restaurant exhibit was led by the inspector general of Chinese Imperial Maritime Customs, Robert Hart, for the International Health Exposition. He brought in Chinese cooks and designed the restaurant after those in China. The goal of the exhibition restaurant was to introduce people to China and Chinese culture rather than to market cuisine, so the dishes were to be Chinese instead of undergoing the processes of simplification and adjustment to local palates. Still the restaurant's menu oscillated between Chinese dishes and dishes that seemed thoroughly European. It was written mostly in French, the language of haute cuisine, and designed by a French cook who had by then lived and worked in China for fifteen years before coming to England for this short-term exhibition restaurant. The typically Chinese dishes included *pullulas à l'Huile* (a type of fried insect), bird's nest soup and *Biche de Mer à la Matelote Chinoise* – sea cucumber in a Chinese wine sauce. Classic European dishes include *Beignet Soufflé à la Vanille*, *Roulade de Pigeon farcie au Pistache* and olives. Interesting proto-fusion dishes include *Sharks' Fin à la Bagration* and *Vermicelli Chinoise à la Milannaise*.

The restaurant was popular and received a lot of media attention. Despite its popularity, the coverage was often ridiculing.[14] This piece from the *Pall Mall Budget* is representative:

LUNCH WITH THE CELESTIALS. If the multitudinous dishes inscribed on the menu of the trial lunch with which the Chinese restaurateurs lately opened their campaign at the Health Exhibition are set before the British public, it is easy to foresee that the British public will be at a great loss which to choose. It is right, therefore, to give a little advice. The hungry Sightseer may with confidence order birds'-nest soup. As served in a tiny slop-basin, it is excellent. It will have a great success in London, and will probably be naturalized in England from and after 1884. Let one only of the party order Shaohsing [*sic*] wine. It is warm like the soup, and also served in a tiny slop-basin. But a taste of it will be enough for each of the guests. It is made from rice, and its flavour is indescribable. Besides birds'-nests the Chinese eat many things which we do not eat. Either of the two following dishes, called respectively, in Franco-Chinese jargon, 'Timbale Biche de-Mer au Madere,' or 'Shark's fin a la Bagration,' will give to any curious barbarian some notion of the skillful manner in which they utilize treasures of the deep which we waste. This so-called

'Biche-de-Mer' is a sea-slug two inches long by an inch thick. It lies at the bottom of the deep seas off the Chinese coast, and looks when dried like a piece of india-rubber, from which protrude rows of short spikes. When cut open it is found to consist of an alimentary canal, surrounded by a tough gelatinous substance of the consistency and colour of india-rubber. This unprepossessing little animal keeps a long time in a dried state. It is cut up and cooked in minute pies. The British public will not find these sea-slug pies so bad as might be imagined, their taste being not unlike that of turtle. The shark's fin, however, is for the more audacious only. It is cartilaginous, and eaten with rice.[15]

While the exhibit restaurant piqued white Britons' interest in Chinese food, it was again a wave of migration coupled with an expansion of overseas experiences that most lastingly changed their eating patterns and established the ubiquity of Chinese restaurants and takeaway places. After the Second World War and into the 1950s, a rise in immigrants from Hong Kong coincided with a British population that had been exposed to Chinese dishes during their time in the Pacific theatre, creating both supply and demand for Chinese restaurants.[16]

Whether in Liverpool or Lima, Havana or San Francisco, the rise of Chinese restaurants outside China follows the patterns of immigrant restaurants that anthropologist Krishnendu Ray identifies: immigrant restaurateurs often rely on networks of capital and low overheads, often supplemented by family labour or their own access to the low-cost labour of new immigrants. Immigrant cuisines often begin in service of fellow migrants, people looking for the food they know and love, or simply people looking for food they can access. However, because

Potsdamer Platz, Berlin: Haus Vaterland, Löwenbräu, 1920.

restaurants are public spaces, people from other groups and places, from the dominant culture or from other marginalized cultures, end up in immigrants' restaurants. Low cost and novelty often drive this customer base, and in turn the new customer base often drives shifts in cuisine. The result is a changing and proliferating restaurant scene that reflects realities of cultural power dynamics, which values aesthetic difference while responding to market pressure. Thus we end up with many genres of restaurants, serving customers' needs and desires, following traditions that lead to both homogenous American Chinese menus and menus that innovate with flavour and texture combinations in new iterations. Discussing the rise of Asian American dining in 2017, Ligaya Mishan describes this latter cuisine

as having an 'attitude that informs and powers it, reflecting a new cockiness in a population that has historically kept quiet and [been] encouraged to lay low. It's food that celebrates crunchy cartilage and gelatinous ooze, that openly stinks, that declares: This is what *I* like to eat. What about you?'[17]

EATING THE WORLD IN THREE FLOORS

As a bustling mercantile city and centre for political power, Berlin has long been home to diners from other places. However, in 1928, in central Berlin a new wonderland of a restaurant opened its doors. It was the continuation of a family restaurant empire as well as a whole new kind of dining experience. Haus Vaterland was an entertainment complex that included a cinema, a 2,500-person café, and twelve regional and international eateries. Serving more than a million guests a year, it drew on the spectacular entertainment culture of amusement parks like Coney Island, with outlandish decor, costumed staff and live entertainment. This theme park of food serves as an instructive example of the restaurant as cultural performance.

Haus Vaterland was one of a style of restaurants that in German is called *Erlebnisgastronomie* (performance gastronomy). At Haus Vaterland, each space allowed the customers to take a trip. When the restaurant complex opened, it had seven themed restaurants: from Germany, the Bavarian Löwenbräu and the Rheinterrasse; the Austrian Grinzinger Heuriger; the Türkisches Café; the Spanish Bodega; the Hungarian Puszta Czardas; and the American Wild West Bar. In the following decade (with the rise of the Third Reich), it added two more German places (the North Sea Bremer Kombüse and the Berlin Teltower Rübchen), an Italian osteria and a Japanese tearoom – the last two likely to honour the other two prongs of the new Steel Axis. In 1929 one would enter the Haus Vaterland and decide where in the world to go. It typified the pleasure of spectacle and the pleasure of engaging with difference. Haus Vaterland was simultaneously breathtaking in its scope, joyous in its celebration of variety and problematic in its approach. It is in many ways a perfect case through which to consider what food culture theorists often refer to as the question of 'eating the other'.

FATHERLANDS, HOMELANDS AND OTHER LANDS

An advertising pamphlet from Haus Vaterland's opening speaks to the ways that it understood Vaterland – fatherland – and the relationship between the fatherland and international engagement and pleasure, proclaiming to harness both the local and the exotic.

Fatherland:
A word that speaks to the heart of everyone, a word that we all know, whether one is from the Holstein Coast, or is at home in Bavaria. A word that means home, that finds a friendly echo in every heart.

Warm and local are the ways that the proud Haus Vaterland greets its guests in the hottest spot in Berlin, the capital city. Day and night it offers the colourful variety of modern, big-city wonders in an ever-changing but inviting atmosphere. The romantic beauty of the world in its crystallized form has found its mirror image here. Everyone will experience enjoyment and happiness.

The great stream of visitors to today's high-flying world-class city, through the West and the City [parts of Berlin] will, at Haus Vaterland on the Potsdamer Platz, experience a surge of pleasure. The business world of the big city has found its new central core, which bestows on Berlin a new high of internationalization.[18]

In this passage, we see a tension or perhaps a marriage between the desire for the local, the idea of home, and a cosmopolitan vision, brimming with excitement. What this looked like in practice was themed settings, entertainment and cuisine. The elaborately decorated dining areas took more from contemporaneous stage and film design than earlier restaurant designs, using painted scenes derived from the place they were to echo. Famous American club owner Barney Johnson described it:

I visited the most famous entertainment palace, Haus Vaterland on the Potsdamer Platz, something out of a De Mille extravaganza. I don't know how many rooms there were. Each room had its own special setting representing different countries, with entertainment to match. There would be an American nightclub with really good jazz and dancing for the patrons, or you could visit an American burlesque show. There was a Turkish cafe serving sweet, strong coffee, complete with belly dancers; a Wild West bar with a band of black musicians dressed up as cowboys; a Spanish room with flamenco dancers and singers; many more such rooms.[19]

The architecture of these eateries, in addition to the decor, was designed to reflect its place of origin: from the heavy Gothic interiors in the Spanish Bodega to the light and elaborate columns and screens of the Turkish café. Each restaurant had performers engaged in music and dance traditions from the country or region they represented.

The serving of Turkish coffee in the Haus Vaterland, interior view, 1938.

Finally, the food included intentional culturally specific dining.

While depicting a familiar German scene (the Rhine between St Goar and the Lorelei), the Rheinterrasse was constructed for a dramatic, immersive cultural dining experience. The two-storey restaurant was set up so that it appeared to overlook the Rhine: murals covered the walls and ceiling; dioramas depicted scenes below. Women dressed as local maidens danced with grapevine hoops. However, the real show of the Rheinterrasse was the weather. A thunderstorm, complete with water (guests were shielded by high glass panes), and simulated lightning and thunder, erupted regularly. At the end, a rainbow emerged.

On the third floor was the Löwenbräu, the Bodega and the Türkisches Café. At the Löwenbräu, waitresses served steins of beer in a large Bavarian beer garden atmosphere. The Bodega had wine barrel tables and chairs, and Spanish entertainment: flamenco, Spanish guitar and other Spanish musical acts. The Türkisches Café was a smaller space; however, it was richly decorated with low stools topped with plush cushions, hookah pipes and waiters in Ottoman clothing, including fezes.

The Grinzinger Heuriger restaurant was decorated so that you could look out and see (in full wall and ceiling mural) the picturesque cathedral, St Stephen's, against a starry sky. The Wild West Bar was a strange wonderland of Americana. Not just a cowboy bar, it was an African American cowboy bar. All of the waiting staff were black; some sources even report that they were former American cowboys. The timing and experience of black American cowboys seems like a stretch; more likely, the waiters were black Germans – including one from Africa, to whom we will later return.

THE MAKING OF HAUS VATERLAND

Haus Vaterland was the brainchild of Leo Kronau, an artistic director across many mediums. In 1905, with a partner, he put on a show at the Hippodrome in London called 'America's Lads in Blue', which included six actors and forty American service members performing a military drill: 'Indeed the spectacle were worth seeing for the infantry drill alone,' one spectator wrote, but that was not all. The show also included a coastal battle – complete with the bombing of a warship – and bareback horse-riding, an animal act and a performance by a German juggler of plates, umbrellas and balls who showcased these feats while balancing an assistant in a chair on his head. Clearly Kronau was a fan of the dramatic and was willing to interpret broadly what entertainment could be, from military precision to classic circus acts.[20]

In the early twentieth century (though we do not have an exact date), Kronau visited Coney Island in the United States. Unsurprisingly, he loved it and began designs to bring a variation – a House of Nations – to Berlin. His plans complete, he sold the idea to the food and entertainment powerhouse at Haus Potsdam, owned by the Kempinski family. The Kempinskis, Berthold and Helena, moved from Posen to Berlin in 1872, and there they reopened their business selling sandwiches, boiled eggs and Hungarian wine. By 1915 the firm owned a number of large restaurants across the city. The Haus Potsdam was built next to the Potsdam train station in 1911 and contained, in addition to some office space, a large UFA film theatre and the Café Piccadilly with a capacity for 2,500 patrons. During the First World War, the Café Piccadilly became, not surprisingly, the Deutsches Kaffeehaus Vaterland. In 1929, with Kronau's input, the Kempinskis began renovating the giant café and cinema at

Haus Potsdam into a gustatory, auditory and visual international theme park that would become Haus Vaterland. Kronau was the first artistic director of Haus Vaterland, but not the last.

In the 1930s, with the rise of the Nazi Party in Germany and its subsequent legislation that led to genocide, Haus Vaterland was confiscated from the firm on 1 May 1937. The Jewish Kempinskis, who had operated Haus Vaterland and funded its transformation into an international eatery and play-place, had been vital members of the Berlin economy for more than sixty years. They were forced to sell the establishment at a very low price to an Aryan family. Many members of the family died in the Holocaust – Richard Unger, the son-in-law of the Kempinskis and head of the firm, and his immediate family did manage to make it to the United States during the war. After the confiscation, in addition to rooms featuring the Axis powers, the complex's logo also underwent a transformation: the original logo included a K with a Star of David suspended from it; in 1935 the star was changed to grapes; by 1943 the K was changed to a B. Despite its seizure, Haus Vaterland remained popular until it was bombed in 1943. Even after the restaurant was gone, the building remained a place of complex cultural intersection: in occupied Berlin, after the war, the building was in the Russian sector but had doors that opened into American- and British-occupied Germany, eventually making it a borderland between East and West Berlin.

WORKING THE SPECTACLE

Haus Vaterland's visual fantasy could act somewhat like the lovely glass-fronted cases of the automat: so arresting and seamless that one could forget about how things got there. The kitchen system was purposefully complex and hidden. Each restaurant had

its own smaller kitchen as well as being connected to the main kitchen by private elevators that opened into the other smaller kitchens on each floor. In addition to the many performance staff, including the costumed waiting staff, Haus Vaterland had many cooks, cleaners and even seamstresses to maintain the abundance of costumes, pillows, curtains and tablecloths that the giant complex used.

The story of a Haus Vaterland employee, Bayume Mohamed Husen, is a good example of how Haus Vaterland appealed to customers' desires for the exotic with often little concern for authenticity or even reality. Husen was originally from Tanzania. He came to Berlin after serving in the German army in his occupied homeland during the First World War. In Berlin he got a job at Haus Vaterland, sometimes wearing a checked shirt and cowboy hat in the Wild West Bar, at other times a fez at the Türkisches Café. His role was to be entertaining, to be the other,

Bayume Mohamed Husen died in a concentration camp in 1944. This *Stolperstein* – stumbling block to commemorate Holocaust victims – sits in front of his home in Berlin, 2010.

and to fulfil the interests, fantasies and orders of diners.

These diners were often part of a burgeoning class of white-collar workers who had more disposable income, but did not come from well-to-do backgrounds. The point of Haus Vaterland was, for all intents and purposes, to obliterate work and normal everyday life. In his sociological study *The Salaried Masses* (1930), Siegfried Kracauer said,

> The fact that nineteenth-century panoramas are coming back into such high regard in all these establishments is related to the monotony in the sphere of work. The more monotony holds sway over the working day, the further away you must be transported once work ends . . . The true counterstroke against the office machine, however, is the world vibrant with colour. The world not as it is, but as it appears in popular hits. A world every last corner of which is cleansed, as though with a vacuum cleaner, of the dust of everyday existence.[21]

At Haus Vaterland, one could travel the gustatory (and spectacular) world in a single American city block or thoroughfare of streets. However, the interpretations were decidedly German and the frame was decidedly one of a worldly cosmopolitan adventure – of touristic travel – rather than an engagement with a variety of different cultures. Haus Vaterland had no pretence of 'authenticity' – it was about an immersive experience of variety as entertainment. We see this kind of performance now in places like Disney's Epcot Center as well as the performance of Japanese-ness in *hibachi* places like Benihana.

GLOBAL NORDIC FOOD

Much of culture-based dining follows immigrants' entrepreneurship and customers' long-standing yet complex investments in novelty; however, there are other paths to global cuisine. One of the most interesting versions of this occurs in the twenty-first century: Nordic food. This case illuminates both long-seated and cutting-edge aspects of the restaurant. The rise of Nordic cuisine did not follow immigrants, but rather industry – two industries to be exact: low-cost furniture and hyperlocal high-end cuisine.

Despite the role of the smörgåsbord in influencing the development of the cafeteria, Nordic cuisine did not become a central part of the dining scene in the way that Italian and French food did. This may be due to the fact that most Nordic countries have not had historically strong restaurant cultures.[22] Nordic restaurants were not part of popular parlance until the 2000s, when intersecting high- and low-end restaurant spaces took the global imagination by storm. Noma, the Copenhagen poster-child of the new Nordic cuisine, opened in 2003. By then, people in Warrington, England, had been eating Ikea Swedish meatballs for sixteen years.

In the 1990s, the Swedish furniture company Ikea decided to revamp its approach to international markets. Over the next two decades, it exploded with stores across the globe. These shops are not simply places to purchase home goods – they are destinations, and as such, they have restaurants. Ikea has been committed to adapting Scandinavian design to a variety of markets, but their food markets play up their Nordic roots. Most people in Mumbai or Philadelphia who have had Nordic food have not bought it from a high-end restaurant, or from a Finnish 'mom-and-pop' diner: they have eaten at Ikea.

The transition into a new market is not always easy (as we saw in the case of McDonald's in the previous chapter). After an earlier unsuccessful attempt at entering international markets, Ikea was committed to inserting itself into markets armed with a sense of what customers would like. They created dishes for specific national clientele. The Malaysian Ikea has curry with tofu; the Jordanian Ikea has a breakfast of fowl, labneh, egg and *mana'esh*; the Canadian Ikea offers haddock and chips. However, at all Ikea restaurants you can get Swedish meatballs and salmon with dill.

As a company, Ikea uses culturally iconic food to reinforce its brand, which projects a notion of simplicity as part of a Nordic aesthetic and temperament. As a branding effort, this has been largely successful; however, running an international restaurant that exports a vision of its home cuisine comes with complications that are different from those faced by local restaurants serving international foods. While Ikea, like Chinese American restaurant owners, might have thought carefully about the palates of its customers, and like the owners of Haus Vaterland, created a unique dining excursion, as a multinational corporation it also has to deal with the laws and regulations governing food distribution in each of its new markets. In Malaysia, the company ran into trouble. It had not misread the market; Malaysian customers streamed into the 1,600-seat Ikea restaurant, and they were keen on the Swedish meatballs. However, the company had not kept on top of its contracts with halal producers, and in 2005 the Malaysian restaurant was raided by the government, forced to forfeit sixty boxes of meatballs and threatened with a large fine because the factories with which they were working had not maintained halal conditions. As with other large companies food-manufacturing blunders (for example, McDonald's 2001 beef tallow debacle[23]), the Ikea

incident flared but did not permanently impact the sales of its meatballs. Factory-produced meatballs, jams and cakes may seem like dubious ambassadors for Swedish food; however, they have become the introduction to Nordic cuisine for millions of people.

At the opposite end of the spectrum from large-scale prepackaged meatball production is New Nordic cuisine. High-end and hand-wrought, New Nordic cuisine exploded around the globe with the rise of Cophenhagen's progressive Noma restaurant in the early 2000s.

In 2003 the restaurant opened with a simple philosophy: all the food served would be hyperlocal. Because of this, the restaurant ended up serving grasses, sea vegetables, tubers from leaf to tip, insects and moss. It also employed methods for preserving and curing that are vital to an area that stays cold and dark for much of the year. In form and cuisine, this restaurant was at once the heart of ethnic dining and its opposite. It was intrinsically based in culture and geography – but that culture and geography was rooted in the place where the restaurant was located. When you ate at Noma, or at other restaurants that embraced what was called New Nordic cuisine, you engaged with the principles of the 2004 New Nordic Manifesto:

1) To express the purity, freshness, simplicity and ethics we wish to associate to our region.
2) To reflect the changes of the seasons in the meal we make.
3) To base our cooking on ingredients and produce whose characteristics are particularly excellent in our climates, landscapes and waters.
4) To combine the demand for good taste with modern knowledge of health and well-being.

Indigenous guide Clifford Coulthard and top chef René Redzepi, of Danish restaurant Noma, forage for food during a visit to Nepabunna land, in Flinders Ranges, Australia, 3 October 2010.

5) To promote Nordic products and the variety of Nordic producers – and to spread the word about their underlying cultures.

6) To promote animal welfare and a sound production process in our seas, on our farmland and in the wild.

7) To develop potentially new applications of traditional Nordic food products.

8) To combine the best in Nordic cookery and culinary traditions with impulses from abroad.

9) To combine local self-sufficiency with regional sharing of high-quality products.

10) To join forces with consumer representatives, other cooking craftsmen, agriculture, fishing, food, retail and wholesale industries, researchers, teachers, politicians and authorities on this project for the benefit and advantage of everyone in the Nordic countries.[24]

For a few years René Redzepi, the head chef and co-owner of Noma, ran his exquisite, expensive restaurant in Copenhagen, abiding strictly to the rules of the manifesto and welcoming a steady flow of customers. In 2007 he ended up on the World's Best Restaurants list; the next year, Noma was Michelin starred (just two). Then in 2010 the restaurant ended up at the top of the World's Best Restaurants list, and was subsequently displayed on magazine covers across the globe.

At this point, what happened with Nordic cuisine demonstrates two competing aspects of the manifesto and of the high-end restaurant scene in the 2000s. Restaurants that served Nordic cuisine opened in major cities across the world, from New York to Shanghai (a phenomenon that some referred to as 'Scandamania'). These restaurants were the embodiment of the manifesto: they often played up the 'purity, freshness, simplicity and ethics' that these initial restaurateurs like Redzepi espoused. The internationally located restaurants used 'Nordic products' and attempted to combine 'Nordic cookery and culinary traditions with impulses from abroad.'[25] They served things like smoked salmon, mushrooms and herbed sauces – even reindeer – and often in simple, stunning geometric presentations that were inspired by nature (using leaves, flowers and ingredients that look like dirt) on rustic dishware. Nonetheless, Nordic cuisine in these places was, in significant ways, the opposite of that embodied at Noma. These high-end restaurants were places that imported foods – an aspect that the manifesto seems to encourage if one is outside of Nordic countries; however, the manifesto is also fully committed to the local and culturally situated food. The manifesto plays up seasonality, the centrality of local producers, animal welfare and environmentalism. These features are hardly unique to Nordic cuisine in the 2000s; these principles had become central in restaurants across the world at that point.

In some ways, New Nordic cuisine is the apogee of twenty-first-century fine-dining trends: fairly obscure dishes that play with texture and taste expectations, drawn from local, individually identifiable sources. It follows the trend towards working with farmers, started by people like Deborah Madison, which evolved into naming farmers explicitly in menus, a nod to both the centrality

of sourcing and changing customer expectations. These are trends that simultaneously believe in cosmopolitan palates (the menu is not necessarily framed by a single historical cultural food tradition) and are committed to local food sources. This attention to food provenance grows from concerns about globalizing, monetizing and homogenizing food production, and beliefs about the taste and cultural value of locally sourced food. Restaurant culture, in these movements, attempts to wield power in ecological and economic issues. The outcome can look like Chipotle or like detailed lists of food sources, leading to satire in which customers ask for the name of the chicken they are about to order; exposés about restaurants not actually contracting with the farmers and producers they name; and to a new crop of young and sometimes urban farmers, who often base part of their business model on the consistent demand of restaurants.

Where does this leave international Nordic cuisine? In Nordic countries, having hyperlocal, culturally specific Nordic food makes sense; however when that Nordic restaurant is in Shanghai, the physically local and the culturally specific global cuisine form a tension. Noma took a different route from its international replicators.

Noma itself expanded outside of Nordic regions, opening up pop-up style short-term restaurants in Japan (2015), Australia (2016) and Mexico (2017). However, New Nordic cuisine in Mexico meant, in this case, using products that are available and sustainable in Mexico. The nomenclature of New Nordic becomes, like the Paris Treaty or the German Historical School, a way of naming an approach rather than a national or geographic origin. This means that Noma in Mexico, Australia and Japan worked to establish relationships sourcing not only foodstuffs but flatware and dishes from local farmers, gatherers and artisans. The Mexico pop-up's menu included bee larvae, while the Australian menu included green ants. Redzepi continues to put the local and sustainable principles of the New Nordic Cuisine Manifesto at the forefront, while other restaurants across the world opt to serve reindeer and dill potatoes.

Eating food from other cultures has, since the first restaurants in China, been a key feature of restaurant dining. By being in a space where there is a set menu of choices and a cook that specializes in what is on the menu, customers have the opportunity to explore culinary cultures – or to taste the culture of their country of origin. The people who run these restaurants craft experiences that blend the familiar and the novel in ways that over time transform many 'ethnic' cuisines into the favourite dishes of other countries.

AFTERWORD

Telling the history of restaurants entices us to the possibilities of the future of dining out. This has long been a subject of interest to businesspeople, cultural critics and all types of diners. The 1980s, for example, saw a surge of interest in futuristic visions of food. Waiters at Disney's Epcot restaurants took orders on handheld computers. Children went nuts over frankly disgusting space ice cream (the astronauts didn't want it), while NASA, working to develop a line of space cuisine that was more like Earth food, took its inspiration directly from archived Moosewood Restaurant menus at Cornell University. Forty years earlier, in 1939, the famous maître d' Oscar Tschirky had already called the bluff of space ice cream: 'I have no sympathy with those who predict a fantastic diet of pills and compressed victuals for the people of tomorrow. The whole evolution of food is against it. Such methods would indeed mean that we were going back to the old idea of eating to live.'[1]

Tschirky correctly identified why the restaurant is so meaningful: it is a place where eating is about more than biology. Like the first restaurants in China, the nineteenth-century dining palaces of Paris and the minimalist vegetarian haven Gesshinkyo, decorating and design – atmosphere – continues to be a central concern for restaurants. Labour, though, changes wildly: over the course of this book, we've told stories of waiting staff seen as both experts and pariahs, and customers seen as waiting staff. We encountered kitchens as places of artistry and as places of mechanization. And there may even be a place for space in the future of dining: we saw how travel birthed and transformed the restaurant for a thousand years, from Chinese merchants to Danish chefs. From the explosion of food trucks, casual eateries and food halls over the past decade to the burgeoning industry of social dining – where strangers pay to eat, as if in a restaurant, in private homes – future labour models, dining rooms, cuisine and kitchen arrangements are likely to be as varied in 2020 Kaifeng as they were in 1020 Kaifeng.

REFERENCES

1 EATING AWAY FROM HOME:
THE LONG HISTORY OF RESTAURANTS

1 Lizzie Wade, 'How Sliced Meat Drove Human Evolution', *Science News* (9 March 2016); Kenneth F. Kiple and Kriemhild Coneè Ornelas, *Cambridge World History of Food* (Cambridge, 2000), p. 1571.

2 Susan Pollock, 'Between Feasts and Daily Meals: Toward an Archaeology of Commensal Spaces', *eTopoi: Journal for Ancient Studies*, Special Volume II (2012), pp. 1–20.

3 Maria Bianca D'Anna, 'Between Inclusion and Exclusion: Feasting and Redistribution of Meals at Late Chalcolithic Arslantepe (Malatya, Turkey)', *eTopoi: Journal for Ancient Studies*, Special Volume II (2012), pp. 97–123.

4 Quoted in Pollock, 'Between Feasts and Daily Meals', p. 9.

5 Quoted ibid., pp. 4–6.

6 James Davidson, *Courtesans and Fishcakes: The Consuming Passions of Classical Athens* (New York, 1998), pp. 43–9.

7 Quoted ibid., pp. 48–9.

8 Ibid., p. 20.

9 Clare F. Kelly-Blazeby, 'Tavernas in Ancient Greece *c.* 475–146 BC: An Archaeological Perspective', *Assemblage*, VI (2001), pp. 69–83.

10 Quoted in Davidson, *Courtesans and Fishcakes*, p. 58.

11 Jodi Campbell, *At the First Table: Food and Social Identity in Early Modern Spain* (Lincoln, NE, 2017), p. 45.

12 Helen Saberi, *Tea: A Global History* (London, 2010); Paulina B. Lewicka, *Food and Foodways of Medieval Cairnes: Aspects of Life in an Islamic Metropolis of the Eastern Mediterranean* (Leiden, 2011).

13 Jacques Gernet, *Daily Life in China on the Eve of the Mongol Invasion, 1250–1276* (Stanford, CA, 1962), p. 50.

14 Beat Kűmin, *Drinking Matters: Public Houses and Social Exchange in Early Modern Europe* (New York, 2007).

15 Cong Ellen Zhang, *Transformative Journeys: Travel and Culture in Song China* (Honolulu, HI, 2011), p. 116.

16 Miguel de Cervantes, *Don Quixote,* trans. Edith Grossman (New York, 2003), p. 29.

17 Miguel de Cervantes, *The History of that Ingenious Gentleman, Don Quijote de la Mancha*, trans. Burton Raffel (New York, 1966), p. 660.

18 Beat Kümin, 'Eating Out Before the Restaurant: Dining Cultures in Early Modern Inns', in *Eating Out in Europe: Picnics, Gourmet Dining and Snacks since the Late Eighteenth Century*, ed. M. Jacobs and P. Scholliers (Oxford, 2003), pp. 71–87.

19 Stephen H. West, 'Playing with Food: Performance, Food, and the Aesthetics of Artificiality in the Sung and Yuan', *Harvard Journal of Asiatic Studies*, LVII/1 (June 1997), pp. 67–106; Gernet, *Daily Life in China*; Cho-yun Hsu, *China: A New Cultural History* (New York, 2012). There are three contemporary accounts written in 1235, 1253 and 1275, the latter two about Hangzhou. West reports that in *Donging meng Hua lu* (about Kaifeng) 'nearly half of the eighty-six entries deal wholly or in part with food or restaurants . . . with the daily life of a leisured and affluent class of consumers in Kaifeng', p. 69. Although there has been some disagreement about the veracity of Marco Polo's account – he clearly does exaggerate at times – Cho-yun Hsu states: 'Marco Polo's account of the flourishing, lively and exciting nature of the nature of cities of Yuan China is in complete accord with Chinese records', p. 289.

20 West, 'Playing with Food', p. 72.

21 Quoted ibid., pp. 73–4.

22 Ibid., p. 71.

23 Ibid., pp. 72, 91.

24 Ibid., p. 92.

25 Quoted in Gernet, *Daily Life in China*, p. 48.

26 Quoted ibid., p. 49.

27 Gernet, *Daily Life in China*, p. 49.

28 Quoted in West, 'Playing with Food', p. 94.

2 THE RESTAURATEUR AND YOU: THE PRIVATE AND THE PUBLIC IN THE EARLY FRENCH RESTAURANTS

1 Quoted in Rebecca L. Spang, *The Invention of the Restaurant: Paris and Modern Gastronomic Culture* (Cambridge, MA, 2000), p. 22.

2 Francis William Blagdon, *Paris As It Was and As It Is* (Paris, 1803), p. 439

3 Spang, *The Invention of the Restaurant*, p. 22.

4 Jean Anthelme Brillat-Savarin, *A Handbook of Gastronomy (Physiologie du goût)*, trans. Charles Monselet (Boston, MA, 1915), p. 299.

5 Blagdon, *Paris As It Was*, p. 441.

6 Caroline Mathilda Stansbury Kirkland, 'Sightseeing in Europe: Glimpses of Paris', *Union Magazine* (November 1848), p. 197.

7 Priscilla Parkhurst Ferguson, *Accounting for Taste: The Triumph of French Cuisine* (Chicago, IL, 2004), p. 95.

8 William Walton, *Paris from the Earliest Period to the Present Day* (Philadelphia, PA, 1899).

9 Blagdon, *Paris As It Was*, pp. 160–61.

10 Marjorie. S. Coryn, *The Marriage of Josephine* (New York, 1945).

11 Shelby T. McCloy, *French Inventions of the Eighteenth Century* (Lexington, KY, 1952) pp. 109–10.

12 Thomas Webster, *An Encyclopaedia of Domestic Economy* (London, 1815), p. 18.

13 Julian Barnes, *Metroland* (New York, 1992), p. 93.

14 Auguste Luchet, quoted in Spang, *The Invention of the Restaurant*, p. 245.

15 Caroline M. Kirkland, *Holidays Abroad; or, Europe from the West* (New York, 1854).

16 Guy de Maupassant, *Bel Ami; or, The History of a Scoundrel* (Akron, OH, 1903).

17 Blagdon, *Paris As It Was*, pp. 442–3.

18 Ibid.

19 Ibid., pp. 441–2.

20 Honoré de Balzac, *A Distinguished Provincial at Paris*, vol. XIII: *The Works of Honoré de Balzac*, ed. George Saintsbury (New York, 1915), p. 18.

21 Spang, *The Invention of the Restaurant*, pp. 133–7.

22 Sam Ward, quoted in Lately Thomas, *Delmonico's: A Century of Splendor* (Boston, MA, 1967), p. 46.

23 Guy Deghy and Keith Waterhouse, *Café Royal: Ninety Years of Bohemia* (London, 1955), p. 27.

3 ELITE EATING AND THE DEMOCRATIZED RESTAURANT

1 James Jackson Jarves, *Parisian Sights and French Principles Seen through American Spectacles* (New York, 1856), pp. 16–18.

2 Andrew P. Haley, *Turning the Tables: Restaurants and the Rise of the American Middle Class, 1880–1920* (Chapel Hill, NC, 2011), p. 22.

3 Ibid., p. 38.

4 Arthur Ransome, *Oscar Wilde: A Critical Study* (London, 1912), p. 153.

5 Guy Deghy and Keith Waterhouse, *Café Royal: Ninety Years of Bohemia* (London, 1955), p. 31.

6 Edwina Ehrman et al., *London Eats Out: 500 Years of Capital Dining* (London, 1999), p. 79.

7 Marie Louis Ritz, *César Ritz: Host to the World* (Philadelphia, PA, 1938), p. 112.

8 John Timbs, *Clubs and Club Life in London; with Anecdotes of its Famous Coffee Houses, Hostelries, and Taverns, from the Seventeenth Century to the Present Time* (London, 1872), p. 1.

9 David S. Shields, 'Anglo-American Clubs: Their Wit, Their Heterodoxy, Their Sedition', *William and Mary Quarterly*, LI/251 (1994), pp. 293–304.

10 Quoted in Timbs, *Clubs and Club Life in London*, p. 127.

11 James R. Smith, 'Tales of San Francisco: The Poodle Dog Restaurant', www.historysmith.com, accessed 1 December 2017.

12 David G. Dalin and Charles A. Fracchia, 'Forgotten Financier: François L. A. Pioche', *California Historical Quarterly*, LIII/1 (1974), p. 20.

13 Smith, 'Tales of San Francisco'.

14 Walton E. Bean, 'Boss Ruef, the Union Labor Party, and the Graft Prosecution in San Francisco, 1901–1911', *Pacific Historical Review*, XVII/4 (1948), pp. 443–55.

15 Corinne K. Hoexter, *From Canton to California* (New York, 1976), p. 8; Haiming Liu and Huping Ling, *From Canton Restaurant to Panda Express: A History of Chinese Food in the United States* (Camden, NJ, 2015), pp. 15–17.

16 'History of the Hotel Metropol', http://metropol-moscow.ru, accessed 28 April 2018. See http://new.metropol-moscow.ru/en/history for the date '1905'.

17 Kelly Erby, *Restaurant Republic: The Rise of Public Dining in Boston* (Minneapolis, MN, 2016), p. 67.

18 'Mrs Blatch to Sue the Hoffman House', *New York Times* (6 August 1907).

19 'Hotels May Bar Lone Women Diners: Jury Quickly Decides Against Mrs Harriet Stanton Blatch, Who

Sued the Hoffman House', *New York Times* (6 February 1908).

20 G. Sudley, *Munsey's Magazine* (1901), quoted in Haley, *Turning the Tables*, p. 157.

21 Haley, *Turning the Tables*.

22 Erby, *Restaurant Republic*, p. 68.

23 Haley, *Turning the Tables*, p. 55.

24 Jan Whitaker, 'Domesticating the Restaurant: Marketing the Anglo-American Home', in *From Betty Crocker to Feminist Food Studies: Critical Perspectives on Women and Food*, ed. Avakian Arlene Voski and Haber Barbara (Amherst, MA, 2005), p. 90.

25 Ibid., p. 91.

26 Haley, *Turning the Tables*.

27 Antonio Mattozzi, *Inventing the Pizzeria: A History of Pizza Making in Naples* (London, 2015), p. 32.

28 Ibid.

29 Simone Cinotto, 'Serving Ethnicity: Italian Restaurants, American Eaters, and the Making of an Ethnic Popular Culture', in *The Italian American Table: Food, Family, and Community in New York City* (Chicago, IL, 2013).

30 *Die Gehemnisse von Philadelphia* (Philadelphia, PA, 1850). Translation authors' own.

4 THE MENU AND THE CHEF

1 Oli Stratford, 'Ferran Adrià and Experiments in Design', *Disegno Daily* (3 May 2013).

2 Gary S. Cadwallader and Joseph R. Justice, 'Stones for the Belly: Kaiseki Culture for Tea During the Early Edo Period', in *Japanese Foodways, Past, and Present*, ed. Stephanie Assmann and Eric C. Rath (Urbana, IL, 2010), pp. 68–91.

3 Gerald Groemer, *Edo Culture: Daily Life and Diversions in Urban Japan, 1600–1868* (Honolulu, HI, 1997).

4 Cadwallader and Justice, 'Stones for the Belly', pp. 71–4.

5 Eric C. Rath, 'Reevaluating Rikyū: Kaiseki and the Origins of Japanese Cuisine', *Journal of Japanese Studies*, XXXIX/1 (2013), pp. 67–96; Eric C. Rath, *Food and Fantasy in Early Modern Japan* (Berkeley, CA, 2010).

6 Antoine Carême, quoted in Sutherland Menzies, 'A Chat About Good Cheer', *Fraser's Magazine*, 24 (1881), p. 763.

7 Ruth Cowen, *Relish: The Extraordinary Life of Alexis Soyer, Victorian Celebrity Chef* (London, 2006).

8 Alexis Soyer, *The Gastronomic Regenerator* (London, 1847), p. 715.

9 'Haute cuisine', in the *Oxford English Dictionary*.

10 Auguste Escoffier, *Auguste Escoffier: Memories of My Life* (New York, 1997), p. 117.

11 Ferran Adrià, Juli Soler and Albert Adrià, *A Day at elBulli: An Insight into the Ideas, Methods, and Creativity of Ferran Adrià* (New York, 2008), p. 272.

12 Silviya Svejenova, Carmelo Mazza and Marcel Planellas, 'Cooking up Change in Haute Cuisine: Ferran Adrià as an Institutional Entrepreneur', *Journal of Organizational Behavior*, XXVIII/5 (2007), pp. 539–61.

13 Salvador Domenech Philippe Hyacinthe Dalí, *Les Diners de Gala*, trans. J. Peter Moore (Cologne, 2016), p. 10.

14 'The Story of elBulli: Our Story from 1961 to Today', www.elbulli.com, accessed 1 December 2017.

15 Ibid.

5 THE MAÎTRE D' AND THE WAITRESS

1 J. Stopford, 'Some Approaches to the Archaeology of Christian Pilgrimage', *World Archaeology*, XXVI/1 (1994), pp. 57–72; Beth Archer Brombert, 'The Pilgrim's Food', in *Medieval Tastes: Food Cooking, and the Table*, ed. Massimo Montanari (New York, 2012), pp. 172–6.

2 Amy Stanley, *Selling Women: Prostitution, Markets, and the Household in Early Modern Japan* (Berkeley, CA, 2012).

3 'Naniwaya Okita Teahouse Waitress', www. metmuseum.org, accessed 1 December 2017.

4 Laura Nenz Detto Nenzi, *Excursions in Identity: Travel and the Intersection of Place, Gender, and Status in Edo Japan* (Honolulu, HI, 2008).

5 J. Weintraub, 'The Restaurants of Paris: A Translation from *Paris à table*', *Gastronomica* (Spring 2014), p. 41.

6 Quoted in Andrew P. Haley, *Turning the Tables: Restaurants and the Rise of the American Middle Class, 1880–1920* (Chapel Hill, NC, 2011), p. 26.

7 George G. Foster, *New York in Slices* (New York, 1849).

8 Abram Child Dayton, *Last Days of Knickerbocker Life in New York* (New York, 1882), p. 110.

9 Dorothy Sue Cobble, *Dishing it Out: Waitresses and their Unions in the Twentieth Century* (Urbana, IL, 1991), p. 207.

10 Karl Gratzer, 'Agents of Change: Inventors, Entrepreneurs, Financiers, and Small Business Owners in the Beginning of the Swedish Fast Food Industry', in *Soziologie des Wirtschaftlichen*, ed. Dieter Bögenhold (Wiesbaden, 2014), pp. 329–60.

11 E. A. Brininstool, 'The Restaurant Girl', reprinted in *The Mixer and Server*, XII (1903), p. 27.

12 'A Bloomer-clad Waitress', *New York Times* (17 November 1895).

13 Andrew Gordon, 'Consumption, Leisure and the Middle Class in Transwar Japan', *Social Science Japan Journal*, X/1 (2007), pp. 1–21.

14 Elise K. Tipton, 'Pink Collar Work: The Café Waitress in Early Twentieth Century Japan', *Intersections: Gender and Sexuality in Asia and the Pacific*, VII (March 2002).

15 Louise Edwards, 'Policing the Modern Woman in Republican China', *Modern China*, XXVI/2 (2000), pp. 115–47.

16 Di Wang, '"Masters of Tea": Teahouse Workers, Workplace Culture, and Gender Conflict in Wartime Chengdu', *Twentieth-century China*, XXIX/2 (1 April 2004), pp. 89–136; Shiling McQuaide, 'The Battle over the Employment of Waitresses in Beijing, China, during the 1930s', *Histoire Sociale/Social History*, XLII/85 (19 November 2010), pp. 65–95.

17 Stephen Fried, *Appetite for America: How Visionary Businessman Fred Harvey Built a Railroad Hospitality Empire That Civilized the Wild West* (New York, 2010), p. 67.

18 Fried, *Appetite for America*, p. 89; Lesley Poling-Kempes, *The Harvey Girls: Women Who Opened the West* (New York, 1989), p. 56.

19 Poling-Kempes, *The Harvey Girls*, p. 84.

20 Ibid., p. 43.

21 Ibid., pp. 39, 43, 94.

22 Ibid., p. 40.

23 Quoted in Audrey Russek, 'Domestic Restaurants, Foreign Tongues: Performing African and Eating American in the U.S. Civil Rights Era', in *Dethroning the Deceitful Pork Chop: Rethinking African American Foodways from Slavery to Obama*, ed. Jennifer Jensen Wallach (Little Rock, AR, 2015).

24 Kerry Segrave, *Tipping: An American Social History of Gratuities* (Jefferson, NC, 1998); David E. Sutton, 'Tipping : An Anthropological Meditation', in *The Restaurants Book: Ethnographies of Where We Eat*, ed. David Beriss and David E. Sutton (Oxford, 2007).

25 Harumi Befu, 'An Ethnography of Dinner Entertainment in Japan', *Arctic Anthropology*, XI (1974), pp. 196–203.

6 ROAD FOOD

1 Psyche A. Williams-Forson, *Building Houses out of Chicken Legs: Black Women, Food, and Power* (Chapel Hill, NC, 2006), pp. 32–4.

2 Anthony Trollope, *He Knew He Was Right* (London, 1869).

3 Madhulika Dash, 'From Railway Mutton Curry to Bedmi-aloo: When Railway Food Was an Affair to Remember', *Indian Express* (30 October 2014).

4 Stephen Fried, *Appetite for America: How Visionary Businessman Fred Harvey Built a Railroad Hospitality Empire That Civilized the Wild West* (New York, 2010), p. 41.

5 Jeri Quinzio, *Food on the Rails: The Golden Era of Railroad Dining* (Lanham, MD, 2014), p. 29.

6 'Paderewski Chef Quits Pullman Job', *New York Times* (3 January 1928).

7 Fried, *Appetite for America*, p. 41.

8 Lesley Poling-Kempes, *The Harvey Girls: Women Who Opened the West* (New York, 1989), p. 31.

9 Fried, *Appetite for America*, p. 49.

10 Ibid., pp. 50, 118.

11 Kara Newman, 'Cattle Call', in *The Secret Financial Life of Food: From Commodities Markets to Supermarkets* (New York, 2013), pp. 91–105.

12 Fried, *Appetite for America*, pp. 65, 93.

13 Ibid., p. 93.

14 Ibid., p. 95.

15 Ibid., p. 94.

16 Poling-Kempes, *The Harvey Girls*, p. 41.

17 Ibid., p. 42.

18 Ibid., p. 46.

19 John A. Jakle and Keith A. Sculle, *Fast Food: Roadside Restaurants in the Automobile Age* (Baltimore, MD, 2002), p. 37.

20 Ibid.

21 Ibid., pp. 44–5.

22 'Plan for State-wide Clean-up Roadside Refreshment Stands', *New Castle News* (6 August 1928), p. 6; '"Hot Dog" Not So Hot', *Freeport Journal-Standard* (14 December 1929), p. 8; 'Save the "Hot Dog"', *Scranton Republican* (27 July 1929), p. 8; 'Feeding Motorists Big Business', *Greenwood Commonwealth* (28 November 1929), p. 4.

23 Andrew Hurley, 'From Hash House to Family Restaurant: The Transformation of the Diner and Post-world War II Consumer Culture', *Journal of American History*, LXXXIII/4 (1997), pp. 1282–308.

24 Herbert R. Lottman, *Michelin Men Driving an Empire* (London, 2003); 'Follow the Guide', www.michelin.com, accessed 1 December 2017.

25 John Colapinto, 'Lunch with M: Undercover with a Michelin Inspector', *New Yorker* (23 November 2009).

26 Duncan Hines, *Duncan Hines' Food Odyssey* (New York, 1955), p. 26.

27 Julian Bond, quoted in 'Recalling "Green Book," Guide for Black Travelers', *New York Times* (23 August 2010).

28 Priscilla Parkhurst Ferguson, 'Michelin in America', *Gastronomica*, VIII/1 (2008), pp. 49–55.

7 THE MACHINE IN THE RESTAURANT

1 Adam Hart-Davis, *Henry Winstanley and the Eddystone Lighthouse* (Gloucester, 1980); Hazel Forsyth, *London Eats Out: 500 Years of Capital Dining* (London, 2003), p. 28.

2 'Staging a Popular Restaurant', *Theatre* (October 1912).

3 'Theft by Women', *Chicago Daily Tribune* (10 October 1895); 'Honesty Not Their Policy', *Chicago Daily Tribune* (12 January 1896); 'Goes on the Cafeteria Plan', *Chicago Daily Tribune* (13 January 1895).

4 Angelika Epple, 'The "Automat": A History of Technological Transfer and the Process of Global Standardization in Modern Fast Food around 1900', *Food and History*, VII/2 (January 2009), pp. 97–118.

5 Carl Wilson, *The Economical European Guide* (Philadelphia, PA, 1913), p. 57.

6 Lawrence P. Spingarn, 'Horn and Hardart', *Salmagundi*, 65 (1984), pp. 119–20.

7 Karl Gratzer, 'Agents of Change: Inventors, Entrepreneurs, Financiers, and Small Business Owners in the Beginning of the Swedish Fast Food Industry', *Soziologie des Wirtschaftlichen*, ed. Dieter Bögenhold (Wiesbaden, 2014), pp. 329–60.

8 Patti Smith, *Just Kids* (New York, 2010), p. 123.

9 'History of Food Chemistry in Germany: Insititut für Lebensmittelchemie', ilc.unihohenheim.de, accessed 29 March 2017.

10 Horn & Hardart Baking Co. v. Lieber, 25 F. 2d 449 (Circuit Court of Appeals, 3rd Circuit 3704).

11 Justin Gifford, '"He Jerked His Pistol Free and Fired It at the Pavement": Chester Himes and the Transformation of American Crime Literature', in *Pimping Fictions: African American Crime Literature and the Untold Story of Black Pulp Publishing* (Philadelphia, PA, 2013), pp. 14–39.

12 Quoted in Karl Gratzer, 'Agents of Change'.

13 Alec Tristin Shuldiner, 'Trapped Behind the Automat: Technological Systems and the American Restaurant, 1902–1991', PhD thesis, Cornell University, NY, 2001, p. 69.

14 Karl Gratzer, 'Agents of Change'.

15 John Daub, 'Japan's All-vending Machine, No-staff Restaurant Serving Up Cheap Eats', www.tokyocheapo.com, accessed 1 December 2017.

16 Sarah Fritsche, 'Fast Food Reinvented? Eatsa, a Fully Automated Restaurant, Now Open', https://insidescoop.sfgate.com (31 August 2015).

17 Saki Matsukawa, 'Japanese Consumers as Technology Innovators', PhD thesis, Texas State University, 2009, p. 26.

18 John P. McDonald, *Flameout: The Rise and Fall of Burger Chef* (2011); Andrew F. Smith, *Food and Drink in American History: A 'Full Course' Encyclopedia* (Santa Barbara, CA, 2013); John A. Jakle and Keith A. Sculle, *Fast Food: Roadside Restaurants in the Automobile Age* (Baltimore, MD, 2002).

19 Hidemine Takahashi, 'It Started in Japan: Conveyor-belt Sushi', *Nipponia*, 15 (2000), p. 18.

20 Adel P. den Hartog, 'Technological Innovations and Eating Out', in *Eating Out in Europe: Picnics, Gourmet Dining and Snacks since the Late Eighteenth Century*, ed. Marc Jacobs and Peter Scholliers (Oxford, 2003), pp. 263–80.

21 Jacques Pépin, *The Apprentice: My Life in the Kitchen* (Boston, MA, 2003), pp. 158–9.

22 See www.facebook.com/pralusgeorges; Amanda Hesser, 'Under Pressure', *New York Times*

(14 August 2005); Scott Haas, 'Better Dining through Chemistry', *Gastronomica*, VI/4 (2006), pp. 74–7.

23 Georgina Ferry, *A Computer Called LEO: Lyons Teashops and the World's First Office Computer* (London, 2003), p. 12.

24 Ibid., p. 120.

25 Ibid., p. 125.

26 J. C. Tweedell, 'A New Ice Cream Installation: England's Leading Restaurateur Finds Many Uses for Refrigeration', *Refrigeration Engineering*, XXIX–XXX (1935).

27 Ferry, *A Computer Called LEO*, p. 125.

8 CHAINS AND LOCAL GEMS

1 George Ritzer, *The McDonaldization of Society* (London, 1998), pp. 9–11.

2 John F. Love, *McDonald's: Behind the Arches* (New York, 1986), p. 11.

3 Ibid., pp. 14–15.

4 Andrew Hurley, 'From Hash House to Family Restaurant: The Transformation of the Diner and Post-World War II Consumer Culture', *Journal of American History*, LXXXIII/4 (1997), pp. 282–308.

5 Love, *McDonald's*, p. 12.

6 Ibid., p. 16.

7 Ritzer, *The McDonaldization of Society*, p. 30; Love, *McDonald's*, p. 18.

8 Love, *McDonald's*, p. 17.

9 Ritzer, *The McDonaldization of Society*, p. 36.

10 Love, *McDonald's*, pp. 21–5.

11 Ibid., pp. 26–9, 40.

12 John A. Jakle and Keith A. Sculle, *Fast Food: Roadside Restaurants in the Automobile Age* (Baltimore, MD, 2002), p. 70.

13 Ritzer, *The McDonaldization of Society*, p. 32.

14 Love, *McDonald's*, pp. 308–10.

15 Ibid., pp. 418–36.

16 James L. Watson, *Golden Arches East: McDonald's in East Asia* (Stanford, CA, 1997), pp. 25–9.

17 Ibid., p. 2.

18 'The Zen of Shojin Cuisine', *Special to The Daily Yomiuri* (30 November 2002).

19 Trish Hall, 'Vegetarianism: More Popular, If Less Pure', *New York Times* (25 March 1987).

20 'The Zen of Shojin Cuisine'.

21 Kelly Horan, 'Vegetables Are Genius: A Zen Chef Cooks toward Enlightenment', *Gastronomica*, VI/4 (Autumn 2006), p. 26.

22 Julian Ryall, 'A Life in the Day: Toshio Tanahashi', *Sunday Times* (18 April 2004).

23 John T. Edge, 'Pig, Smoke, Pit: This Food's Seriously Slow', *New York Times* (9 June 2009).

9 GLOBAL DINING

1 Krishnendu Ray, *The Ethnic Restaurateur* (London, 2016), p. 11.

2 Ibid., p.12.

3 Adam McKeown, *Chinese Migrant Networks and Cultural Change: Peru, Chicago, and Hawaii, 1900–1936* (Chicago, IL, 2001).

4 Isabelle Lausent-Herrera, 'Tusans (tusheng) and the Changing Chinese Community in Peru', *Journal of Chinese Overseas*, VII/1 (2009), pp. 115–52.

5 Andrew R. Wilson, *The Chinese in the Caribbean* (Princeton, NJ, 2004), p. 148.

6 Andrew Coe, *Chop Suey: A Cultural History of Chinese Food in the United States* (New York, 2009), p. 97.

7 Ibid., p. 104.

8 Ibid., pp. 109–10.

9 Ibid., p. 104; Haiming Liu and Huping Ling, *From Canton Restaurant to Panda Express: A History of Chinese Food in the United States* (Camden, NJ, 2015), pp. 18–28.

10 As quoted in Coe, *Chop Suey*, p. 157.

11 Coe, *Chop Suey*, p. 166.

12 Ibid., p. 170.

13 Ibid., pp. 222–40.

14 J.A.G. Roberts, *China to Chinatown: Chinese Food in the West* (London, 2002), pp. 141–3, 156.

15 'Lunch with the Celestials', *The Pall Mall Budget* (11 July 1884), p. 14.

16 Roberts, *China to Chinatown*, pp. 159, 172.

17 Ligaya Mishan, 'Asian-American Cuisine's Rise, and Triumph', www.nytimes.com (10 November 2017).

18 Translation by Elliott Shore.

19 Dan Morgenstern, '"I Saw Gypsy Rose Lee Do a Political Striptease"', in *Cafe Society*, ed. Barney Josephson and Terry Trilling-Josephson (Urbana, IL, 2009), pp. 18–22.

20 *The Times* (8 May 1905), p. 1; *Illustrated Sporting and Dramatic News* (29 April 1905), p. 10.

21 Siegfried Kracauer, *The Salaried Masses: Duty and Distraction in Weimar Germany*, trans. Quintin Hoare (New York, 1998). pp. 92–3.

22 Henry Notaker, *Food Culture in Scandanavia* (Westport, CT, 2009), p. 133.

23 The company claimed it had switched to vegetable oil in 1990, despite still using beef tallow. It was subsequently sued, and faced the outrage of vegetarians and Hindus worldwide. See Luke Harding, 'Hindus Angered by Burger Chain's Beef Lie', www.theguardian.com (24 May 2001).

24 'The New Nordic Food Manifesto: Nordic Cooperation', www.norden.org, accessed 26 April 2017.

25 Ibid.

AFTERWORD

1 Oscar Tschirky, 'Promise for the Epicure', *New York Times* (5 March 1939).

BIBLIOGRAPHY

Adrià, Ferran, Juli Soler and Albert Adrià, *A Day at elBulli: An Insight into the Ideas, Methods and Creativity of Ferran Adrià* (New York, 2008)

Assmann, Stephanie, and Eric C. Rath, *Japanese Foodways, Past, and Present* (Urbana, IL, 2010)

Beriss, David, and David Sutton, eds, *The Restaurants Book: Ethnographies of Where We Eat* (Oxford, 2007)

Campbell, Jodi, *At the First Table: Food and Social Identity in Early Modern Spain* (Lincoln, NE, 2017)

Cobble, Dorothy Sue, *Dishing it Out: Waitresses and Their Unions in the Twentieth Century* (Urbana, IL, 1991)

Cowen, Ruth, *Relish: The Extraordinary Life of Alexis Soyer, Victorian Celebrity Chef* (London, 2006)

Davidson, James, *Courtesans and Fishcakes: The Consuming Passions of Classical Athens* (New York, 1998)

Ehrman, Edwina, Hazel Forsyth, Lucy Peltz and Cathy Ross, *London Eats Out: 500 Years of Capital Dining* (London, 1999)

Ferguson, Priscilla Parkhurst, *Accounting for Taste: The Triumph of French Cuisine* (Chicago, IL, 2004)

Freedman, Paul, ed., *Food: The History of Taste* (Berkeley and Los Angeles, CA, 2007)

——, *Ten Restaurants That Changed America* (New York, 2016)

Fried, Stephen, *Appetite for America: How Visionary Businessman Fred Harvey Built a Railroad Hospitality Empire that Civilized the Wild West* (New York, 2010)

Haley, Andrew P., *Turning the Tables: Restaurants and the Rise of the American Middle Class, 1880–1920* (Chapel Hill, NC, 2011)

Jacobs, M., and Peter Scholliers, eds, *Eating Out in Europe: Picnics, Gourmet Dining and Snacks since the Late Eighteenth Century* (Oxford, 2003)

Jakle, John A., and Keith A. Sculle, *Fast Food: Roadside Restaurants in the Automobile Age* (Baltimore, MD, 2002)

Kumin, Beat, *Drinking Matters: Public Houses and Social Exchange in Early Modern Europe* (New York, 2007)

Lewicka, Paulina B., *Food and Foodways of Medieval Cairenes: Aspects of Life in an Islamic Metropolis of the Eastern Mediterranean* (Leiden, 2011)

Liu, Haiming, and Huping Ling, *From Canton Restaurant to Panda Express: A History of Chinese Food in the United States* (Rutgers, NJ, 2015)

Pillsbury, Richard, *From Boarding House to Bistro: The American Restaurant Then and Now* (Boston, MA, 1990)

Pollock, Susan, ed., *Between Feasts and Daily Meals: Towards an Archaeology of Communal Spaces* (Berlin, 2015)

Ray, Krishnendu, *The Ethnic Restaurateur* (London, 2016)

Shore, Elliott, 'Dining Out: The Development of the Restaurant', in *Food: The History of Taste,* ed. Paul H. Freedman (Berkeley and Los Angeles, CA, 2007), pp. 301–32

——, 'Modern Restaurants and Ancient Commensality', in *Between Feasts and Daily Meals: Towards an Archaeology of Communal Spaces*, ed. Susan Pollock (Berlin, 2015), pp. 277–88

Spang, Rebecca L., *The Invention of the Restaurant: Paris and Modern Gastronomic Culture* (Cambridge, MA, 2000)

Thomas, Lately, *Delmonico's: A Century of Splendor* (Boston, MA, 1967)

Watson, James L., *Golden Arches East: McDonald's in East Asia* (Stanford, CA, 1997)

West, Stephen H., 'Playing With Food: Performance, Food, and the Aesthetics of Artificiality in the Sung and Yuan', *Harvard Journal of Asiatic Studies*, LVII/1 (June 1997)

ACKNOWLEDGEMENTS

We would like to thank all of the people in libraries, archives, museums and historical societies who made this work possible through preserving and providing access to these stories. Brandon Wicks and Maria Sturm encouraged us along the way with their thoughtful responses and editorial eyes, for which we are deeply grateful. We want to thank Trevor Muñoz and Lisa Shore for their wonderful editorial assistance, Moritz Shore for his technical assistance, and the many friends and colleagues who answered our questions and pointed us to sources. We would like to thank Michael Leaman for his invitation to write this book, and we are indebted to Paul Freedman, the editor of *Food: The History of Taste*, who gave Elliott the opportunity to write about dining out in the West. Thanks to the libraries and librarians of Bryn Mawr College, the University of Pennsylvania and Emory University; and to our wonderful colleagues at the Council on Library and Information Services, whose vision for libraries fosters a global cultural heritage community.

PHOTO ACKNOWLEDGEMENTS

The author and the publishers wish to express their thanks to the below sources of illustrative material and/or permission to reproduce it.

Alamy: pp. 20 (Gado Images), 36 (Interfoto), 105, 183 (Heritage Image Partnership Ltd), 190, 194 (Everett Collection Historical), 197 (Kees Metselaar); Americasroof: p. 199; Mark Bellis: p. 204; August Berlin: p. 223; Bibliothèque nationale de France: pp. 46 left and right, 47, 56, 60, 71, 72, 83, 84; Bibliothèque nationale et universitaire de Strasbourg, Strasbourg: p. 96; Bodleian Libraries: pp. 97, 98 (Internet Library of Early Journals); Boston Public Library: p. 154 (Tichnor Brothers Collection); The British Library, London: pp. 76, 165; Bundesarchiv, Koblenz: p. 118; Eatsa: p. 178; Égoïté: p. 35; Luis García (Zaqarbal), 11 September 2009: p. 11 (left); Getty Images: pp. 22 (Photo by Austrian Archives/Imagno), 23, 59 top (DeAgostini/Biblioteca Ambrosiana), 34 (DEA/J. M. Zuber), 48, 49 (Photo by Museum of the City of New York/Byron Collection), 88 (John McDonnell/The Washington Post via Getty Images), 104 (Felix Man/Picture Post), 109 (Photo by Samuel Aranda), 130 (Bettmann), 155 (Photo by Apic), 164 (Photo by Keystone View/FPG), 168, 219, 221 (Photo by Ullstein Bild/Ullstein Bild via Getty Images), 169 (Bettmann), 170 (Universal History Archive/UIG via Getty Images), 212 (Photo by Nathaniel Hoffman/MCT/MCT via Getty Images), 226 (Lisa Maree Williams); The J. Paul Getty Museum, Los Angeles: pp. 68, 82, 115, 150; Immanuel Giel: p. 25; Imperial War Museum, London: pp. 184, 189; Steven-L_Johnson: p. 177; Kansas Historical Society: p. 126; Library of Congress, Washington, DC: pp. 79, 80, 81, 134, 142, 143, 144 top and bottom, 149 top, 151, 152, 153, 163, 181, 193, 210, 216; London School of Economics: p. 123 (The Women's Library); Louvre Museum: p. 13 right; McCord Museum of Canadian History, Montreal: p. 141; Mary Evans Picture Library: p. 59 bottom; Metropolitan Museum of Art, New York: pp. 12 top and bottom, 13 left, 15, 17, 18, 38, 45, 58, 63, 69, 89, 90, 91, 92, 93, 94 top and bottom, 95, 114, 116 top and bottom, 129, 136, 137, 209; Moonik: p. 31; Musée Escoffier de l'Art Culinaire: p. 101; MZSL/Ofner Károly: p. 140 top; National Archives, Washington, DC: p. 191; National Gallery of Art, Washington, DC: pp. 117, 138; National Library of Norway, Oslo: p. 122; National Palace Museum, Taipei: p. 19; The New York Public Library, New York: pp. 84, 214 top and bottom (The Miriam and Ira D. Wallach Division of Art, Prints and Photographs), 157 (Schomburg Center for Research in Black Culture, Manuscripts, Archives and Rare Books Division), 158 (Schomburg Center for Research in Black Culture, Photographs and Prints Division), 166, 215 (General

Research Division); Marie-Lan Nguyen: p. 11 right; Ribberlin: p. 55; Clem Rutter, Rochester, Kent: p. 179; Stockholm Transport Museum: p. 167; United States Patent and Trademark Office: p. 149 bottom; Victoria and Albert Museum, London: pp. 21, 52, 67, 73; Bohao Zhao: p. 140 (bottom).

INDEX